The Chicago Marathon

The

Andrew Suozzo

Chicago Marathon

University of Illinois Press

Urbana and Chicago

Photo on page 62 courtesy of
Frank Wheby.
All other photos courtesy of
The LaSalle Bank Chicago Marathon.

© 2006 by the Board of Trustees
of the University of Illinois
All rights reserved
Manufactured in the United States of America
1 2 3 4 5 C P 5 4 3 2 1

♾ This book is printed on acid-free paper.

Library of Congress Cataloging-in-Publication Data
Suozzo, Andrew G.
The Chicago Marathon / Andrew Suozzo.
p.   cm.
Includes bibliographical references and index.
ISBN-13: 978-0-252-03168-7 (cloth : alk. paper)
ISBN-10: 0-252-03168-7 (cloth : alk. paper)
ISBN-13: 978-0-252-07421-9 (pbk. : alk. paper)
ISBN-10: 0-252-07421-1 (pbk. : alk. paper)
1. LaSalle Bank Chicago Marathon—History. I. Title.
GV1065.22.L37S86   2006
796.42'52—dc22   2006020763

Dedicated to all
who make the Chicago Marathon
the great race it is today.

contents

preface

In 1995, late into my forty ninth year, I rediscovered running—largely as a matter of chance. Rather than pay a hefty gym initiation fee to use a chain's facility during a brief summer seminar stay in Paris, I chose jogging as a cost-free way of controlling my weight. Shortly upon my return to Chicago, I took up running more seriously and succumbed to the lure of racing by completing the Motorola Half-Marathon that September, thus returning to competition after a hiatus of more than thirty years from high school cross country. I achieved only modest results (1:32:32), but they were enough to make me consider more. The temptation to run the Chicago Marathon that October—and to complete this formidable ordeal before my fiftieth birthday—was irresistible. Against the advice of some seasoned fellow runners, but with encouragement from a colleague and a good friend, both experienced marathoners, I stuffed my wristband with cab fare and, prepared for any physical failings, set off for the Chicago Marathon, untrained, terrified, and utterly determined to finish. At the time, I did not suspect how close to typical my case was. Unaware that ever more runners in the coming years would make the marathon their first race, I imagined my own situation as somehow aberrant, unique, and a bit crazy. Little did I suspect that reaching middle age or a decade milestone like fifty often creates the need in people to prove they are still physically vital. In any event, to reduce the psychological immensity of the distance, I broke up the course into seven-mile segments (my maximum training mileage). After mile 14, I knew I would make it. Nearing mile 20, I asked another runner when to expect to hit the wall. He responded that if I hadn't hit it, it didn't exist. Good advice! I finished in an unimpressive 3:21:11, my second-to-worst time ever, but rarely have I felt such elation. Decades of chain smoking had been swept away, and I had qualified for Boston on my first try. I was hooked on marathoning.

I became a very competitive runner, able to place in the regional age-group circuit and occasionally capable of winning my age group in individual races. I devoured running magazines like *Runner's World* and *Running Times*. I trained seriously, learned many techniques, and endured frequent injuries almost from the onset. Nonetheless, I bounced back from these multiple injuries and even a stroke (which was not running related). It would take me four years to reach the goal I formulated after that first marathon: breaking three hours. It would take a full eight years before I would place in my age group in the Chicago Marathon. I remained focused on improving my times, and enjoyed the friendly rivalry with men my age.

However, academic training taught me to look far beyond my own preoccupations. Indeed, as I contemplated the amazing growth of the Chicago Marathon even since my own involvement, I was astonished by the magnitude of the event and its impact on the city. I knew that marathoning was a national and international phenomenon, that running was emerging as a mass sport in nearly every developed country, and, given certain specific characteristics of running, that this new prominence suggested a major shift in values. Because Chicago has in the past decade reaffirmed a position it had temporarily lost as one of the world's premier marathons, I knew that I was in a unique position as a runner, a running club member, and a marathon supporter to observe this development and to discover in the outstanding example of Chicago the emergence of an extraordinary urban dynamism as well as new values and goals—in fact, to witness the dramatic transformation of a sport. Thanks to the help of many contacts, I was able to study what the marathon meant for the city, its business community, and its runners, local, national, and worldwide.

Soon I found myself giving a course on the marathon and its impact on the city. Teaching also stimulated my desire to give lectures and write about the marathon. My trial-balloon article, "The Chicago Marathon and Urban Renaissance," was well received, winning the Russel B. Nye Award from the *Journal of Popular Culture*. This good fortune and, ironically, a severe case of plantar fasciitis that put an end to all competitive running for 2004 gave me both the motivation and the much needed leisure to complete this book, which has been in the works since 2001. I hope that readers will find some inspiration in discovering the complexity of collective effort that makes the modern marathon a reality. It is also my intention to call attention to the Chicago Marathon in particular, which I feel is undiscovered in relationship to its New York and Boston counterparts, and to claim for the city the prestige it deserves as one of the greatest and fastest marathons in the world, a marathon that flourishes thanks to the dedication and generosity of its citizenry.

Despite the current marathon craze, the race itself has been the object of little serious study. Sandy Treadwell's *The World of Marathons* (1982), a rather early work on the subject, offers only brief accounts of major world marathons, not an analysis of their workings. Fred Lebow's autobiography, *Inside the World of Big-Time Marathoning* (1984), supplies an executive race director's perspective of the New York City Marathon. Tom Derderian's *Boston Marathon: The First Century of the World's Premier Running Event* (1996) provides intriguing portraits of professional runners and marathon victors but keeps to that focus. His latest work, *The Boston Marathon: A Century of Blood, Sweat, and Cheers* (2003), tells the story of the towns along the way, but it is not a work of analysis. It is Pamela Cooper's *The American Marathon* (1998) that provides the only academic analysis of U.S. marathon history. The work, however solid and enticing, offers a relatively brief overview (181 pages) of the marathon in this country and does not discuss the Chicago Marathon. Cooper's work is clearly an invitation to other authors to expand our knowledge of the subject. John Bryant's *The London Marathon: The History of the Greatest Race on Earth* was published in 2005 and, while not an academic study, is a lively and informed book that suggests a broad audience for marathon literature.

In writing this work on the LaSalle Bank Chicago Marathon, I have had to rely not only on written, largely journalistic sources but also on the testimonials of many individuals. In the latter situation, I have for the most part allowed them to speak for themselves, consciously limiting my commentary and attempting to respect the informant's point of view, in part as an act of gratitude for the kind assistance the individual afforded in supplying vital information for the book. In some cases, I cannot verify particular assertions, but I chose to report them. Discerning readers should bear this in mind and make their own judgments.

I have organized the book by grouping the components that make up the marathon into five parts. Although personally highly enthusiastic about the marathon, I am attempting to supply a description and an analysis of the event, not a promotional treatise. After a broad introductory chapter that outlines some of the key features of the marathon today, I supply a short history of the Chicago Marathon. Then I look at the practices of race management and follow this with a description of the grassroots support from local and regional runners, who provide the bulk of race volunteers. I examine the profound influence of corporate sponsors, most particularly LaSalle Bank, and the de facto sponsorship provided by the city itself. I consider the immense importance of the marathon for charity fundraising and discuss how the media is enlisted to publicize and valorize the event. I devote the final four chapters to the runners themselves, with an emphasis on amateurs rather than professionals. If my efforts prove worthwhile, readers should have a broad view of the effort, time, and emotion that goes into a major urban marathon and will gain an understanding of one of the world's truly great races, the Chicago Marathon.

acknowledgments

This book could never have been written without the help of Carey Pinkowski and David Reithoffer. I thank Carey for opening every door, which enabled me to gather vital information on the workings of the Chicago Marathon. I am also indebted to him for his comments on the original manuscript. Though a busy race director, he found the time to read and annotate key aspects of the text. I express my gratitude to David for his introduction to Carey, his constant support, and his invaluable assistance both in Chicago and in France in meeting key people and securing permissions.

Also critical to this book was the assistance of Liz Kiser at the Chicago Marathon office. Liz patiently tracked down missing runners, provided and sent marathon photos, and handled the office permissions.

Likewise, I must thank my colleague Clara Orban, who handled the mailing and receipt of a flood of permission-related correspondence in Chicago while I was away managing a university program abroad. I am also grateful to my departmental chair, Mark Johnston, for reading my first chapter and to DePaul staff members Nick Marotta and Analuz Duran for assisting me with sundry time-consuming clerical matters.

I would also like to acknowledge my debt to former marathon press officials Robin Monsky and Tom Smithburg, who arranged lecturers' visits to my classes. These lectures inspired me to think first about an article and then about a book on the Chicago Marathon. Thanks are likewise due to Shawn Patt, who now handles press matters, particularly for granting me press credentials to the 2004 Chicago Marathon.

For critical readings, inspired suggestions, and unfailing encouragement, I thank my old friend and former marathoner, Stephen Blumm. I am also indebted to Terry Nicola, M.D., for the medical perspective on running that he has shared with me. I also drew energy and resolve from the encouragement I received from Tom Bestul, Passcale-Anne Brault, Pasquale Larotonda, Ruth Lowe, Carl Petry, and my brother, Paul Suozzo, during the writing of this book.

More generally, I wish to express my appreciation to Mark Nystuen, executive vice president of LaSalle Bank, for his support and for looking over the LaSalle portion of the text, and I would like to express my enduring gratitude to the numerous kind people whose interviews and lectures make this book a reflection of the extraordinary diversity and mix of talent that breathe life into the Chicago Marathon.

I note the generosity of DePaul University for allowing me to teach about the Chicago Marathon and for assisting my research with a competitive leave grant in the spring of 2001.

Lastly, I would like to thank University of Illinois Press acquisitions editor Laurie Matheson for her assistance and support from the initial proposal through the publication process; Rebecca Crist, managing editor, for her expeditious handling of the text; and Dennis Roberts for his selection and arrangement of illustrations.

the chicago marathon

Perhaps the LaSalle Bank Chicago Marathon's most dramatic moment: the massive start, with runners in the tens of thousands surging forward.

PART I

The Race Then and Now

In 1999, Khalid Khannouchi broke the world record in Chicago in an astounding 2:05:42.

the marathon:
from myth to actuality

Classical antiquity knew no such race as the marathon. Even the historical sources referring to Pheidippides' mythical run are scant and suspect.
The first text that mentions one "Phidippides"[1] is Herodotus's *Histories*
in the fifth century B.C.E. Pheidippides, a day runner by profession, was
sent as a herald to southern Greece to gain Spartan assistance in the war
against the Persians. Herodotus never mentions Pheidippides at the
battle of Marathon or his death as the heroic bearer of joyous tidings of
the Athenian victory. Pausanias, who wrote around 174 C.E.—some six
hundred years later—basically repeats Herodotus's account; likewise, he
has nothing to say about the battle of Marathon or the death of Pheidippides (Pausanias, *Attica,* xxviii, 4–7, 149; *Arcadia,* 6–7, 169). In this text,
the runner's name is transliterated differently as "Philippides."

The first and only reference to the Pheidippides legend as we know it comes from Lucian, who wrote some five hundred years after Herodotus. In this account, devoted to greetings, Lucian cites a "Philipiddes" as the courier who brought the news of the victory from Marathon to Athens. Upon arrival, he addressed the magistrates with "Joy to you, we've won" and then promptly died, presumably of overexertion (Lucian, 177). A slightly earlier version of this story is available in Plutarch's *Moralia*. The author, however, names a different courier: "most historians declare that it was Eucles who ran in full Armour, hot from the battle, and bursting in at the doors of the first men of the State, could only say, 'Hail! we are victorious!' and straightway expired" (Plutarch 503, 505).[2]

Thus, the specific legend of the Marathon run is based on only a few lines of two classical sources that were written many centuries after the Athenian victory. This has not stopped contemporary authors from embroidering the tale and making groundless assertions,[3] despite the widely known lack of evidence about Pheidippides.[4] Robert Browning's nineteenth-century poem "Pheidippides" may well be the source of much contemporary confusion, as it conflates Herodotus's account of the courier's truly epic run to the Spartans and Lucian's account of the aftermath of the battle of Marathon. It is likely Browning's richly poetic imagination that created the image of the noble Pheidippides hurling down his shield at the end of the battle and running back to Athens only to die in the exultation of victory:

> . . . "Rejoice, we conquer!"
> Like wine through clay,
> Joy in his blood bursting his heart, he died—
> the bliss! (Browning, 227)

The modern—indeed, the first—marathon ever to exist was created at the end of the nineteenth century as perhaps the noblest event of the first Olympiad of the new era. It was the result of the collaboration between two Frenchmen, Pierre de Coubertin, founder of the modern Olympics, and the classical philologist, Michel Bréal. It would be appropriately dubbed "an invented tradition."[5]

The first marathon was about twenty-five miles and was won, to the delight of the local populace, by a Greek athlete, Spiridon Louis. Greeks also took second and third place, although the third-place runner was disqualified for cheating. The time of the first marathon champion was quite slow by today's standards (2:58:50 for 40 kilometers or nearly 25 miles[6]); in fact, it was quite amazing that any of the runners actually managed to finish the race. It seems that the Greeks, fueled by a spirit of fervent patriotism, were the only runners who prepared themselves with any seriousness.[7]

The first Olympic marathon generated strong interest in this footrace throughout much of the world. In the ensuing years, marathons were held in most western countries and sporadically throughout different regions of the United States. Chicago, St. Louis, and the New York area all had marathons that came and went. These races included very few runners. The whole notion of the marathon as a mass event does not really begin to develop until the 1960s in the United States— and even that date may be an overstatement.

This initial marathon growth in the 1960s was fueled by a new health consciousness that identified jogging with fitness. This new identification would merge with Cold War concerns in triumphant fashion with Frank Shorter's gold medal in the marathon of the 1972 Munich Olympics. In many ways, Shorter personified the convergence of several trends. A Yale graduate, he clearly represented the upper-middle class in the athletic arena. Victorious against the communist enemy, he also personified the American struggle against the highly competitive socialist republics of the east. Further, he projected an accessible image of health—not necessarily marathon victory—to upper-status Americans. Shorter had been preceded in the American public's consciousness by Amby Burfoot, the winner of the Boston Marathon in 1968, referred to as "Burfoot of Wesleyan" by the *New York Times*. Burfoot, formerly the editor-in-chief of *Runner's World,* also encouraged William Rodgers, fabled marathon victor during the 1970s and fellow Wesleyan alumnus, in his running (Cooper, 130). Burfoot had served in the Peace Corps in El Salvador after graduating from college, thus fusing the idealism of the Kennedy tradition with running acclaim. These male champions, all from New England, would be complemented by an illustrious female runner from Maine, Joan Benoit Samuelson, who for many years held the U.S. women's record, which she achieved in the 1985 Chicago Marathon. Like her male counterparts, Samuelson had graduated from a respected New England school, Bowden College. Clearly, this new set of middle-class, attractive, well-educated, distance-running champions had a direct impact on those Americans who had the means and the leisure to take up running. Henceforth, a new type of runner—the long-distance runner—would fuel the emerging running boom.

This new type of runner quickly became part of a mass movement rather than a professional elite. Sandy Treadwell sees the 1976 New York City Marathon as a watershed in marathon history—the race that began popularizing big-city marathons for masses of people (Treadwell, 19–21). Perhaps *the* critical event in marathon history occurred in 1975 when the legendary Ted Corbitt was trying to promote a marathon for teams from each of the city's boroughs. George Spitz, a running enthusiast and activist, altered Corbitt's idea and rushed to the New York Road Runners Club (NYRRC) president Fred Lebow with the idea of a five-borough course, which Lebow, in horror, initially rejected as unmanageable. But Spitz continued to press his idea, and Lebow, after presenting what he viewed as impossible terms, discovered that the city fathers were willing to meet them. Thus, the five-borough marathon was born, and the following year's 1976 race, with 2,000 entrants, was four times the size of the inaugural year's. No longer a Central Park event, the new marathon symbolized the unity and scope of New York City. It had become an urban festival.

By the early 1980s, the New York City Marathon confirmed that rapidly expanding fields of entrants were a genuine trend: in 1971, there were only 127 starters and 55 finishers; in 1981, some 4,000 runners finished the race. The New York City Marathon also highlighted another trend—that running was an upper-middle-class activity that attracted well-paid, urban professionals.[8] The middle-class admirers of the marathon champions of the 1970s and 1980s began to emerge in force. The growing participation in marathons was strikingly evident in Chicago as early as 1977, when the newly founded Mayor Daley Marathon (the original name of the Chicago Marathon) drew a field of 4,200 runners, positioning itself as a strong rival of New York.

The growth of the field of runners and spectators has been nothing short of amazing. With only a few thousand participants in the early 1990s, the Chicago Marathon's field began to grow exponentially in the later part of the decade and into the new millennium: in 1995, registration numbered some 9,000; by 1999, it had climbed to over 29,000 with nearly 25,000 finishers; by 2003, it reached 40,000 registrants, its cap in 2004 and 2005. In 1995, a runner could register on the eve of the marathon; in 2004, marathon registration closed in August. In nine years (from 1995 to 2003), the Chicago Marathon increased by nearly 450 percent from an already substantial base—a growth rate that would make any CEO euphoric! Chicago is typical in this respect: large urban marathons in New York, London, Paris, Berlin, and Honolulu experienced explosive growth in the late 1990s and early 2000s with between 30,000 to 40,000 registrants. New York and London, because of their exceptional appeal, had to impose caps earlier than Chicago. This is a far cry from the beginning of the century when the newly invented marathon drew minuscule fields. The modern mass marathon is quite another phenomenon; it is an event that enlists the energies of entire cities and celebrates not only athletic accomplishment but also the vitality and dynamism of the cities that sponsor it.

The extraordinary situation usually referred to as the second running boom calls for an explanation. Some of the factors that propelled marathon running into such prominence were already in place earlier in the century; others have to do with broader, more recent value shifts that have dramatically increased the growth potential of marathons.

One of the most significant positive changes in this sport's growth was the association of distance running and good health, a notion that, as indicated earlier, began to emerge in the 1960s and reached a wider audience throughout the ensuing decades. As more and more people in affluent countries struggle with their weight, the growing threat of heart disease, and the general atrophy that comes from sedentary jobs and lives, they see running as an ideal activity to counter the physical deterioration that marks modern professional life. This positive association when applied to the marathon is largely an uncritical one because, although the general practices of jogging, distance running/racing, and training up to about twenty miles are considered healthy for physically fit people, running a marathon is emphatically not a healthy practice. It exceeds the body's limits. Nonetheless, so powerful is the notion of general fitness as a benefit of running that it is simply carried over to the marathon, which is often viewed as some kind of ultimate confirmation of top physical condition rather than the act of attenuated self-destruction that it actually is—at least for most mortals.

The marathon also has a particular appeal not only as a form of maintenance but also as an assertion of recovered health, of a physical rebirth. There are numerous personal stories of individuals suffering from obesity who have overcome serious weight problems by training for and running a marathon. Oprah, the media star and Marine Corps Marathon finisher, is perhaps the most celebrated example of this kind of personal transformation. But she is hardly alone; many people with life-threatening conditions such as heart disease have recovered from their afflictions and have provided triumphant proof of their fitness by completing a marathon. Here, time usually has little importance. Completing the ordeal is the paramount issue. The marathon thus represents a kind of certification of fitness, proof positive that an impaired individual can overcome adversity and prevail. The marathon assumes a metaphorical dimension; it is an assurance of the individual's ability to succeed in the inevitable future struggles that life will present.

This sense of physical triumph holds a powerful attraction for the middle-aged. Here, running the marathon assumes the dimension of a revolt against aging, a refusal to be consigned to the easy chair, and an assertion that a physically active life is as much their right as that of twenty-year-olds. It also implies a redefinition of the body culturally assigned to the aging individual. The marathon becomes an opportunity to explore the individual's potential to exceed the supposed limits of the body. Although even the young experience this testing, it is more dramatic for people already beyond youth in a culture that dismisses them as unworthy of consideration as physical entities. For the middle-aged woman or man, running is an act of defiance and a demand for cultural revision—a trend that is bound to continue as the population ages and simultaneously refuses to be deprived of the physical stimulations arbitrarily reserved for youth. In this age of erectile dysfunction drugs, it is hardly surprising and indeed is expected that the marathon will continue to exert increasing appeal on the graying population. The baby boomers are not a population segment that will vanish meekly into obscurity.

Whether for the middle-aged or those in the full bloom of youth, running exerts a powerful appeal in its admirable simplicity and accessibility. Despite the escalating cost of shoes, shorts, and numerous accessories, it remains a relatively affordable, uncomplicated sport that can be practiced alone or in a group. Running is a natural behavior, and although training and coaching can improve it, human beings do not need to be taught how to run. It can be a competition, a group social event, or a solitary activity. A healthy person of almost any age and of either sex can practice it. It is devoid of the violence found in many sports and is often associated with friendliness and courtesy. The introduction of competitions based on sex, age class (usually five-year segments), and weight (Clydesdale/goddess) means that, more than in almost any other sport (barring serious injury or other medical problems), individuals may continue competing throughout their lives and even with bodies clearly not designed to excel at racing, as in the case of the heavier subdivisions of a Clydesdale/goddess competition. The synergy generated by nearly universal accessibility to attenuated competition ensures this health-enhancing sport the potential for dynamic growth in the foreseeable future. But this growth is largely fueled by a noncompetitive, group-oriented participation, this kind of participation is linked to the current value shift that emphasizes inclusiveness rather than personal distinction.[9] As American and world society continue to celebrate the virtues of diversity in the new millennium, a sport that emphasizes mass participation rather than excellence and concomitant exclusivity will grow. Viewed from this perspective, the marathon becomes not so much a contest, but rather a mass celebration in which thousands of extremely diverse individuals engage in a vast urban procession.

Americans have become acutely sensitive to the multiethnic and multiracial nature of their society. The all-white, suburban society depicted in 1950s sitcoms like *Father Knows Best* and *Ozzie and Harriet* has long since vanished as the stereotypical representation of America. People are quite aware that, to survive, our society must embrace diversity or tear itself apart. Although the marathon remains a predominantly white sport,[10] the body types and abilities of people who run it now span almost every imaginable category. Hence, the marathon (and other footraces as well) has increasingly become the domain of the nonathlete, the ungifted, marginally competent amateur. This participation is staunchly defended by writers like Bingham and, to some extent, even Galloway, who validate noncompetitive performances.[11] This development is a manifestation of a growing hostility toward excellence. It has become far more important in our society that everyone who trains can become a participant, that all who finish should be considered victors. This tendency is similarly reflected in the educational system by grade inflation and social promotion. We place a high value on inclusion; the desire not to offend or leave out takes precedence over acknowledgment of significant achievement and criticism of poor performance. This collapse of standards is essential to marathon growth and its transformation into a happening that is far broader than a professional competition. Mass urban festivals cannot really afford to be picky.[12]

This mass inclusiveness is also aided by how individuals measure performance in the marathon. Although top professionals compete for first place and serious amateurs strive for distinction overall and in their age categories, most runners compete at most against a few friends—if anyone. The real competition for the great mass of runners is against themselves. Therefore, whether one is a penguin or a relatively strong middle-ranked runner, participants will be looking to beat their own personal records (PRs) or particular course records. Chicago's extraordinarily fast, flat course has an extra draw in this respect. Despite an official closing time of six and a half hours, finishing chutes are left open to what can only be described as walking times (8 hours plus). This tolerance allows a "competition" of sorts and a sense of fulfillment for even those who have walked the marathon—a tendency that has now come close to general acceptance.[13]

On the other hand, this inclusiveness is far more restrictive than it initially appears, for the marathon's current appeal is largely directed toward the urban middle class in the renascent cities of North America and other major cities throughout the world. Most marathons offer a predictable composition: a handful of elite runners, largely East and North Africans, followed by a huge army of domestic middle-class runners peppered with other middle- to upper-middle-class runners from various affluent countries. In the United States and specifically in Chicago, this means a predominantly white marathon. This uniformity of class and, to a large degree, race is marked by a great diversity of age and a near equality of the sexes within the interior of these categories. Thus, even with the caveats we have indicated, the marathon continues to attract enormous numbers because the participants are largely economically secure and thus better positioned to gratify their desires.

The lure of the marathon is especially powerful for young urban professionals. Indeed, this group, male and female, constitutes the largest percentage of marathon runners. The reasons for the power of this appeal are hardly surprising. The lives and general culture of these urban professionals tend to push them toward marathoning. The race embodies middle-class virtues that they cultivate: discipline, long-range planning, and deferred gratification.[14] Indeed, the analogy between the marathon and the lifestyles of so many of its participants is a point that has not been lost on advertisers. It was evoked in 2004 by an Oppenheimer Fund television commercial depicting an ongoing "marathon" and comparing it to financial planning. During the same period, Pacific Life used an urban footrace as a metaphor for investment strategies. The young are encouraged to invest for the long haul and to understand foot racing in those terms, however alien they may be to real athletic achievement. In short, the young are targeted by a world of figures and financial advice that promises them riches from intelligently placed, long-term investments. They are constantly tempted not only by instant riches but by the more reassuring notion that sensible, rational steps taken at this stage of their lives will provide handsomely for them to enjoy retirement and even early retirement in admirable wealth and comfort. All this is bolstered by a sense of uniqueness at being Generation X, now the digital generation—as if the historical accident of being born at a fortunate time made them better than the other human beings who preceded them. This culturally condoned arrogance as well as a firm belief in the rewards of rational, long-range planning feed marathon running. Together, these factors help create a large pool of entitled people with the self-assurance necessary to believe in their physical ability and the social conditioning to expect benefits from long-range planning. One result is the extensive training (usually a minimum of fifteen weeks for a seasoned runner and at least twenty for a novice) needed to run a successful marathon. Only a general mind-set that is fixated on future, highly personalized rewards could call forth the masses who participate in today's marathon.

The city itself, whether Chicago or elsewhere, consciously targets these young professionals. American cities began to stage a recovery in the 1990s—that is, concurrently with the second running boom—and they began to reassert their appeal to the suburban population, especially to the young (and still childless) and the elderly (and free of their child-raising duties), who, in the case of young people, either went directly to or stayed in the city after graduation or, in the case of older people, returned to the city to enjoy its cultural vitality. It was during this time of recovery that Chicago, after a period of uncertainty and decline, began to recover momentum. The city's policy of sponsoring numerous free public spectacles and of converting the lakefront into a cultural and sports playground has given urban life a new attraction that has brought about the redevelopment of former fading neighborhoods. In this new context of celebration, the marathon figures as both the symbolic and real pursuit of individual pleasure—ironically occurring as a collective activity—and social distinction in the postmodern playground that the successful city has become.

The marathon also serves as the focus of broader, more socially conscious endeavors. It ignites the enthusiasm of numerous altruists who tie the marathon to their personal efforts to raise funds for specific causes. Charity fundraising has become a significant aspect of the event. Here, marathoning appeals to deep, enduring archetypes—to notions of sacrifice and pain to achieve a noble cause. In a sense, the marathoners become their own sacrifice: their pain and their agony are the offering that will somehow placate the forces of illness; their heroic deeds become in some way instrumental in effecting a cure. On a more practical level, they raise money to promote further research or aid in the care of the suffering patients they have sponsored or commemorated; they heighten public consciousness about the impact of specific diseases or conditions and the need for funding to fight them. The marathon gives them the opportunity for drama and heroism in what could be perceived more mundanely as routine fundraising. It confers an epic dimension on their strivings while simultaneously personalizing their efforts as they are directed to help individuals with names and personalities, often children engaged in a genuine struggle for survival. The marathon thus becomes a metaphor of each stricken individual's situation. The physical efforts of the runners meld with the struggle of each patient. In short, the runners' efforts are exorcisms of illness and death and a commemoration of those who could not be saved. This commemoration is in itself a mitigated triumph over death. The marathon from this perspective taps deep resources of personal generosity and the abiding goodness and selflessness people feel within themselves, and allows them to exteriorize these qualities in a physically dramatic fashion that permits identification with less fortunate human beings.

Perhaps the single most long-term contributions to marathon growth are those measures, legal and social, that have led to the inclusion of women in races. Women most likely will soon constitute the majority of U.S. marathon fields. The inclusion of women into running in general and marathoning in particular is recent. In the late 1960s, women were still crashing the Boston Marathon. Although there was never any official discrimination against women in the Chicago Marathon, the women's fields were initially significantly smaller than the men's. Today, the evidence of this historical sexism is glaringly evident among older runners where, in the veterans category, men often outnumber women by about five to one. What is far more striking and indicative of the successful integration of women into the race is that the field of women in their twenties has now begun to outnumber the men's for the first time in marathon history. The same numerical superiority is not evident for women in their thirties, although the drop-off rate (not overwhelming) may be attributed to deferred childbearing and child raising. What remains clear, however, is that young, professional women see marathoning as a recreational option. It is worth recalling that the women's marathon was only officially included in the Olympics in 1984. Women who were born in that year have now reached the younger age groups of marathon competition. That factor alone may be significant in their numerical superiority in the 20–24 and 25–29 age groups.[15] Younger women benefit from the battles fought by their older predecessors whose victory to be part of marathon competition was so complete that the new generation is often unaware that their prerogatives were ever contested. A new sense of equality as well as a more athletic conception of the female body than the hourglass, Marilyn-Monroe physique[16] allow female runners easy psychological and official access to marathon participation. The outstanding achievements of recent women champions in a race only a few decades ago thought to be beyond the physical abilities of women provide inspiration and confirmation for younger women runners. No woman has to ask herself if the marathon is beyond the physical capabilities of her sex, which was the received truth forty years ago. Indeed, in this new affirmative psychological climate, women are now ubiquitous in running events and people the jogging trails in every major urban area. They now dominate most group training programs.[17]

The proliferation of training programs, ranging from the 5K to the marathon, is a new and significant contributing factor to the growth of marathon running. These training programs may be charity related, as in the case of Chicago's official charities; individually initiated, as demonstrated by journalist Eric Zorn's FOOLS;[18] privately conceived, for-profit training programs; or low-cost multioptioned packages offered by running associations such as the Chicago Area Runners Association (CARA) that sponsors training throughout the Chicago area and is often used by charity fundraising groups that do not have their own trainers. Perhaps individuals are seeking an escape from the isolation of the workplace and new options for social bonding with a clearly defined and formidable undertaking in view. These training groups are inspired by the marathon but also feed marathon growth because, as runners in training share their enthusiasm with others, they make many converts along the way, especially when they are viewed as ordinary human beings rather than as top athletes who dedicate their lives to such rigors.

———

In the closing section of this chapter, it seems appropriate to evoke one aspect of the marathon that always held great potential to attract runners—the race's particular liminal or threshold status. By an act of serendipity, this liminal race is also the only race bearing a mythical name rather than an actual distance to identify it.[19] Unlike any lesser race, the marathon is universally viewed as a truly exceptional challenge. Race statistics make it clear that this challenge is highly prized. In this regard, racing fields from Chicago, which are typical of other urban areas, become highly informative. The Chicago area hosts many dozens of races annually. These range in distance from the 5K to the 50K. Running fields vary with the popularity of given races, but 5Ks like the Why Me Race Against Breast Cancer draw thousands of runners. The 2003 LaSalle Bank's Shamrock Shuffle saw nearly 16,000 finishers, making it the world's largest 8K. The 2003 Chicago Half-Marathon (not even a regional circuit race) saw 5,658 finishers. The 2003 LaSalle Bank Chicago Marathon had 40,000 registrants and some 33,000 finishers—making it the world's third- or fourth-largest marathon, depending on whether one chooses to use registrants or finishers as the defining statistical measure. Most strikingly, the 2003 Chicago Lakefront 50K had only slightly over 120 finishers—an extraordinary falloff from marathon participation.

Although it is clear that races in Chicago draw huge fields of runners, there is an obvious hierarchy. The marathon dominates all other races in its power to register tens of thousands of participants. The 50K, on the other hand, distinguishes itself by its inability to attract more than a handful of competitors. In fact, its numbers resemble more closely participation in marathons before the running boom of the 1980s. What can explain this extraordinary drop-off in numbers in a race that is only some eight kilometers longer than the marathon? Why does the marathon attract more runners than races that are clearly less demanding—in fact, a great deal easier for the ever-increasing numbers of walkers, joggers, and noncompetitive runners who now populate the marathon? As indicated above, these statistics are not confined to the Chicago area. Rather, they illustrate a general trend: hearty registration in races shorter than the marathon, immense marathon registration, and infinitesimal participation at longer distances.

Possibly the best explanation for this otherwise baffling success is the threshold or liminal nature of the marathon. Although the classical history of the marathon would seem to be largely the stuff of nineteenth century fantasy, its association with the heroic death of the runner has considerable significance. All running is physically taxing, but most running, under appropriate circumstances, is healthy. The marathon, as has been stated, is not. From one perspective, running a marathon is an exercise in masochistic stupidity. The human body is not designed to function properly beyond a twenty-mile run. Thereafter, instead of consuming fat and glucose, the body actually cannibalizes itself, using muscle tissue for power through the last agonizing six miles. In more recent medical theory, international endurance expert, sports doctor, and author of *Lore of Running* Tim Noakes speculates that the issue may not be glycogen depletion but rather muscle damage that causes people to "hit the wall." The intense discomfort experienced by runners may be the brain's way of telling them to stop before they damage their muscles (Matt Fitzgerald, 14). Whether one accepts the older hypothesis (glycogen depletion) or the new one, the issue remains the same—the latter stages of the marathon do often involve physical harm to the runner. The marathon is long, unbearably so for most people. It is thus a test of will, of resolution. It is the only massive physical ordeal that most individuals will encounter in their otherwise highly sedentary existence. It is a proof of heroism, a flirtation with and a defiance of death. 5Ks, 10Ks, and even half-marathons are mere trifles when compared to this protracted and agonizing effort that takes the body—and, most emphatically, the mind—beyond the threshold of its natural limits. It not *a* test; it is *the* test. Those who announce that they have run a marathon know that they have made a powerful statement about their will and determination. Substituting a shorter distance would simply not resonate. Conversely, runners seem to realize instinctively that they have no need to go any farther to prove they have passed the ultimate test. Longer distances seem more a testimony to a kind of addiction or obsession. They are superfluous once one has proven oneself in the marathon.

The world public—at least that public wealthy enough to seek out the kind of sports that please it—has shown a growing interest in extreme sports: sky diving, bungee jumping, eco-challenges, and the like. Participation in these sports remains restricted, whatever fascination they hold. Although many of these sports flirt with death, they cannot be staged on a stupendous scale with the same ease as the marathon, which facilitates a mass collective liminal experience. The newer extreme sports also lack the "tradition" so graciously concocted for us by de Coubertin and Bréal. The marathon is ennobled by its classical aura that confers a prestige heavy with the weight of millennia. The stark, epic, and eloquent voices of Greek antiquity—Homer, Herodotus, Xenophon, Sophocles—echo through the centuries and inevitably associate themselves with the word "marathon." The combats of the *Iliad, The March of the Ten Thousand,* the *Histories,* and so many other works are part of the resplendent culture that brought us the tale(s) of Pheidippides. In such a context, the mythic value of the word "marathon," the unintended gift of the children of "gray-eyed Athena," is incalculable. Invented tradition reveals itself as extraordinarily effective in popularizing a sport.

Human beings seem to harbor a need to inflict pain upon themselves—not gratuitously, but to prove that they can surpass the frailty of their bodies, that they are expressions of a sovereign and indomitable will, that they possess a determination powerful enough to defy the limitations of the flesh. Endowed with an imaginary but noble tradition, the marathon, the very evocation of victory even in death, is ideally suited to offer this kind of transcendent ordeal—one that happily involves no harm to others and rarely inflicts lasting damage on the individual participant.

The marathon takes runners past landmarks modern and noteworthy, from dizzying skyscrapers to the historic Chicago Theatre.

two

a brief history
of the chicago marathon

Chicago's marathon grew out of the planning of a small cadre of people devoted to making the race a reality. These individuals brought with them an interest in sports, medicine, the parks, and urbanism. Among them were Wayne Goeldner (physical education director of the Hyde Park YMCA), Sharon Mier (director of women's sports at the Loop Center YWCA), Wendell Miller (founder of Midwest Masters Running Club and member of Club North Shore), Noel Nequin (director of cardiac rehabilitation at the Swedish Covenant Hospital), Bill Robinson (executive director of Friends of the Parks), and Erma Tranter (then a graduate student of urban studies) (Hall, 14). These early enthusiasts soon discovered they faced a major political obstacle in the person of Ed Kelly, then park superintendent. Kelly refused permission to run in the parks or along the lakefront. He apparently clung to the earlier view of runners as undesirables, a near-criminal element.

Fortunately for the birth of the Chicago Marathon, Kelly did not reign supreme. The original organizers contacted Lee Flaherty, owner of Flair Communications and an avid runner himself. Flaherty was politically connected and was able to get then Mayor Daley interested in the marathon. Unfortunately, Daley died in the meantime, but Flaherty and a few others were able to secure a meeting with the new mayor, Bilandic, also a runner. He approved the race and told Kelly to go ahead with the marathon. A permit was then issued and Kelly became a friend of the marathon.

The way had already been prepared because Nequin had succeeded in organizing the Ravenswood Bank Lakefront 10–Mile Run in May 1977. This race far exceeded expectations because it drew over 1,000 runners instead of the 200–300 expected (Chicago Marathon, "History"). Mayor Bilandic and his wife actually handed out medals at this event. This combination of political sanction and popular support buoyed the confidence of the founders of the marathon, for it confirmed that long-distance running did have a powerful appeal.

Perhaps characteristic of the naïveté of the times, the original founders of the marathon had no sponsor—something that greatly surprised Flaherty. When no sponsor came forward, Flaherty put up the money and the Mayor Daley Marathon took place on September 25, 1977. Interestingly, the marathon drew 4,200 runners and saw 2,128 finishers (Chicago Marathon, "History"), which made it one of the nation's largest marathon at its very inception. Thus, even early on, Chicago was relatively well poised to vie for dominance in American marathon running. In 2000, it would be the nation's second largest after New York's. Chicago's first marathon was a costly endeavor for Flaherty; it fell $65,000 short, and he paid the expenses.

The 1978 marathon illustrated the tensions between business sponsorship and runners. The first marathon had been viewed as a people's race, launched by running enthusiasts and idealists. It drew on the earlier tradition of marathon running that was very informal and makeshift. Flaherty, who was footing the bill, had his own ideas as to how the race should be run. He wanted higher fees: $10 instead of $5 and a later starting time, from 8:30 to 10:30 A.M. This meant a real clash of interests and principle. Most runners had emerged from a background of shoestring budgets and volunteerism. A doubling of fees (and $10 was worth a great deal more in 1978) meant a departure from a democratic race, open to those of very modest means. The change in time was fraught with medical risk: the possibility of a late start on a warm September day posed the danger of severe heat exhaustion, even death. To Flaherty, a later start would enjoy better viewership.

Thus, even early in the history of the Chicago Marathon, business interests had already quashed the more social orientation of its idealistic founders. Although today's marathon treats its participants with great concern, its orientation is very different from a "people's marathon." It is a business offering a quality product aimed to please its clientele, but not an event whose primary concern envisages any societal mandate.

But the marathon's disgruntled founders did not passively accept the dominance of business interests. The 1978 dispute spurred them to create the Chicago Area Runners Association (CARA), which sought to approach running from the runner's perspective; that is, to ensure that races met certain essential standards of quality, such as proper water stations and rational starting times. CARA enjoyed enormous success and became the runners' umbrella organization for the Chicago area, but, at the time of Chicago's second marathon, it remained a small organization of dissident idealists (or realists, if one considers the health of runners the primary concern). CARA runners did participate in the 1978 marathon, but with 500 to 2,000 runners (depending on one's sources) wearing black armbands. This race was still called the Mayor Daley Marathon and was sponsored by Flaherty. The heat took its toll: some 300 runners were treated for heat exhaustion and blisters; ten were hospitalized. Despite the temperature problems, the race was a success, although Flaherty was criticized by the media for crass over-commercialization. The rift between CARA and the marathon endured for some years, although, eventually, mutual interest would lead them to cooperate.

In 1979, Beatrice Foods became the race sponsor, providing the deep pockets needed to ensure the race's financial stability. Political régimes had changed. Jane Byrne had ousted Bilandic as mayor, and she wanted a race that presented Chicago as an international city. Thus, with solid corporate backing and a new, ambitious mayoral administration, the race was renamed, at Flaherty's suggestion, "America's

Marathon."[1] But the 1979 and 1980 marathons remained the people's marathon in the sense that they were largely mass gatherings of amateur runners. Rain diminished participation in the former, and the finish times of the latter, though better than the year before, were modest by racing standards. Chicago was simply not a world-class marathon in performance; it could not yet attract the field of professionals needed to change its image.

This situation changed rather suddenly with the appointment of Bob Bright as race director in 1982. Bright, who was removed in 1988 for using marathon funds for his own purposes (dog sledding in Alaska; Hall, 17), had the necessary funding to recruit top athletes. In 1982, the greatly enhanced prize money at Bright's disposal led to world-class times with Greg Meyer's 2:10:59 and Nancy Contz's 2:33:23. Meyer was the last native-born American male to win the race. Thereafter, excellent runners from throughout world came to Chicago. In 1983, part of a field of 7,000 participants, Joe Nizau of Kenya and Rosa Mota of Portugal set new course records. Thus, by the early 1980s, Chicago had already achieved prominence as one of America's most important marathons. In 1984, Beatrice doubled its purse to $250,000, exceeding New York's by $50,000. Steve Jones, a Welsh RAF plane mechanic, obligingly broke the world record in 2:08:05 and received a handsome cash award of $174,000, although his record stood for only a month. Jones remarked that when he was 100 yards from the finish line, he "looked up at the time with the seconds ticking off and with the wind blowing in my face I gave it one final burst because I felt the record was in my grasp" (UPI, October 22, 1984). Rosa Mota once again broke the woman's course record. Mota remarked, "My only concern was to go as fast as I could and I was rewarded with my best personal marathon record" (UPI, October 22, 1984).

This race marked the increasing rivalry between New York and Chicago. Both marathons were trying to recruit the best runners, and Chicago sometimes met with rejection. In the case of Italy's Giuseppi Gerbi, Bright claimed that the former had chosen New York because he felt that he had a good chance of third there as opposed to fifth in Chicago (Rosenthal). He gave the impression he was winning the struggle with Lebow: "'It's not totally apparent now,' Bright said. 'There is no formula for instant success. But the tables are turning. If we can run a high-caliber race each year, maybe they will keep turning'" (Rosenthal).

The 1985 America's Marathon was particularly impressive. Jones returned to break his own record but missed a new world record by two seconds. Jones apparently did not realize how close he was. "About halfway down the stretch, I saw the clock and I realized it was so close, within my grasp. I didn't know how fast I had to run" (McDill, October 21, 1985). Joan Benoit Samuelson, recruited with great calculation by Bright, set the course record with 2:21:21, which remained the woman's course record until 2001 and the women's American record until Deena Kastor broke it in 2003. As Philip Hersh wrote, "No invitational marathon ever had assembled a women's field like the 1985 America's Marathon/Chicago: Joan Benoit Samuelson, winner of the debut Olympic women's marathon in 1984; Rosa Mota, 1983–84 Chicago champion and Olympic bronze medallist; and Ingrid Kristiansen of Norway, fourth at the Olympics, who had set a world record of 2:21:06 earlier in 1985 at London" (Hersh, "9th Chicago Marathon," 10).

Bright, in his friendly rivalry with Lebow, was determined to use the power of capital to outspend and outrecruit New York. Benoit acknowledged this transformation after her 1985 victory by stating that "Beatrice has turned America's Marathon into the world's marathon. This is where the competition is" (Treadwell, 64). Despite Benoit's superlative performance, she was never to break the 2:20:00 barrier. Chicago had proven her best try.

The 1986 race was a bit anticlimactic in comparison with 1985's. Although a field of 8,000 participated with some forty world-class marathoners among them, the times were slower than the previous year's. Toshihiko Seko finished in 2:08:27 and Ingrid Kristiansen in 2:27:08 despite relatively good running conditions (overcast skies and temperatures in the mid-fifties). Seko was nonetheless particularly pleased because he had dedicated the race to his coach, Kiyoshi Nakamura, who had drowned in a fishing accident in 1985. "This race was Mr. Nakamura's dream," Seko asserted. "I was running it with him" (Litke). Kristiansen felt that she had lost her concentration and would have run harder had Joan Benoit Samuelson, who was sidelined by injuries, been there (Litke). Unfortunately, bad news was just over the horizon: Beatrice, that most generous of sponsors, was about to withdraw from the marathon.

Before discussing the vacuum created by Beatrice's departure, it is worth remarking just how significant a wealthy sponsor is to a race. Chicago had no trouble drawing impressive numbers of runners in the late 1970s and 1980s, but it simply could not become a world-class race without an infusion of capital from a powerful sponsor. Flair Communications could not afford to foot the kind of bill it took to draw elite runners. Chicago, in this sense, was no different from other emerging marathons; in fact, it was typical. Even proud Boston would have to boost its prize money. New York relied on solid and savvy sponsorship such as Avon to grow to its world-class status. The Paris Marathon has moved from city ownership to private corporate ownership with heavy reliance on corporate sponsors. Examples to this effect can be cited ad infinitum. The truth is, the word's fastest runners, by and large, are drawn to the highest fees. There is nothing shocking about this; it mirrors all other professional sports. But what occurred in the late 1970s and early 1980s was twofold. The marathon emerged simultaneously as a mass-participation sport and as a professional sport. Suddenly, marathon champions could actually envisage making a living from their running—something largely unthinkable prior to this. Corporate sponsorship would allow a class of professional athletes to flourish, and this elite segment of runners would be international. The practical result would be the near disappearance of American males as victors of major marathons. The overall picture, which is utterly typical of Chicago, is really one of a dual race: masses of amateurs in the thousands and a tiny handful of professional elite men and women who have any real hopes of placing. The infusion of capital makes the simultaneity of the modern marathon possible, allowing it to be at once a minority competition and a mass happening.

In 1987, Beatrice Foods dropped America's Marathon to sponsor the Western Open golf tournament, and the former literally ceased to exist. In its place was a half-marathon held on October 25 without prize money. The gracious Steve Jones, twice victor of America's Marathon, returned to run and win the race in 1:04:20; Kim Ballentine won the women's division in 1:18:20. Without financial backing, Chicago was temporarily eliminated from world status competition.

But Chicago revived immediately the following year when the Heileman Brewing Company took over as sponsor. The race became the Old Style Chicago Marathon and saw a 2:08:57 victory by Alejandro Cruz, who broke the Mexican national record with his time. Lisa Weidenbach won in 2:29:17, the fifth American woman to break the 2:30 barrier. The women's story for 1988 was particularly interesting: the first three had all been passed over for the Olympic Games in Seoul. Weidenbach was the only one not to complain about her exclusion; she had placed fourth in the U.S. trials. Second-place Emma Scaunich of Bologna was still trying to figure out why the Italian Federation had not selected her. Alternate Paula Fudge of the U.K. had been deprived of the chance to substitute for her twin and qualifier Ann Ford, who had failed to inform her twin sister in sufficient time that an injury would keep her from competition. With too little time to prepare, Fudge had chosen Chicago. In a salute to the sponsor and to her competitors, Weidenbach remarked, "I think the three of us should go home and drink a lot of Old Styles"(Hersh, "Top 3 Women's Finishers," 16).

For the 1988 race, journalist Philip Hersh analyzed in some detail Chicago's relatively poor spectator turnout in comparison with Boston and New York (Hersh, "Civic Apathy"). He pointed out that few in the city cared about the marathon and that even race founder Lee Flaherty admitted, "It's still not happening." Hersh argued that the problem with Chicago was that two-thirds of the race happened outside populous neighborhoods. Citing Tony Reavis, who had covered several marathons for Chicago, Hersh argued in favor of putting the marathon where people lived. Reavis remarked, "Lake Shore Drive is wide open and fine for TV, but who lives there?" Hersh argued against restricting the marathon to the city and perhaps starting it in Highland Park (a northern suburb). Hersh also cited Lebow, who said that in New York, they bring the race to the people. Hersh presented New York's five-borough marathon (as opposed to the former loop course in Central Park) as an expression of this commitment. Hersh also interviewed Greg Meyer, a midwesterner and former Chicago champion, who opined that the Midwest was more blue-collar and more interested in football, baseball, and basketball. He felt that when people in the neighborhoods came home from work, they didn't see running as a hobby, and that this attitude spilled over even to people with white-collar jobs. Unlike Boston, Chicagoans did not see runners as real athletes. Reavis confirmed Meyer's evaluation, remarking, "Chicago is still a meat-and-potatoes town. Subtle sports don't sell real well here." Hersh also noted that the Chicago Area Runners Association had grown out of a dispute between the local running community and marathon organizers, whereas the New York Road Runners had staged the New York City Marathon only after twelve years of prior existence.

Hersh's analysis indicates the spectator support problems that bedeviled the Chicago Marathon throughout more than half its history. The race was never transformed into a point-to-point course starting in the northern suburbs as suggested in his article. For one thing, that would have repudiated any sense of a course that celebrated the city proper. Indeed, the current buckle race remains closer in spirit to New York's five-borough model, although Hersh alluded to it to argue for the suburban strategy. The upsurge in spectator interest and citywide support that became apparent by the late 1990s surely reflects in part demographic shifts in the city; the white-collar neighborhoods of Lincoln Park and Lakeview provide a substantial running population for the marathon. The attention the race now draws has finally established it as a genuine city event, but population gaps between some of the neighborhoods in the southern portions of the course still leave empty places even with a million spectators.

In 1989, a year that saw particularly warm, humid weather for the race, registration continued to increase, with 8,529 starters (Chicago Marathon, "History"). The impact on the male runners was obvious; Paul Davies-Hale finished in 2:11:25, the slowest time since 1981. The weather, however, did not stop Lisa Weidenbach, who won the women's race with a personal best of 2:28:15 to become the first repeat winner in the marathon's twelve-year history. Weidenbach attributed her taking the lead to the support of family and friends. Weidenbach remarked, "They were corralled at the 18–mile mark and that's where I had a surge of adrenaline and took the lead" (Young, 11). Weidenbach, though reluctant to plug a product, stated that Gatorade provided needed sugar at the twenty-mile mark: "without it, I think I'd still be chugging to the finish line" (Young, 11).

Chicago that year had not been selected for random drug testing by the U.S. track federation, something that bothered race director Tim Murphy, given the $350,000 purse. He announced his intent to test independently if testing were not guaranteed for the 1990 race (Hersh and Young). This lack of testing underscores that marathoning wasn't yet understood properly as a big-time sport even by professional running associations. The problem of crowd support also continued from 1988, as "spectator interest in the race remained occasional at best" (Hersh and Young, 11).

The 1990 race featured a dramatic finish-line duel between Antoni

Niemczak of Poland and winner Martin Pitayo of Mexico (2:09:41) with only 0.49 seconds separating the two (Hersh, "Marathons Need Finishing Kick"). Despite the relative weakness of the field, the race even confounded Hersh's own dire predictions—to the journalist's satisfaction. Aurora Cunha took first place among the women with 2:30:11. The race was nonetheless plagued by sponsorship problems. The owner of Heileman Brewing Company was witnessing the collapse of his financial empire and was on his way to jail. He paid only half of the agreed-upon $1.2 million to sponsor the race (Hall, 18). The race was able to go on with the help of other sponsors, but it was marred by race founder Lee Flaherty's strong accusations against former race director Bob Bright, who claimed he had a "firm" commitment of $500,000 to stage another race in the fall of 1991, outside city limits, if necessary (Hersh, "Marathons Need Finishing Kick"). Flaherty had accused Bright of financial malfeasance with the seven Chicago marathons he directed. Flaherty also angered the Heileman Brewing Company by announcing prior to the race that it would not be involved in 1991 sponsorship, which turned out to be true despite the company's denials.

A new race director (and current executive race director as of this writing) arrived in 1990, Carey Pinkowski. A native midwesterner from Hammond, Indiana, Pinkowski would eventually be a major actor in enabling the race to realize its potential. In 1990, however, Pinkowski, hampered by a halved budget and involved in the early process of building strong alliances with the local running community, was just learning the ropes of race management. All was not smooth sailing. The diminished race purse meant that the New York/Chicago rivalry had temporarily ended in victory for New York, which Hersh predicted "will be overrun with Olympic medallists, world champions and top-ranked runners next Sunday" (Hersh, "Problems Keeping Marathon," 5). Pinkowski did heal the gap with CARA (Chicago Marathon, "History"), but he took a lot a flack from professional runners prior to the race. Two-time champion Lisa Weidenbach was particularly critical, stating, "I think Carey Pinkowski lacks the skills to deal with elite athletes . . . I personally was turned off by his treatment. When I call him, he makes me feel like I'm wasting his time" (Hersh, "Problems Keeping Marathon," 5). Weidenbach, however, tempered her criticism by adding, "It's not all his fault. Carey has too many responsibilities. He has taken over the jobs of two or three people" (Hersh, "Problems Keeping

Marathon," 5). Lisa Kindelan also dropped out of the Chicago Marathon in protest of treatment by Pinkowski, according to Weidenbach. There were complaints about not following through and about money, which, given the sponsorship problems, would have limited any race director's abilities to make commitments. In any event, Pinkowski disagreed with Weidenbach's view that he had been insufficiently active in pursuing elite athletes. In January 2005, he remarked to me that he was forced to slash all the frills (including prize purses and parties) for the 1990 race; he could not meet Weidenbach's financial demands. He also noted that Hersh interviewed some fifteen athletes for that race but only presented the views of Weidenbach and her friend Kindelan. Weidenbach went off to Japan to run a marathon for a higher fee, and then returned to run the 5K that was held in conjunction with the Chicago Marathon. Pinkowski's current success both in selecting talented relative unknowns as marathoners and in modifying recruitment policies to promote a faster race suggests more the quandary of a young director in a difficult situation beyond his control than any professional ineptitude. In 1990, Pinkowski displayed his talents as a healer of the breach between marathon officials and CARA. His talents as a recruiter would become evident later.

In 1991, Heileman Brewing Company was no longer a sponsor, and prize money was scarce (a mere $7,500 for the male and female winners versus $30,000 the previous year). The times for both the male and female winners under such circumstances were the slowest since 1981. On the other hand, Pinkowski was able to recruit Joseildo Silva of Brazil, who won in 2:14:13. Although the time was not impressive, Silva was at the time an undiscovered runner, who could at least set a credible pace when the competitive field was severely diminished by the meager purse. Silva was actually quite perplexed by the lack of competition, which he had been counting on to push him to a better time. In fact, he remarked, "Without competition, I couldn't run fast" (Johnson, "Silva Wins," 11). He apparently didn't realize the impact of diminished sponsorship.

Journalist Hersh, who clearly put the blame for the race's eclipse on lack of money, once again examined the sponsorship crisis. "Chicago's race is now poorer, in terms of prize money, than the Twin Cities and Columbus Marathons, which offer $200,000 and $145,000 respectively" (Hersh and Johnson, 1). Hersh referred to Flaherty, who mentioned some ten sponsors now handling the marathon. Hersh also cited Lebow's assertion that Flaherty's relentless attacks on Bob Bright, fired after 1988, had also harmed the search for sponsors. Hersh cited Italian track and field expert Gianni Merlo who spoke of Chicago's attempt to buy tradition. In the latter's analysis, that lasts as long as the buyer has money, whereas places like New York already possess it. Amby Burfoot, also cited by Hersh, remarked that, "In some regards, Chicago seems to be backpedaling, and that is a shame" (Hersh and Johnson, 1). Hersh concluded with the grim observation, "To the elite marathoning world, the race has died already. Race organizers insist reports of its demise are premature" (Hersh and Johnson, 1). Obviously, the greatness and stature of Chicago were very much in play.

In 1992, the marathon was still without major sponsorship, and Pinkowski had to use all his talents just to get passable runners. The results reflected the limited budget with the male winner, Jose Cesar De Souza, finishing in 2:16:14, and the female champion, Linda Sommers, in 2:37:41, the slowest times since 1981. Journalist Len Ziehm noted that although the marathon lacked sponsorship dollars and national exposure, this would be the first race to have Spanish radio coverage (Ziehm, "Flaherty May Reveal Future"). Both the *Chicago Tribune* and the *Chicago Sun-Times* noted the surprise caused by Eddy Hellybuyck, hired as a rabbit, who took third place (Hanna, "Top Marathon Finishers"; Ziehm, "Cashing In"). Despite the poor sponsorship situation, the race was well attended with a field of 8,214 runners (Chicago Marathon, "History").

The following year, 1993, was a very significant one for the Chicago Marathon. Flaherty decided to sell the marathon. Major Events, Inc., headed by Chris Devine, who, like Flaherty, was a marathon runner, purchased it. Devine would bring in what was to become the most significant sponsor—and later owner—of the race, LaSalle Banks,[2] which, with a coalition of lesser sponsors, was able to up the prize money to $20,000 for the winners. Journalist Len Ziehm attributed the larger purse to the efforts of Pinkowski, Tom Cooney, and Robert McAuliff, marketing director of Major Events (Ziehm, "It's a Time-Tested Marathon"). The race itself was held after a three-inch snowfall with continuing intermittent snow and mid-thirties temperatures throughout the day. Times were understandably modest, although Brazilian victor Luiz Antonio Dos Santos's 2:13:14 represented the best time since 1990, as did Finnish women's victor Ritva Lemettinen's 2:33:18. Unfortunately, the latter was disqualified for being illegally paced by men (a violation of U.S. Track and Field Rule 66)—one of Pinkowski's tougher decisions. Lemettinen regained her prize money on appeal, and the rule was later changed as a result of the controversy. Both victors suffered from the cold. Dos Santos's interpreter indicated that he was very cold and that "he put on unusual clothes. He never wore that much before" (Hanna, "Brazilian, Finn Kick," 11). Lemettinen was reported to have remarked that she might not come back because of the weather (Hanna, "Brazilian, Finn Kick"); however, she told reporter Bob Richards, "In Finland we have had weather like this for two weeks already . . . I am used to it" (Richards, "Dos Santos Snow Job," 2).

By 1994, the combination of Pinkowski's skilled race management and the greater economic role of LaSalle, which became title sponsor in that year, produced an upsurge in what was now called the LaSalle Bank Chicago Marathon. The bank had signed a three-year agreement as title sponsor in July, which helped double the purse to $200,000 and enabled Pinkowski to recruit aggressively (Johnson, "Chicago Marathon Can Bank"). The winner's prize was increased 50 percent to $30,000, and the field included Boston Marathon record holder Cosmas Ndeti (2:07:15), who was eying the world record. Clearly, the male field was outstanding. The runners were also there in force—some 12,000 starters for a new course beginning in Grant Park (Caro). Chicago had recovered its world status.

Victors Luiz Antonio Dos Santos (2:11:16) and Kristy Johnston (2:31:34) did not dazzle anyone with their times. As reporter Hersh pointed out, there were already twenty-five men's times as fast or faster than Dos Santos's; likewise, Johnston's was only the twentieth fastest by a woman (Hersh, "Thorns, Not Laurel Wreath"). Worse, Cosmas Ndeti, who had been paid $50,000 to run in hopes of challenging the world record of 2:06:50, had done no such thing. Hersh also expressed his exasperation with local television coverage, pointing out that only 24 of the 131 minutes of actual race coverage had been devoted to Dos Santos. He noted that "the rest of the time was filled with vapid features on local color and back-in-the-pack runners, sinfully stupid side-of-course interviews . . . and commercials" (Hersh, "Thorns, Not Laurel Wreath," 8)

A new challenge for the Chicago Marathon was posed by the Olympic trials, which made it difficult to attract world-class runners in 1995. Consequently, LaSalle and the other sponsors supplied total prize money of $250,000, upping the winner's purse from $30,000 to $35,000. The registered runners were numerous, increasing to 13,000 for the marathon and 5K. The marathon had 8,641 finishers and the 5K had 2,563. Eamon Martin won over a diminished field in an exciting finish during which he dashed past Carlos Bautista in the last 200 yards for a 2:11:18 victory. Martin had used his track experience in the 5K and 10K to snatch victory from Bautista (Johnson, "'Sprint' Key"). Ritva Lemettinen won her second Chicago victory in 2:28:27 with only thirty-five men ahead of her; she dominated the women's field from nearly the start (Ziehm, "Lemettinen Left All Alone"). Local runner, seventy-five-year-old Warren Utes, was clearly eyeing the national record for his age group when interviewed (Richards, "Marathoner"), and he followed through with his seventh national record with 3:18:07 (Chicago Marathon, "History"). Clearly, the size of the field suggested that the race was once again growing to huge proportions, and that Chicago was positioning itself to challenge for world supremacy.

At this point in the race's history, it was evident that Pinkowski had emerged as a successful race director. Reporter K. C. Johnson compared the executive race director to the late Fred Lebow, whom the reporter saw as a gregarious, tireless promoter of New York City's marathon. In contrast, Johnson quoted Pinkowski, who described himself as "an operational guy at heart" (Johnson, "Marathon Director Waits," 7). The reporter stressed Pinkowski's success at building a field, quoting Los Angeles Marathon champion Mark Plaatjes who said, "The main thing Carey does well is put the field together with chemistry. . . . In most of his fields, many runners have a chance to win. That's very difficult to do, but since Carey ran himself and is a fan of the sport, he can relate" (Johnson, "Marathon Director Waits," 7).

In 1996, LaSalle took the final step in sponsorship—it bought the race from Major Events and increased the purse to $275,000. With its long-term commitment, LaSalle had restored the financial underpinnings that had made the marathon great during the Beatrice period. The richer purses elicited improved male performance: Paul Evans won in 2:08:52, the eighth-fastest time in the world for that year. The unusually tall Marion Sutton won the women's race in 2:30:41. Sutton was exceptionally pleased because she had been passed over for the British

Olympic team even though she had beaten one of the women chosen to represent her country. Her performance left no doubts about her abilities and was also her personal best (Johnson, "Sutton Avenges"). Evans's victory was not without drama. Around the twenty-one-mile mark, he became disoriented and didn't know which way to turn. He overcame the problem and logged the best race time since 1986 (Nickel).

Local support was also increasing. The feud with CARA had ended and that organization initiated marathon-training classes that year. Enrollment reached nearly 700. Financially and socially, the marathon was in an extraordinary position. As Pinkowski stated at the time, "We've accomplished what we set out to do five years ago. We've rebuilt from the ground up. We're all the way back" (Ziehm, "Chicago Marathon Gets 10–Year Deal," 36).

By 1997, there could be no doubt that the marathon had regained its former stature; it was a "return to the golden days," as Hersh's prerace article trumpeted (Hersh, "Return to the Golden Days," 12). Prize monies were increased to $300,000, with an additional $197,000 in time bonuses—a special Chicago/Pinkowski feature that rewards exceptional time performances even when runners fail to place. This incentive drew a very strong field that would be led by Pinkowski discovery, Khalid Khannouchi, who won in 2:07:10, setting course, debut, and North American records in the process. Khannouchi took home the $50,000 winner's purse plus an additional $50,000 in bonuses. His time actually "exorcised the ghost" of marathons past. Since assuming the race directorship, Pinkowski had constantly heard about Steve Jones's great 1985 time. Khannouchi had beaten Jones by three seconds (Johnson, Hersh, and Myslenski).

American men actually performed extremely well in this race: Jerry Lawson finished in 2:09:35, breaking the American record he had set in Chicago the year before, and Todd Williams finished in 2:11:17. The quality of the male field was evident in that five men had arrived in less than 2:09 and eight under 2:10. This kind of elite male performance signaled the complete return of Chicago to world-class status. Marion Sutton, despite a nosebleed, also won again, finishing under 2:30 in a personal best of 2:29:03. The sub-2:30 performance brought her a $4,000 bonus. The registrants and finishers signaled the ever-growing popularity of the Chicago Marathon: 16,372 signed up and 14,322 completed the race.

Joan Benoit Samuelson also returned to Chicago, the scene of her greatest marathon time triumph (the women's American record of 2:21:21 achieved in 1981 and still holding strong in 1997), in an attempt to break the American women's masters record. Unfortunately, a cramp dashed her hopes. Benoit Samuelson described the pain as feeling "like a bullet had gone right through my calf" (Johnson, Hersh, and Myslenski, 6). She nonetheless finished with her typical pluck and promised to return, which she did both as a commentator and participant.

The following year, 1998, once again saw outstanding times and record participation. Ondoro Osoro of Kenya won the race in 2:06:04, garnering several records: world debut, course, and Kenyan and North American national records with the third-fastest performance in history. Osoro, who had not expected to win, announced "I am a lucky man today" (Myslenski, "It Turns Out," 3). He earned $105,000 with a time bonus, profiting from an increase of nearly 500 percent in purses over the past few years. Four male runners finished in less than 2:08. The female competition was also particularly exciting with Kenyan Joyce Chepchumba's 2:23:57 victory—it was the fourth-fastest women's time in 1998. Chepchumba's winnings totaled a hefty $85,000, again a substantial increase of award money from just a few years earlier.

That year's race saw a continuing increase in registrants—17,731 runners started the race and 17,204 completed it. This time, the race used the ChampionChip, a relatively new device in running, to ensure exact times and competition statistics, thus maintaining itself on the cutting edge of the technological front. The now-ubiquitous chip was introduced to allow runners to know the actual time it took them to complete the course rather than the time from the official start of the race. The new device recorded the times of nearly 3,000 more finishers than the previous year.

The 1998 race unfortunately brought the marathon's first death: Kelly Barrett, a forty-three-year-old mother of three and Chicago Heights native. Barrett died from "an irregular heartbeat caused by a combination of unusually small coronary arteries and imbalance of sodium and potassium in her bloodstream" (Manier and Deardorff, 1). She was properly trained; ironically, drinking too much water may have triggered her condition. The death renewed a long debate about marathon safety.[3] As of 1998, there had been only four or five road-race runner deaths out of some 6.3 million finishers (Manier and Deardorff). The victim's brother understandably expressed his anger at the loss of his sister, but noted marathon writer Hal Higdon pointed out the health benefits, such as losing weight and smoking cessation, that often accompany marathon training. David Patt of CARA emphasized proper training before attempting the race (Manier and Deardorff).

The 1999 race was the most triumphant of all Chicago marathons to date, both in numbers of participants and achievements. Khalid Khannouchi broke the world record with an astounding 2:05:42. Khannouchi had not been initially optimistic; taking into account the cold and windy weather, he remarked, "I thought maybe I could run 2:07. I didn't think there was any way there would be a world best today" (Hamel, "Khannouchi Blows Past," 3). He actually had been behind for most of the race and only caught the lead runner, Moses Tanui, at mile 25. Tanui placed a very credible second in a deep professional field. American David Morris finished fourth in 2:09:32 with an American record for the race. Joyce Chepchumba again won the woman's race. After tripping earlier, she defeated opponent Margaret Okayo by one second, finishing in 2:24:59.

The two winners were richly rewarded: Khannouchi collected $65,000 for his win, a $100,000 bonus for his world record, and a new Volkswagen Beetle (VW supplies the race's pace cars). Chepchumba with her combined winner's prize and time bonus won $80,000. The overall prize money—$715,200—was the largest in marathon history, indicating once again the importance of capital in making a truly successful marathon (Chicago Marathon, "History").

Numerically, the race was also an incontestable success—29,256 runners registered, 25,145 actually started, and 24,654 finished. More than 2,000 international runners participated, and spectators numbered over 800,000. The century thus closed on a marathon that was utterly triumphant—the fastest in the world, with a deep elite field and tens of thousands of runners. The Chicago marathon was truly a mass phenomenon.

The 2000 marathon, though less spectacular in records, drew a vast field of 27,956 finishers, making it the fourth-biggest marathon in history, once again confirming that Chicago's growth was not a momentary flash in the pan. Khalid Khannouchi won his third Chicago Marathon in 2:07:01, but was unable to better his world record. As a recently naturalized American citizen, he was, however, able to beat

David Morris's American race record and achieve an as-yet-unbroken American record. The American field was particularly strong, with four men placing in the top twenty. The new American Khannouchi was seized with emotion. After praying, he picked up the U.S. flag and suddenly sat down and cried with his back against a finish chute barrier. Khannouchi stated, "It's hard to describe what I was feeling . . . I felt a lot of pressure before the race. I hoped I wouldn't have a bad day. I didn't want to embarrass the crowd as a favorite son of Chicago and as an American" (Hersh, "Showing His New Colors," 1).

The woman's race featured an outstanding performance by Catherine Ndereba with 2:21:33, the fastest woman's time in 2000. Ndereba, who shattered her personal record by almost five minutes, felt vindicated after failing to make the Kenyan Olympic team (Garcia). Ndereba also got some help from her friend, Lornah Kiplagat, who led for almost twenty-two miles and also cut almost three minutes off her previous best. The gracious Kiplagat had no complaints and declared, "I am absolutely happy with the results" (Garcia, 3). Eying the future, Ndereba was already contemplating a new world record.

Sadly, the 2000 marathon saw the second death in the twenty-three years of the event's history, when veteran runner Dan Towns, a geologist from Edmond, Oklahoma, collapsed shortly after the twenty-mile mark and died of coronary arteriosclerosis a few hours later at Mercy Hospital. Although he was given on-the-spot aid quite rapidly from medical personnel—a doctor and nurse were running right behind him (Roeper)—it took some time for the ambulance to get through the crowds and no defibrillator was immediately available (Wilson). Journalist Richard Roeper editorialized about the death, reminding people that it was inappropriate for those critical of running to seize upon it: "Fitness does not always mean the same thing as good health; aerobic perfection does not fix a heart problem. The death of Dan Towns, like the relatively few number of deaths that have occurred during previous marathons, is not an indictment of the sport, nor should it be the object of a macabre embrace by anti-runners" (Roeper, 11).

The 2001 race saw an ever-increasing field of some 37,500 registrants and some 950,000 spectators. The size of the crowd once again confirmed the popular support for the race. A victory by pacer Ben Kimondiu (2:08:52) came as a surprise, but the real story was the victory of Catherine "the Great" Ndereba, who managed to overcome the first women's world record under 2:20—which had been set only the previous month in Berlin—with a stunning 2:18:47. Her victory gave Chicago, for the time being, temporary world supremacy with both the men's and women's records. The massive registration marked Chicago as the fastest-growing marathon in the world. The race proved an affirmation of the human spirit as it occurred in the wake of the September 11th terrorist mass murders. It also indicated the extraordinary economic power of the marathon; it temporarily filled the city's hotels, which had been experiencing a catastrophic decline in bookings provoked by the September atrocities.

Kimondiu's victory was especially surprising in that he beat Paul Tergat, who would take the world record two years later at the Berlin Marathon. Kimondiu was somewhat awed by his victory over his fellow Kenyan. He remarked, "I never dreamed of beating him, but I have dreamed of running a big race" (Ziehm, "Stunning Victory," 85). The amazing Ndereba, surprisingly, was not daunted by Takahashi's breaking the 2:20 barrier with a 2:19:46—it was more of an encouragement to her. She stated, "Once this barrier disappeared, I could see women running 2:16 or 2:15" (Hersh, "Amazing Finishes," 1). Her actual race was also a surprise. She ran off pace, especially because she couldn't see the first two mile markers and didn't realize that she was running too slowly. She did the first half in 1:10:14, not the 1:09:53 she had projected. Undeterred, she ran the second half in 1:08:33 (Cheung). Chicago's bragging rights as the world's fastest marathon course were now incontestable.

Sadly, this great day for women's running was marked by the marathon's third fatality, twenty-two-year-old Luke Roach, who died of heat exhaustion only four blocks from the finish line (McCann).

The 2002 marathon—its twenty-fifth anniversary—saw the number of spectators nearly reach a million. It was a rather blustery, cool day, but the level of performance was exceptionally high. Khalid Khannouchi nearly reached his former world-record performance at Chicago with 2:05:56, and Paula Radcliffe set an extraordinary women's world record of 2:17:18. Khannouchi also became the marathon's fourth-time winner. Chicago once again remained home to the men's and women's records, with the women's record broken twice in succeeding years. Radcliffe's record (one minute, twenty-nine seconds faster than Ndereba's time) was the most dramatic improvement since Ingrid Kristiansen had lowered Joan Benoit Samuelson's time by one minute, thirty-seven seconds in 1985 (Ginnetti and Hamel). Women were now logging astonishing times on an annual basis. In fact, even second-place Catherine Ndereba's 2:19:26 was the fourth-fastest women's marathon time in history (Hersh, "Like a Broken Record"). The marathon thus showed that it could now attract massive numbers of finishers and offer a consistently outstanding level of performance. As the *Chicago Tribune* editorialized,

> It's clear that if you want to set a marathon record, or see one set, your best bet is not New York or Boston, which have older and more famous races, but Chicago. That's especially impressive considering that the Chicago Marathon was once so financially troubled that it wasn't held at all in 1987. But since its founding in 1977, it has grown into the third-largest marathon in the world, with 31,584 runners taking part this year. ("The Marathon at Its Peak," 28)

The 2003 Chicago Marathon marked the introduction of a registration cap in September when 40,000 entrants had signed up. The registration prompted *Tribune* reporter Alison Neumer to write a column entitled "Too Popular?" She reported that without the cap, marathon officials estimated there would have been another 10,000 registrants (Neumer). Clearly, there would be limits even to Chicago's quest for the world's largest race. There were challenges and disappointments for the race that year. Khalid Khannouchi, who was nursing an injury and eyeing Olympic competition for the United States, was forced to drop out. In Berlin, shortly preceding the Chicago race, Paul Tergat, who had chosen Berlin over Chicago to avoid competing with Khannouchi, broke the men's world record. By this time, Chicago had already lost the men's record to London—to none other than Khannouchi himself. Khannouchi's absence and Tergat's new record diminished Chicago's hopes of being home to the men's fastest marathon. Paula Radcliffe, who had subsequently broken the women's world record of Chicago 2002, also decided not to compete in Chicago. The men's and women's competitive fields were thus painfully diminished, but Evans Rutto won the race with a men's world record marathon debut time of 2:05:50—still one of the best performances in the world, whether for a beginner or experienced runner. Veteran Russian woman runner Svetlana Zakharova won the women's race in 2:23:07. Generous additional prize money of $115,000 went to thirty-nine American runners who met Olympic trial–qualifying times.

The women's race was particularly dramatic: Russian Svetlana Zakharova overtook the leader, Romanian Constantina Tomescu-Dita, in the twenty-fifth mile. The leaders of the women's field were all Eastern Europeans (Russian, Romanian, and Latvian), prompting journalist Bob Richards to call the race "the unofficial Eastern European 'championships'" (Richards, "Zakharova Finally Catches," 92). The male champion, Rutto, realized that the men's lead runners were not moving quickly enough. He responded with relentless pressure and a final 10K of 29:26 to achieve his record debut run (Freedman, "Beginner's Pluck?").

Tragically, the marathon's fourth death occurred during this race: that of twenty-nine-year-old Rachel Townsend, who had been named academic All-Big Ten in field hockey in 1993–1994 ("What Killed Runner?"). The demise of a physically fit young woman caused great dismay. She was cared for at the medical tent at the finish line, near where she collapsed. Dr. William Roberts, president-elect of the American College of Sports Medicine, who was present at the tent, stated that "the response to this woman was almost instantaneous. . . . They did everything possible to try to save her" ("What Killed Runner?" 3). Later tests would reveal that Townsend had an undiagnosed heart problem.

The race's popularity was in no way diminished in 2004. On this occasion, the entry cap of 40,000 was imposed on August 19th. Spectators once again reached the one million mark. The chief goal this year was to regain the male world record. There was little-to-no hope of achieving this goal with the women's field, which lacked such greats as Paula Radcliffe and Catherine Ndereba. Evans Rutto set out with the men's record in mind; by the half, which he completed in 1:02:18, it seemed that Rutto was well on his way (Freedman, "Encore Performance"). He maintained a fearsome, record-setting pace until mile 20; then, the wind kicked in. As Rutto remarked, "A guy [on the lead truck] kept telling us about the world record, but at 20 miles the wind became very strong. That changed everything" (Ziehm, "Kenya's Rutto," 102). Rutto finished in 2:06:16, but that proved twenty-six seconds slower than his winning time in 2003. Pinkowski concurred with Rutto's analysis, remarking, "I thought he could pull it off, but that's the marathon. You never know when Mother Nature might kick in" (Ziehm, "Kenya's Rutto," 102). Khalid Khannouchi, recently recovered from his injuries, only managed a fifth-place finish, to the disappointment of his many Chicago fans.

The women's race, though far from record pace, was perhaps the most exciting for personal drama. It featured a rematch between defending champion Zakharova and 2003 runner-up Tomescu-Dita, who in that year saw victory snatched from her grasp by a surge from her Russian adversary around mile 25. This time it was different. Tomescu-Dita retained her lead throughout the race and finally won in 2:23:45. The real surprise was that she had won battling a bad cold contracted during a two-day delayed flight from New Delhi, where she had been ordered by the Romanian track federation to run the World Half-Marathon Championships a week earlier (Richards, "No Svet"). Both Richards and Garcia and Freedman reported that this battle with the Romanian government could have cost Tomescu-Dita her right to run Chicago.

The 2005 marathon had an exceptional men's field and an American star for the women's. Given runners like two-time race winner Evans Rutto and second-fastest men's marathon champion Sammy Korir, there was reason to hope for a new world record. This, however, was not to be as the wind once again took its toll. In a Kenyan sweep of all the top ten places, Felix Limo, who won at Rotterdam and Berlin in 2004, took first in 2:07:02, fast enough to earn a $30,000 sub-2:07:30 bonus to add to his $125,000 winner's purse. It was also the fastest marathon time of the year to date. He was followed relatively closely by Benjamin Maiyo (2:07:09) and Daniel Njenga (2:07:14). Limo, who sealed his victory only near the end of the race, declared, "When there is a tough battle, you don't show people you are shy; you show that you are strong" (Richards, "Fellow Kenyans," 114).

The story of the day was Deena Kastor's victory (2:21:25)—an agonizing and costly one. Through mile 18, she ran with 2004 champion Constantina Tomescu-Dita, but she then took the lead in a failed effort to be the first American woman to break 2:20:00. The last five miles were particularly painful, as her feet, legs, and back all fought against her. Only her strength of will allowed her to keep first place by five seconds over a closing Tomescu-Dita. Kastor made it clear how costly the victory was in her postrace remarks. She stated that she was thinking, "This is going to be the ugliest mile of my life," and added, "I kept digging down, digging down and really used the last bit of energy I had" (Myslenski, "Sprinting, Struggling," 2).

The women's field was, nonetheless, largely a very happy one: Kastor, because she had won and become the first U.S. woman to win a major event since Christy Johnston's victory in Chicago in 1994; Dita-Tomescu, because she had achieved a PR and broken the Romanian women's record that she herself had set in London (2:21:30 versus 2:22:05); and fourth-place Colleen De Reuck, because she had demolished the American women's masters record previously held by Jenny Spangler (2:28:40 versus 2:32:29) (Myslenski and McCarthy). Kastor had actually "book-ended" her year with first place in both the spring Shamrock Shuffle 8K and the Chicago Marathon; she had become a city favorite.

For the third year in a row, the race once again saw an early closing of registration, capped at 40,000; it included over 33,000 finishers, making it once again one of the world's very largest marathons. Its times, though not world records, were outstanding. An estimated 1,200,000 spectators lined the course, testifying that the city's population had now fully embraced the marathon.

The Chicago Marathon now seems to have reached its maximum field—barring some adjustment by using waved starts—but becoming the world's largest marathon does not seem necessarily that simple, even with the ever-accelerating pace of race registration. Chicago's challenge—if it is to surpass New York, which surpassed London in 2004—lies in part with its extraordinary number of no-shows at the starting line. Many options are possible to deal with this—including making qualification more difficult and thus more prized through either a lottery or some kind of qualifying times. Both solutions are probably unlikely given the preference for openness and easy accessibility that has marked Chicago's marathon.

The larger questions that loom before Chicago are issues of maturity, prestige, and continuity. The marathon seems to be moving with ease into a situation of greatness. It has survived the crisis of sponsorship, and now, after losing Beatrice Foods and the Heileman Brewing Company, it enjoys solid financial backing with its sponsor and, most important, owner, LaSalle Bank, which is owned in turn by ABN AMRO. The marathon also enjoys full community support; it can count on an enthusiastic populace and city administration that is quite aware of the marathon's benefits and fully committed to its staging. The marathon's prestige draws a worldwide field, but it must compete particularly with London and Berlin for prized records; in addition, it must compete with those cities as well as with New York and Paris to lay claim to the title of the world's largest marathon. However, the Chicago Marathon is now well established. Even if it never becomes the world's largest, even if it only occasionally or never reclaims any world records, it can still be expected to draw tens of thousands of runners who come, not so much because they can expect to be in the same race as world champions, but largely because they are fired up by the thought of participation in an event of such magnitude and because they are aware of Chicago's reputation as a tourist destination of note.

Hordes of runners move under the Gehry pedestrian bridge at Millennium Park. Staging a race for thousands of runners can be a monumental organizational task.

PART II

Staging the Event

Following months of race preparation, executive race director Carey Pinkowski (right) enjoys watching the finish line with Norm Robbins, CEO of LaSalle Bank, and Ed Curran of CBS.

three

the race director

Marathon race directors are a relatively new breed. Even the idea of the existence of a career in marathon race management would have seemed a peculiar notion during most of the twentieth century. Despite the longer history of Boston's marathon, modern marathon race management did not really exist on any significant scale until the 1980s. It became a matter of absolute necessity in the 1990s. Because of the relatively sudden emergence of the marathon as a mass phenomenon, race directors are largely self-made men who found their way into management positions.[1] One might describe New York City's Fred Lebow as the creator of the mass marathon, the first race director of a new phenomenon.[2] Carey Pinkowski, the executive race director of the LaSalle Bank Chicago Marathon, knew the famous Lebow and learned from him. There is thus a certain continuity between the New York and Chicago marathons, despite their friendly rivalry.

Pinkowski's involvement with running began early. He ran high school cross-country and track in Hammond, Indiana—essentially Chicago's far south side. He was twice the Indiana state champion both in the mile and in cross-country (2.5 miles). He attended Villanova University outside Philadelphia on a track and cross-country scholarship. After college in 1983, he actually ran the Chicago Marathon in 2:20:48, taking twenty-fifth place overall. In this sense, he is much closer to London's race director, David Bedford, former world record holder in the 10,000 meters, than Lebow. Pinkowski's performance marked him as a truly exceptional athlete, someone who could understand the marathon as a professional runner rather than a manager who could only grasp vicariously the marathon experience at this highly competitive level. In short, Pinkowski's own background makes him well suited to identify with the aspirations of runners and thus to communicate effectively with elite performers. It also gives him a sharp eye for potential stars, the ability to recruit an as-yet-unnoticed champion.

The proximity of Villanova to New York would be critical in creating an early connection between Pinkowski and the first mass marathon. While still a student, he took the train from the Villanova campus to watch the New York City Marathon in 1977, 1978, 1979, 1980, and 1981—at the very start of the new marathon phenomenon. He met and was "amazed" by the celebrated Fred Lebow. Pinkowski also had the opportunity to meet running greats Bill Rodgers, Gary Bjorkland, and Frank Shorter. He again used the term "amazed" in reference to meeting them and the people behind them. So from the beginning, he was at the very least "a casual observer" of the new kind of marathon that was being created in New York and the other races with which Lebow surrounded it. Pinkowski was already in a sense being schooled by the master. Under Lebow's visionary guidance, he was quickly gaining a managerial perspective that complemented the knowledge he already possessed as a semiprofessional runner.

After college, Pinkowski moved to Oregon to continue training, with an ambition to become a professional runner. He was sponsored by Nike in the early 1980s—the time of such races as the Cascade Run-Off 15K, the Gapiralla 15K (Tampa), the Cherry Blossom Ten Miler, and the Peach Tree Road Race in Atlanta. In fact, he looked at these races and thought he could do them a little bit differently. It is obvious that, although his primary concern was his own running, Pinkowski was evolving into a race manager. Repeating his New York experience of being a "casual observer," he would always come to Chicago to watch the marathon. In 1984, he saw Jones break the world record, saw him just miss a new record in 1985, and watched the race again in 1986. He remained involved with races around Chicago like the Distance Classic and the Turkey Trot. His racing, however, had become hampered by injury problems. He had done all the necessary work to become a professional runner but, although certainly an excellent runner, he was not obtaining the results he needed to continue that difficult path.

It was the intervention of a Villanova friend working for Adidas that would steer Pinkowski in a different direction. The friend asked Pinkowski to help him with promotional consulting work in a regional program, which led to Pinkowski meeting Lee Flaherty of Flair Communication. In 1989, Flaherty approached him about doing an operational piece for the event, working with the community. Things just seemed to click for Pinkowski, who really hit it off with the local community. A year later, in 1990, Flaherty asked Pinkowski to become the race director. In all, Pinkowski worked with Lee Flaherty from 1989 through 1992. In 1993, the marathon was facing severe sponsorship problems, and Chris Devine and Major Events bought the rights. Pinkowski joined this group and got an equity interest and incentives to work on the events; he worked for two years in that position.

Pinkowski's race-building strategy would differ somewhat from Flaherty's. Flaherty had always sought to recruit one sponsor, to make the race a corporate event. He had utilized the resources of Beatrice and the companies under its umbrella and tried to position the event as a piece of corporate advertising or promotion. But Pinkowski felt that the marathon had to have a solid foundation that went beyond a corporation; he fully understood the dire consequences of Beatrice's corporate withdrawal in 1987 and the difficulties that persisted until 1988 with the arrival of Old Style (Heileman Brewing Company) as a single sponsor, which would also withdraw its support.

Pinkowski met with LaSalle as early as 1994 and, even at that time, the corporation was interested in doing something less traditional, more multifaceted, and with a community relations dimension— something that its own employees might get involved in. LaSalle's values in sponsorship would later lead to the kind of community interaction that Pinkowski had sought in order to make the marathon into something extraordinary.

Pinkowski already had clear ideas as to why Chicago was exceptionally well situated for a world-class marathon. First of all, he felt that its geographical location in the center of the Midwest was ideal—not to mention that he considered the city to be "marvelous." Second, he felt that the venues were extraordinary: particularly Grant Park, which is not only beautiful but also spacious enough for the marathon start and finish. (The fact that there is no need to bus people out to the start continues to be a plus.) Furthermore, the diversity of the neighborhoods represented another appealing feature for Pinkowski. Finally, he also appreciated the flatness of the course and its suitability to generate world-record times, as in the case of Jones, Samuelson, Khannouchi, and, more recently, Ndereba and Radcliffe.

Pinkowski was convinced that all the elements were present to make Chicago into a great marathon, but the pieces of the puzzle still had to be fitted together. He was aware that the event lacked an identity. It was originally called the Mayor Daley Marathon, then rather pompously America's Marathon, and later the Old Style Chicago Marathon. There were even a couple of years when Chicago wasn't really connected to the marathon. The first two years Pinkowski worked on the marathon were very difficult. Old Style's sponsorship eliminated schoolchildren because of the relationship with alcohol, and the Heileman Brewing Company was headquartered in La Crosse, Wisconsin—which did not forge bonds with the city. Although Beatrice was headquartered in Chicago, its name did not actually become identified with the marathon. Despite the initial problems stemming from sponsorship, Pinkowski's optimism about Chicago as an ideal venue for a marathon remained high. He was (and continues to be) particularly appreciative of the Daley administration's efforts in making Chicago a fascinating place to live. At the time, Pinkowski understood that Chicago was thought of as a dark, gray, dingy industrial city where people went for conventions. Today, Pinkowski sees how the city has established itself as a cultural center—a great place to visit even "when you're not going to look at electrical outlets at McCormick Place." Pinkowski realizes that the success of Chicago as a tourist destination and the success of the marathon go hand in hand. He has watched the city undergo a complete transformation in the last eleven years and become an excellent place to shop and visit with beautiful parks and top-notch restaurants, hotels, museums, and theaters. The change in the perception of Chicago has helped as much as any factor the growth of the marathon. It was a change Pinkowski had hoped for and knew was desperately needed during the difficult years of the late 1980s and early 1990s, when the survival and revitalization of the marathon were his top priorities.

Pinkowski is aware of Chicago's now-established stature as a major international marathon; he believes that "you have to consider Chicago one of the top four marathons in the world." He knows that this has happened in a relatively short period of time, since about 1996: "our reputation and the experience not only for the elite athletes but for the general participants rival that of London, New York, [and] Boston."[3] In terms of its position in the world hierarchy of marathons, he places London as number one and sees Boston, New York, and Chicago as sharing the number-two slot. He pointed out that (at the time of the interview) Boston was 106 years old, New York 32, London 30,[4] and Chicago 24 (with half of that time in difficult circumstances). Clearly, one sees that his interpretation of the situation reflects his ambition, but it also indicates the extraordinary rapidity of Chicago's ascension.[5]

Like all race directors, Pinkowski faces different periods of stress that are, in part, created by the varying rhythms of planning. He would like to have meetings in January and February for the October marathon, but there are certain times of the year when people aren't in the right mind-set. The police have a full schedule throughout the summer. The gist of this is that a director really can't start most of the planning until eight or nine weeks prior to the event. There are also frequent changes that undo previous efforts. For example, in June 2001, the course was measured. In August, the staff realized that, as a result of construction projects, they would have to go out, remeasure, and redo the entire course. Pinkowski notes that whenever you try to do things early, you have to go back and start over again. As the race date nears, concentrated, stressful effort thus becomes an inevitable part of the planning.

Pinkowski finds that when planning for a marathon that takes place at the beginning of October, the tension begins in early August, with the following four weeks being the most stressful. Fortunately, he has a highly competent staff that he empowers and relies on completely. Pinkowski is an easygoing, pleasant person, but even he recognizes that, as the race date draws near, it is impossible to remain low-key: "As much as any race director would like to be calm, cool, and collected before the event . . . it's just crazy; it's just the nature of the animal."

Pinkowski's broader experience allows him to do another kind of preplanning for the marathon. The prime example is Pinkowski's eight-year involvement with the Shamrock Shuffle, now the world's largest 8K. LaSalle Bank purchased the event in 2000 from the Chicago Area Runners Association, and currently Pinkowski produces and directs it. He views the Shamrock as "just an extension of the marathon." This spring event kicks off the Chicago running season (this kickoff used to be the March Madness Half-Marathon, which is a small event in comparison to the Shuffle and has since opted out of the CARA circuit races). Pinkowski remarks that it is like an entitlement: a company that is a marathon sponsor is also a Shamrock sponsor. He views this race as a nice exercise to test out technology, such as innovations in communications and timing systems. The Shamrock thus becomes a warm-up for the marathon for him and his staff.

To bring the Chicago Marathon to the level of prominence and size that Pinkowski wished to achieve, he knew it would be essential to create a strong, enduring association of volunteers. Pinkowski felt that during the early 1980s, people were not invited to participate in the marathon; it was a corporate event. He chose to let people know that the marathon was in trouble and that it was an event they could elevate, that they could make into something great. Pinkowski was aware of the powerful commitment of most runners to the sport. "Most people that run or have run," he states, "have a real, intrinsic connection to the sport. They want to be part of that process. They want to contribute." He knows that most people who are invited to work at the aid stations view this activity as fun, despite the fact that it is very hard work and genuinely inconvenient: volunteers need to get up in the middle of the night and ready their stations before the day has dawned. Pinkowski notes that the majority of Chicago volunteers has either run a marathon or has a loved one, friend, or family member that has run or runs the marathon. "There's a real connection there, a real sensitivity," he emphasizes. The volunteers clearly understand the effort that goes into a marathon, and they truly enjoy being part of it. Pinkowski feels that people in Chicago are especially cooperative when asked to help. "We're still a Midwest city. They just want to be part of the process, a lot of them have been working for eleven years, and our relationship hasn't changed."[6] Pinkowski still calls up the volunteers who run the aid stations. When they used to bring him twenty-five volunteers, now they come with 250. "It's become a tradition, a date on their calendar." Pinkowski is a grateful man, and he indicates how he and his staff try to reciprocate in any way they can. He realizes that it has now become almost an honor to be part of the volunteer crew. Pinkowski cites New Balance's contribution (jackets and hats for the volunteers), but he also refers to the marathon's own prize for the best aid station. Pinkowski points out that all of the volunteer coordinators know each other and have become friends over the years. Some do not see each other until the annual coordinators' meeting; for Pinkowski, this function serves as a conduit between the running community and the marathon staff.

Pinkowski credits a number of specific individuals with being instrumental in helping him meet the running community: George Cheung, David Reithoffer (most specifically for his help in France), Stewart Schulman, Beth Onines with the Alpine Runners, Patricia Dean with the Arlington Trotters, and Linda Sikora with Quaker Oats. By way of an example, Pinkowski cites Tom Minichiello, who used to work with the Alpine Runners and then moved out to the western suburbs where he founded the Fox Trail River Run. Minichiello also wanted a marathon water station. When Pinkowski stated that he needed 150 people, Minichiello called back a few days later with 300 volunteers. Pinkowski emphasizes that there is a real camaraderie out there. The volunteers genuinely enjoy the fact that they're part of the marathon.

The response Pinkowski gets from runners outside the Chicago area confirms his impressions: these people comment on the enthusiasm emanating from the aid stations that helps to propel them through their marathon, whether it be a three-, four-, or five-hour effort. Pinkowski muses that this phenomenon is attributable to the Chicago Marathon's philosophy, or perhaps that it's simply grounded in midwestern helpfulness.

In his 2001 interview, Pinkowski was ready to compare Chicago volunteers to those of any other race, but he had the Boston Marathon in mind as a model of general community enthusiasm, which he wanted to improve in Chicago. His focus was on "connecting the community to the event." He wanted it to attract the same kind of areawide attention as the Cubs and White Sox games do—he wanted the marathon to be part of the general consciousness of Chicago residents. (Two years later, by the time of his 2003 interview, Pinkowski clearly thought that was the case.)

Assisted by his communication manager, Pinkowski follows a two-pronged strategy (defensive and proactive) to improve neighborhood participation in the marathon. The defensive dimension is to warn neighborhoods well in advance about prospective road closings and other marathon-related developments that may affect their lives. The proactive strategy includes meeting with neighborhood groups who want to be part of the marathon to provide them with signs, t-shirts, coffee for the course, and so on. This strategy also includes helping the neighborhoods promote their retailers and restaurants. Cooperation also extends to working with local schools like Nettlehorst, where in 2003 elite athletes came to visit the children, and institutions of higher learning, such as the Moody Bible Institute and the Illinois Institute of Technology (IIT). The Moody Bible Institute broadcasts the marathon from its site along the course and it allows people to register for free parking along what is considered a prime viewing area. In fact, Moody had already spontaneously taken many helpful measures, including providing portable toilets, before a planned cooperative arrangement was reached. IIT uses the occasion to draw attention to itself as a fine architectural school along the marathon route. The marathon is also working with Malcolm X College and the University of Illinois at Chicago. It has also extended its help to DePaul University in creating a special course on the marathon as a civic event.

Besides contacts with runners, the general community, and local institutions of learning, Pinkowski had to reach out to the city's politicians if the race were to be a success. Initially, when the marathon did not enjoy its current prestige, Pinkowski could expect a mixed reception: some aldermen would yell at him, while others would be generous with their time. The latter was the case for Bert Natarus (Forty-second Ward), who has been particularly supportive of the marathon. In the past, Pinkowski would let the aldermen know which streets he was going to close and so on, but, as time moved on, such precautions became unnecessary as the aldermen began to view the vast coming together of people for the marathon as a political opportunity. Wards that used to be somewhat negative now have cheering aldermen because they realize that the residents in their wards are participating in the event, whether as spectators, volunteers, or runners.

Pinkowski was able to gain access to the mayor's office through the intervention of alderman Kathy Osterman, who was special events director at the time. Pinkowski salutes the deceased Osterman as a dynamic and open-minded person. During this period, Mayor Daley had made it quite clear that he wished more major events to be developed. Jim "Skinny" Sheehan, who would move on to become assistant director of McCormick Place, was an assistant of Osterman's. Sheehan eventually became director, and, most important, he was (and remains) an avid marathon runner himself. He became most instrumental in helping Pinkowski deal with the city-related side of organizing the marathon. Pinkowski feels that Sheehan ran a lot of interference for him or, at the very least, he took the time to educate the other city departments about the marathon. For Pinkowski, Sheehan's key contribution was to enlighten the administration by explaining the successes that were the New York and Boston marathons. Thereafter, things went very easily.

Pinkowski also has to be attentive to sponsorship. Initial sponsorship had been a problem with both the desertion of Beatrice and Old Style. At the time of the interview (August 2001), the situation had changed radically: the marathon had thirty-five sponsors at different levels than LaSalle, the race owner. Some are suppliers, proprietary owners, or official sponsors. Many of the relationships have been long-term. Some sponsors like American Airlines have been working with Pinkowski since he was at Flair. In 2001, Pinkowski had worked with the same woman at LaSalle for the past eleven years. Gatorade had also been with the marathon for eleven years. Pinkowski felt that the marathon was fortunate in making contact with New Balance. After three years of working with the marathon, New Balance had signed a five-year extension of their contract in 2001. Pinkowski had also made the first approach to Volkswagen for sponsorship—a move that had proved most successful by 2003. By 2001, Pinkowski relied on a sponsorship coordinator responsible for most of the initial contacts.

Pinkowski notes that sponsors have been "folded" into the marathon at a similar connection to their volunteer groups. For instance, the women from American Airlines would come down and do the gear check. The sponsors view this as a team process; they are determined to make the marathon a phenomenal event—one that elicits loyalty from their personnel. Pinkowski also directly contacts potential sponsors at the Super Bowl and at the PGA golf tournament. He attends such functions to learn how other sporting events handle things.

Pinkowski normally follows up a marathon with consumer research. After the 2003 race, marathon officials commissioned a study to talk to participants from all over the world and the United States to develop a profile of their perspective on the event. Part of the research includes discovering which sponsors were the most visible, whether participants use any of the sponsors' products, and whether they have used them since the event. Apparently, there were actually people who bought Volkswagens after seeing them at the Expo, although VW viewed the Expo as more of an occasion to service their customers rather than make sales. In any event, Pinkowski must know the marathon's impact on his sponsors' sales and status if he is to continue to do his share of sponsor recruitment.

Maintaining all of these elaborate connections is highly burdensome for one individual. Pinkowski is fortunate to have a strong backup in his general manager, Mike Nishi, who describes his job as a little of everything. Nishi sees himself as the one who makes sure that nothing falls through the cracks. His duties are essentially more operational: he must implement marketing, oversee changes on the course, and work with television companies, among other things. He is there to realize Pinkowski's ideas, to know what the staff can do within a year's time frame, and basically to function as the reality-check man.

Nishi's duties are precise and meticulous. He intervenes with volunteers in the case of operations-based issues. He participates in their race-day preparation meetings that cover such nitty-gritty issues as the supplies they will receive, the ways communications will function, and the uniforms that will be distributed. In short, he makes a comprehensive review of everything that will need to be taken care of on race day. For that day, Nishi coordinates group-leader activities at the finish line where issues like the distribution of Mylar blankets and medals come to the fore. High pressure begins for Nishi in late July. August and September are for executing ideas—August is no time for new ideas; they must wait for the next year. Throughout August and September, Nishi checks to make sure all the critical elements of the marathon are being carried out—confirming hospitality, supplies, and operations vehicles.

Perhaps Nishi's most demanding duty is the preparation of operations binders that cover different areas and needs: medical, key staff, and aid stations. He provides specific information for these distinctive groups and eliminates the outdated material in the binders on an as-needed basis. His goal is to make the binders user-friendlier and effective for key people as well as enable them to document information to help improve the next year's marathon. To this effect, there are static binder sections that include staffing with a complete overview of individual responsibilities. These are being transferred to an electronic format and include digital images of individuals such as delivery-truck drivers and aid-station directors to simplify the identification of key staff in the inevitably hectic atmosphere of race-day morning.

Nishi is acutely aware of the need to utilize evolving technology. The more quickly staff can communicate during the marathon, the more quickly operations can function. Soon all of Nishi's binders will be stored and organized on handheld personal digital assistants (PDAs). All of the key staff binders, first available on desktop and then transferred to PDAs, have time lines so that those in positions of responsibility can see what's happening and answer questions even if they are not directly involved in an activity. Nishi notes that because of Hewlett Packard's cooperation, the marathon staff has dramatically expanded its computer base. For 2004 they would be using over 120 laptops on the course, in Grant Park, and in the hotels to extend their wireless network, which in turn meshes with Nextel, which provides chip points, timing, and wireless scoring. Nishi was very pleased that the marathon had passed from landlines to the use of remotes and wireless transmission to the timing trailers in Grant Park. In practical terms, this means that all runners, not just professionals, can obtain speedy, accurate results.

Nishi works in a collaborative fashion with Pinkowski. They discuss everything involved with the marathon. Both of them try to take in the ideas they receive from staff and volunteers, to evaluate what works, to see what benefits the event, and to determine what can be used in the future. Nishi thinks that their ability to listen to people explains why the marathon has grown so quickly. He feels that he and Pinkowski are open to constructive criticism. They work with Mark Nystuen, the event chairman, who prefers not to focus on their successes but rather pay attention to what they can improve. Nishi says that the mantra is candor in order to do things better. He describes their activity with a theatrical metaphor: "We create the stage and the platform for everyone to perform."

Nishi's own connection with running and the marathon, like Pinkowski's, goes back a long way. In high school, he worked part time as a gopher at Flair, marathon founder Lee Flaherty's company. In 1990, he was given a full-time position working with Pinkowski on the marathon, and that relationship continues to this day. His early work experience in which he did basically everything was ideally suited to his current role of general manager. Nishi, like Pinkowski, was involved in running in high school. He is a committed marathon runner. His previous best was in New York in 1990 at 2:56; surprisingly, after training with a "great local marathoner," Howard Kambara, Nishi managed an impressive 2:45 in the 2001 Boston Marathon. Though not a professional, he is clearly an outstanding amateur marathoner. Thus, both he and Pinkowski understand the race from the inside, as runners.

Nishi also reveals a deep and genuine commitment to the marathon. When he asks himself why he does this year in and year out and where the passion comes from, he thinks of how many lives he and the marathon staff impact. He speaks of the many emotions he observes in people as they cross the finish line. He knows that his efforts enable people to make their dreams come true. As Nishi puts it, "You're part of helping them achieve a goal that can last a lifetime." An executive race director can thrive with a second-in-command who is so highly motivated.

Thanks to Nishi's careful scrutiny of such matters, Pinkowski is freed from the need to pay excessive attention to the complex minutiae of race management and can turn to larger issues, particularly Chicago's relationship to its competitors. He does not, however, worry about rivalry from the world's great marathons. In many ways he feels they complement each other, but he is convinced that they also do compete. They try to innovate and to one-up each other. They also copy each other immediately. He cites the example of his kidding with Allan Steinfeld at the Chicago Marathon. Pinkowski asked, "What are you doing with that camera?" He noted that, all of a sudden, the same things done at the Chicago finish appeared in New York, for example, the "Jumbotron" at the finish line in the Chicago 2000 race was duplicated in New York. On the other hand, Pinkowski first saw the Jumbotron in Boston. Chicago also imitated the VIP canopies observed in London. London race director Dave Bedford studies the finisher medal racks. Race directors talk to each other about legal issues and other matters; they all interact. They cooperate in approaching the International Amateur Athletic Federation (IAAF) about stringent drug testing. Drugs remain a dark cloud that hangs over the sport, so the race directors collectively signed a letter and sent it to the IAAF and the Olympic Committee stating that they would support any testing for erythropoietin (EPO) or anything enhancing the oxygen content of the blood. This cooperation clearly shows that the world's great marathons are not marked by cutthroat competition. Pinkowski realizes that their growth is mutually beneficial; he believes that if there are more people running in New York, there will be more people running in Chicago and vice versa. The different marathons all feed off one another. Indicative of this spirit of cooperation is the fact that marathon directors all have each other's home phone numbers. Clearly, there are more than enough runners to go around—and these are runners who enjoy marathon tourism—thus ensuring participation beyond their home cities or regions.

Pinkowski sees no major threat to the continued growth of the marathon, but there are always concerns, the principal one being an event that would compromise the course itself. What Pinkowski does not fear is a diminution in the crowd-drawing appeal of marathons. Despite the economic downturn already developing in 2001, Pinkowski noted that the Chicago Marathon was fortunate in that new sponsors had joined that year. He also noted that, although the marathon is an old sport, from the media's perspective, it is a new one in that it has only recently become the focus of national attention. This favors the marathon, as advertisers and television producers are always looking for a new activity to promote their products and stations. In 2003, Pinkowski alluded to the growing attention paid to running on television, citing Miranda in *Sex and the City* and Nate in *Six Feet Under,* both HBO hit series. In the former, Miranda joins a ten-minute-per-mile training group but eventually moves into a nine-mile group to escape from a man she has been involved with; in the latter, the older brother runs when he needs to get away. Pinkowski also cited an *NYPD Blue* episode in which two detectives, the types one would expect to meet in a bar, are instead in their sweats about to go out for a run.

Beyond the media, Pinkowski also feels that fashion plays a role in the promotion of running. The angular, long look has come back, and so has the miniskirt: a physique and a style that favor runners' builds. Pinkowski also believes that people are far more informed about running and that there has been a shift in attitudes. He refers to the old notion of "the loneliness of the long-distance runner" and how people viewed marathoners as if they were crazy or simply loners. He realizes that with training programs and information available on the Internet, the marathon has become a social activity. Pinkowski states that one need only look to the Chicago lakefront to see hundreds of people training for the marathon or running in general. Pinkowski believes that good marketers are quite aware of that.

Pinkowski also manifests a broad understanding of the growth of running and marathoning over the past few decades. Like most commentators, he points to the running boom generated by Shorter's Olympic performances in 1972 and 1976. He feels, however, that marathons were ignored all the way through the early 1990s, but now declares that we have ten times the amount of people who ran previously. He is acutely aware of the decline in average performance. Pinkowski indicates that in the early 1990s, the average finishing time was 3:25:00 and that now it is about 4:30:00. He notes that people are much better trained and that, even with greater numbers of runners, injuries are far fewer. He underlines the more festive nature of the marathon by pointing out that the largest beverage consumption at the finish line is beer. He also points out that of 2,400 people signed up for training in Chicago for 2003, 2,100 had no previous marathon experience, and that 1,900 had never run a road race. As executive race director, he must take into account this changing demography and differing expectations centered on the marathon. If anything, he must remain flexible and adaptable to changing trends.

In addition to marketing to amateur and first-time marathoners, Pinkowski must know how to market the marathon to the world's elite runners. In the early 1990s, most races simply paid runners to show. To gain a recruitment edge, Pinkowski developed another enticement: he offered performance bonuses. Thus, runners had greater incentives to finish well rather than just show. This practice tends to attract very strong fields once professional runners know that they can earn bonuses even if they do not place. Although Pinkowski's initial strategy has continued to draw the world's elite, he must continuously refine his tactics. In 2003, the prize money available to athletes was approximately $800,000. The winner, a virtual unknown from Kenya, Evans Rutto, won some $410,000 for an under-2:06:00 run. The marathon now offers a $100,000 bonus for a world's record, plus $100,000 more if the record is broken by more than twenty-five seconds. Rutto, a first-time marathoner, enjoyed additional bonuses in accumulating his total prize package. Pinkowski was, however, somewhat frustrated that year. First of all, the former world-record holder, Khalid Khannouchi, had to cancel his run because of injury. His foremost adversary, Paul Tergat, had declined to run Chicago because he wanted to avoid competing with Khannouchi. Tergat surprised many race watchers by breaking the world record in Berlin just before the Chicago Marathon. Obviously, having this record set on another course frustrated Pinkowski, who was quick to point out that had Tergat won in Chicago, he would have earned $750,000 more in prize money than he did in Berlin. It certainly pays to highlight these differences when one wants to lure the world's greatest runners. Tergat's record makes it clear how difficult a task it is to keep the world's greatest in one race. Currently, Chicago, London, and Berlin are in constant competition for world records as all three have some of the flattest and fastest courses with which to tempt professional runners.

Despite such difficulties, Pinkowski remains positive about his experience as race director. In regard to his own efforts, he describes the marathon as a "personal and professional triumph," but he modestly qualifies that the marathon was like a beautiful automobile pointed in the wrong direction. He feels that what was needed to make it a success was exposure and proper direction. Pinkowski sees his persistence as the key factor in turning things around: "I think of the one thing I did, I hung in there and just kept it going." He had to struggle to keep people committed, and he found this extremely difficult for a long time. He was maligned and even laughed at. People thought he was crazy, but now, he points out, some of those people call him and want to go to the VIP tent on the finish line or want tickets to the tent because their daughter or cousin is running.

Keenly aware of the human contact it took to move the marathon forward, Pinkowski tries to remain as accessible as possible. He goes to the premarathon expo and sits there and talks with people. He likes to spend an hour or two answering the phone. "That's your direct line of information," he states. "It gives you a really good feel of what people are thinking." He gets a direct, personal notion of how people view the city and the marathon. People often ask where they should stay and what they should do. Pinkowski gets a kick out of responding to these inquiries. His style eschews the aloofness of the professional manager, which makes him all the more effective.

Pinkowski thinks that a successful marathon requires remaining connected to the participants. He believes that it is essential that each individual feels special, whether it's a three-, four-, five-, or even six-hour runner. This seems particularly important to him today when the marathon experience is not as competitive as it once was when people were trying to qualify for the Boston Marathon. Now the challenge is to showcase the neighborhoods, because marathoners are looking at them. In fact, they're running with camcorders, cell phones, and the like. More people are running and running more slowly, and they're enjoying it.

Pinkowski, however, believes that there should be limits to the time allotted to run a marathon—for him, six-and-a-half hours are quite sufficient. Beyond six hours, he notes that the race becomes more like a walk, although he does cherish the ambition to walk the race just once to see what he can do during it. He notes that the marathon could even be held for nine hours, but he adds that one must be cognizant of the needs of the residents of Chicago and the traffic patterns. In short, his realism checks any further expansion of marathon time limits.

Pinkowski sees the marathon as having arrived; his goal expressed in his 2001 interview for the city's population has been met. Chicagoans are now making the same associations with the marathon as they do with the Bulls, the Bears, or the Black Hawks. Pinkowski thinks that Chicagoans can sometimes be tough, but that they can also be very generous, very loving. He thinks he has experienced both sides of that. He believes that much of the good relations he enjoys today go back to communicating with people, a practice that brings him back to the time he was starting his efforts. Pinkowski states that he is grateful to have been around running all his life and to be able to make a living from it.

Briefly then, a successful marathon director is a communicator. He has an essentially gregarious nature and genuinely enjoys contact with others. At the moment, being a marathon director is something beyond a profession. It's a calling and something each individual designs for him- or herself, relying on his or her personal resources and adaptability. In a period when management has become more aloof, race directors like Pinkowski represent a different breed. While hardly ordinary individuals, they must represent themselves as being closely linked to the running community and ready to socialize with all who participate in the marathon. In a certain way, race direction calls for individuals with all the talent and acumen of managers as well as a unique flair for interpersonal relations. In a society in which class distinctions are becoming sharper and the gap between the wealthy and the ordinary citizen looms ever wider, race directors present a friendly countermodel that is well suited for the marathon as an expression of urban pride and unity.

The prize-wining Frontrunners aid station offers humor and fantasy with its Oz theme in 2003. Such local organizations are fundamental to the marathon's success. (Courtesy of Frank Wheby)

four

grassroots support

Marathons do not occur out of the blue; they presume a running community that will support them. Boston's grew under the aegis of the Boston Athletic Association, while New York's emerged from the New York Road Runners Club (NYRRC). These great marathons were able to draw on a strong, organized community of runners, and these clubs ensured both the runners and the volunteers needed to make the marathon work. The Chicago story is somewhat different, in that its marathon emerged with the help of local runners as a kind of modest, grassroots project without powerful club support at a time when an umbrella running association did not yet exist. Even more curiously, the second running of the Chicago Marathon led to a rift between the original planners and the sponsor/owner, who was focused on attracting publicity to the race. It was this quarrel that gave birth to the Chicago Area Runners Association (CARA), and it would take more than a decade before relations really evolved into the synergy they represent today. In particular, it was the intervention of executive race director Carey Pinkowski in the late 1980s that led to a dramatic improvement in relations, although to this day it is the marathon that calls the shots, and CARA has little choice but to follow. But at this point, the interests of CARA and the marathon are so completely intertwined that a real struggle between the two is difficult to imagine.

The former CEO of CARA, David Patt,[1] is in an excellent position to appreciate CARA's relationship with the marathon and to comment on the transformation of running during the past decade and the effect of that transformation on the marathon. CARA functions as an umbrella organization for all the running clubs in the Chicago area. Its CEO must be especially mindful of what Patt sees as its four principal concerns: racing, training, education, and social activities. All have a direct bearing on the marathon. With some 7,600 members in the fall of 2003—when Patt discussed the organization—CARA had become a vital institution and commanded the attention of serious runners throughout the region. Patt indicated that the average age of CARA members was thirty-nine, while new members averaged thirty-two. Most of CARA's members were and still are suburbanites, but an astonishing one person out of every ninety-eight people living in Lincoln Park, a very affluent and densely populated north-side Chicago neighborhood along the lakefront, is a CARA member—which is the highest percentage of runners in any community. In that sense, CARA faithfully reflects running demographics; namely, runners who come largely from the wealthier segments of the population. The organization is also equally split between male and female with the preponderance of new runners being female. This development directly typifies the trend in running throughout the United States; this trend is seen throughout much of the rest of the world as well.

Of the four concerns noted above, Patt sees racing as the most important. By racing, Patt is referring to the circuit and registered races. Briefly, circuit races include a set of over twenty races in which runners score points in a competition to win their five-year age group categories and Clydesdale categories. The Chicago Marathon has always been one of these races. The Chicago Marathon, however, differentiates itself from the others in that it offers neither a CARA race registration discount, nor any other special registration privileges normally accorded to CARA members. This is largely a reflection of the vastly greater magnitude of the Chicago Marathon in relationship to all other circuit races, most of which have several hundred to a few thousand runners as opposed to the Chicago Marathon's 40,000 registrants. The only other circuit race of truly huge numbers (about 22,500 registrants in 2005) is the Shamrock Shuffle, also owned by LaSalle Bank. This race belonged to CARA before the organization sold it to LaSalle. That sale of the race comprises in itself a clear statement about the relationship between CARA and the LaSalle Bank Chicago Marathon.

CARA's responsibility in the domain of racing is fairly complex. Since its sale of the Shamrock Shuffle, the organization neither puts on its own races nor does it hire itself out to produce races for other groups. Instead, it has shifted its focus to quality control for its circuit and registered races. Quality control is a broad issue: it includes features like the starting line, finish chutes, water stations, race marshals, traffic control, the accurate reporting of times, the actual race courses, and race information. Quality control for all of these issues is handled via online surveys, letters from CARA members, and the judgment of CARA's board of qualified runners. CARA can assert considerable power over local races. An example of this was its threat to reject the Chicago Distance Classic as a circuit race for 2004, when its membership sent in indignant reviews of the course and race management. The race owner, well-known John Bingham, author of the "Penguin Chronicles" in *Runner's World,* had to implore the CARA board for a second chance. CARA's power, however, does not really extend to the marathon because even the denial of a CARA endorsement could not stop this race. Its international dimension is such that it is a law unto itself—a greater power than CARA. Censuring it in any way would harm both organizations. In fact, because LaSalle Bank owns the two largest races on the circuit—races with a combined population many times larger than the sum of all the rest of the circuit races, it could be said that LaSalle is in an excellent position to dictate to CARA. But cooperation, not conflict, has produced the most effective relationship.

In maintaining the quality of racing, CARA must also strive for diversity in distances among its circuit and registered races. CARA must be especially careful that racing is not reduced to 5,000- and 10,000-

meter races. Given that these distances are among the most popular and easiest to put together, race directors are understandably tempted in that direction. The Chicago Marathon obviously fills a critical niche by being the only marathon on the circuit; it plays an essential role in sustaining the diversity of the circuit and privileging long-distance running.

In the area of racing, CARA offers several possibilities for individual runner recognition. There is a normal circuit consisting of 103 kilometers as the sum of various races. By completing this distance through circuit and registered races, a runner receives an award at the annual CARA banquet. In a sense, this is intended as encouragement for the many runners who have no hopes of ever receiving any competitive place award. There is also a noncompetitive long-distance circuit, which is a combination of any five designated races ranging from ten miles through the 50K. The Chicago Marathon is an optional race for both of these circuits. Beyond the overall awards (first ten male and female runners on the circuit, age-graded top ten, runner of the year, masters runner of the year, and veteran runner of the year) are the five-year age-group categories, which offer first- through third-place plaques. The age-group awards have the particularly important function of stimulating competition among even the oldest of runners, who would have been excluded decades earlier. The marathon occupies a special place in this award competition because it is the longest race of the circuit and, for most people, the biggest challenge. It offers no extra points beyond any other race, but serious competitors can assume that not all their age-group rivals will want or even be able to compete, given the difficulty of the course. This tends to motivate those who choose to run the marathon because they are aware that they may gain a competitive advantage.

It is training, however, and not racing that is CARA's biggest operation, and the marathon plays a major role in generating business in this area, as it requires the most protracted preparation. CARA's training program directs itself to very broad running options. There is a pre-running group; beginning, 5K, 8K, and 10K training; half-marathon training from March through June; and, of course, a marathon-training program from June through October. CARA's marathon program is widely utilized by charity runners who are sponsoring individual children at Children's Memorial Hospital. Its marathon-training programs now extend to suburban locations, and these programs have become increasingly popular with the many runners who want to run the marathon without any previous experience. The Chicago Marathon is the direct beneficiary of CARA's programs as well as other charity-driven training programs in the area. CARA does not suffer in this either; all its training programs are profitable and the organization re quires no sponsors, and much of the actual training is carried out by volunteer runners.

Education is both part of the training programs and a complement to them. Nutrition and women's issues figure as key educational concerns; in fact, there are many clinics especially for women. CARA also features celebrity runners for brown-bag lunches. Hal Higdon, who supervises the Chicago Marathon training, meshed well with CARA, and he has become part of CARA's education and training program. It is probably most accurate to say that CARA training and education are, with the exception of occasional presentations, largely fused, and that education is a fundamental dimension of training.

Socially, CARA's biggest event is its annual awards banquet, which honors all of its membership and represents the culmination of the previous year's racing. Much of the real socialization, however, occurs long before the annual banquet. That socialization springs in part from the training programs and from racing itself, when different clubs and regular runners, both club members and unaffiliated, meet each other on a regular basis. Friendships, based on mutual interest and admiration, develop both collectively (in the case of interclub socialization) and individually. Runners and their supporters acquire a much broader sense of community in the competitive structure constructed by CARA and the individual race directors. It is this wider community, which would be difficult to imagine without CARA, that provides multiple levels of support for the marathon: the running clubs who staff the aid stations, the local competitions, and a broader population of volunteers who are associated with nearly every aspect related to the production of the Chicago Marathon. CARA has experienced enormous growth from its marathon-related training and charitable activities and the marathon derives much of its local people power and civic passion from CARA in this productive symbiosis.

It should come as no surprise that several of the marathon aid station directors are prominent, highly active CARA members; indeed, the two functions are complementary. But the aid stations embrace a vaster segment of the population, one that includes nonrunners who are drawn to the marathon for reasons of personal loyalty and civic pride. The marathon, perhaps more than any other sport, provides a compelling demonstration of the city's ability to function as a cohesive unit, proof that Chicago's diversity need not imply divisiveness. Its aid stations permit a friendly rivalry among the city's different communities without losing track of the ultimate message of unity. Although many sports communicate urban solidarity by pitting one city against another and others divide by opposing different areas of the city, such as the Cubs and White Sox in Chicago, the marathon, most especially in its aid stations, stresses harmony, working in unison to realize a large, challenging goal.

In this sense, the marathon mirrors the official policy of the Daley administration, which is to celebrate diversity. Although this coordination with the mayor's policy was not consciously planned, it reflects a confluence of public and private aspirations that ensure Chicago's dynamism. The actual course, shaped like a buckle to encompass the bulk of Chicago's constituent communities, includes seventeen aid stations at relatively equal intervals over the 26.2–mile distance. Originating in the Loop, it heads north through affluent Lincoln Park; back down to the city center through upscale residential and business areas; past the restaurants and shops of Greektown; continues past what is left of "Little Italy"; then to more economically modest communities like Pilsen, currently the heart of the Mexican American and Mexican community; through Chinatown; up a segment of southern Michigan Avenue, which includes part of the African American community centered on the south side; and then back to Grant Park. None of this is accidental. Executive race director Pinkowski has not opted for an all-northern course from the Loop precisely because such a choice would largely eliminate the Latino, African American, and Chinese communities.

The Chicago Marathon is clearly following a well-established formula first perfected in New York by Fred Lebow; namely, the five-borough marathon. Although the practice actually developed from a misunderstanding and met with Lebow's initial opposition, once assured of city cooperation, New York City's grand impresario energetically pursued it, even when he needed to negotiate with thugs to ensure the safe passage of marathoners through their turf.[2] Lebow correctly realized that this passage across the city actually affirmed the vibrant diversity of the metropolis, making the course an act of tourism for the visitor or rediscovery for the New York City native. The course also appealed to rising ethnic pride and, in many cases, to the ethnic nostalgia of people who were already one or two generations removed from immigration.

Pinkowski had already witnessed the New York City Marathon during his student days at Villanova. The lesson of a course charged with urban symbolism was not lost on him; when he returned to Chicago, he reinforced and developed this strategy. Chicago would thus follow a pattern similar to New York's, but it would be unfair to exaggerate Lebow's role here because the showcasing of urban diversity was already developing elsewhere to some extent concurrently with the early years of Chicago Marathon; for example, Los Angeles seems to have experienced a similar development in regard to ethnicity without consciously following the New York model (Merle, 44). It was probably a near inevitability that the United States' three most populous cities should highlight diversity in their aid stations, although New York City has the honor of having articulated the policy the earliest, and the impact on Chicago from Lebow to Pinkowski is quite direct.

The Chicago example of valorizing diversity in its aid stations is nonetheless quite dramatic. These stations are large-scale affairs requiring minimally 200 volunteers, but many reach 450. Besides seeing to hydration in the form of water and Gatorade, occasionally in finger-numbing cold, thus literally keeping runners alive, station volunteers offer entertainment and often badly needed encouragement as runners wend their way along the course. First aid is also available at these stations. Beatrice created the original ethnic stations in an effort to boost the rather feeble numbers of marathon spectators in early years. With the sponsor's funding in 1985, then–race director Bob Bright was able to recruit neighborhood captains and offer such exotic spectacles as a Greek belly dancer, Chinese dragon dancers, Scottish bagpipers, and a Jamaican reggae band along the course (Treadwell, 66). The aid stations have evolved into more genuine, less commandeered attractions that better characterize some of the neighborhoods. Testimonials from selected station directors convey some sense of the variety of people who manage these stations and provide a glimpse into the diversity and aspirations of the volunteer population. With the exception of the Frontrunners aid station, which until 2005 had always won the marathon prize for best aid station and that serves as a point of reference for many other stations, the presentation of aid station directors follows their distribution along the course.

David Reithoffer, founder and organizer of the Frontrunners' aid station (Aid Station #4), also wears the hat of chief recruiter of French runners (formerly the largest group of foreign nationals, numbering 800 in 2000). Fluent in French, president of Chicago's Groupe Professionnel Francophone, a competent violinist, and a successful real estate agent, Reithoffer has been involved with the Chicago Marathon since 1996. A gay male and father of two daughters whom he raises conjointly with their lesbian mother, he illustrates in his very person some of the human diversity that makes the marathon work. His work as aid station director requires his attention throughout nearly the entire year. Hardly is one marathon over before Reithoffer begins announcing his recruitment drive to fellow Frontrunners at their biweekly runs starting at the totem pole in Chicago's Lincoln Park. Curiously, Reithoffer does not run himself; physical injury has restricted him to race walking, for which he holds a gold medal from the New York Gay Games. Reithoffer's first association with Frontrunners (whose official name has been changed to Chicago Frontrunners/Frontwalkers) was as a walker. The club nevertheless accepted him and eventually elected him president. His position within the club eventually led to his volunteer work with the Chicago Marathon. Reithoffer's long-term commitment is both an honor and a burden that is hardly free of tension. Any aid station manager is at the mercy of the reliability of volunteers and the various services that deliver supplies. In 2000, for instance, the water truck got lost and barely arrived in time for the volunteers to set up before the race. Despite such aggravations, Reithoffer continues to work for the marathon in many volunteer dimensions. He explains his attraction to a second, largely voluntary career in terms of the atmosphere at the Chicago Marathon. To him, it is very much a community, a family. It is indeed a labor of love. In fact, this is one of the paradoxes of the marathon—it draws the volunteer talent of many competent individuals who are attracted by its atmosphere of cooperation and friendliness, people who could otherwise be earning substantial revenue for the time they are giving away. Reithoffer attributes much of this positive atmosphere to the influence of executive race director Pinkowski, whose interpersonal skills elicit cooperation among a host of different station directors.

Reithoffer acknowledges that the Frontrunners' aid station has taken on a life of its own. Annual themes such as "Y2 Gay," "Under the Big Top" (equivocal pun fully intended), "Oz," and "Village People" (2004) are proposed and developed by club members. A standard feature of the station besides a barrage of costumes and music is its male-drag cheerleaders whose styles have ranged from bouffant hairdos to beards. Because this aid station is located early in the race, after its closing the cheerleaders are regularly bussed to the finish for photo ops—something quite popular with female runners. The drag cheerleaders are largely doctors, lawyers, and other professionals who, in the spirit of carnival, assume their temporary personae for race-day morning. At least one has run the marathon in 2:45. Some club members have reservations about what appears to be pandering to heterosexual stereotypes of gays, and analogies can be made to the criticisms raised by gay critics regarding the stereotypical depiction that marks the television show *Queer Eye for the Straight Guy*. Reithoffer, a subtle man, is entirely aware of this drift of thought, but he points out the strong positive effect the aid station has on runners, its uplifting humor, and the outstanding contribution of the gay community to the success of the marathon. Indeed, so successful is the Frontrunners' aid station that, until 2005, it had never lost the competition for best aid station. In 2004, to encourage some of the understandably frustrated aid station directors, the marathon instituted second- and third-place prizes. The Frontrunners easily won first place and its $1,000 prize on that occasion.[3]

The unifying appeal of the aid stations reaches well beyond the city to suburban running clubs. These are also present in considerable numbers, adding to the volunteer power of the marathon. Pat Onines, a veteran of twenty-five years of running and a self-described "back-of-the-pack runner," has organized Aid Station #1 since 1991. He does this for his club, the suburban Alpine Runners, and he enjoys backup support in recruitment from fellow club members. He is also a member of the board of directors of the Chicago Area Runners Association, and thus even in his person he is an expression of CARA support for the marathon. Unlike the more ethnic water stations, his station does not seek to put on a show. The purpose is to provide fluid to the great rush of marathoners at the beginning of the race. He takes for granted that the Frontrunners will win the prize for the best show and instead focuses on providing essentials. He also enjoys the fact that his station's location in the race allows him to finish early and actually catch the winners as they come in. Particularly striking in his account is the role that club loyalty and personal loyalty play in running these stations. He acknowledges his pride in association with Alpine Runners and with Carey Pinkowski. In regard to Pinkowski, he remarked that he would do anything that he asked for the marathon. The respect and the affection that the executive race director commands seem to be the glue that holds much of the aid station direction together. Onines also acknowledges the work of Mike Nishi, Pinkowski's associate, in perfecting the marathon through his preparedness for any eventuality. He also feels that Pinkowski in particular has made the marathon a "good time" for everyone. Clearly openness and universal participation are seen as key values. Onines did not focus on professional performance—which does not imply that he is indifferent to it. What his emphasis does indicate is the "value shift" of the modern marathon to community support and celebration. But in Onines's case, the cohesion is now regional rather than citywide; it becomes an extension of the city into the suburbs and thus dissipates some of the traditional hostility between city and suburbs; instead, they function in unison, manifesting regional pride.

Director of Aid Station #3, Trisha Dean is an accomplished veteran of many long-distance runs, among which she counts thirty marathons, including a number of Chicago Marathons and some Ironman Triathlons. She characterizes herself as an "endurance runner"—hardly a claim that one could dispute. She was involved with the aid station in 1986 (but she wasn't captain at that time) and became involved on a regular basis as director ever since Carey Pinkowski launched his direct appeal to the running clubs in the Chicago area. She has seen the race evolve through its many phases: a people's race, a professional race, a barely surviving race. Initially, her club worked different miles, including the twenty-fifth, but time and experience have led her to request a station location earlier along the course; for the past few years, she has managed the station on Cannon Drive near the zoo in Lincoln Park only six miles into the race—something that allows her group to finish early, a consideration that seems to be a priority among veteran directors.

Dean does not feel that organizing the aid station is that hard a task—at this point, she has it all down. Nonetheless, she begins recruiting early in August and has good success in getting high school volunteers, especially, but not exclusively, from her own school in Buffalo Grove. Normally, she can count on assistance from some 200 people; about half of her volunteers are high school students. Parents, however, take over the management of specific setup tasks. Nonetheless, with all the potential for confusion, she finds race morning a bit scary.

Dean is not concerned with competing for the aid station prize. She does not feel that her group is homogeneous enough to work effectively for the prize—an attitude shared by Stuart Schulman of the Lincoln Park Pacers. Her club, the Arlington Trotters, is not large enough to staff the station by itself, and the high school students who provide such effective and enthusiastic help are also from different suburban schools. The interaction just isn't there the way it might be in a larger, more closely knit club. She prefers to focus on good service to the runners.

What motivates Dean to do the aid station year in and year out? Beyond the obvious tenacity of an accomplished endurance runner, she feels a sense of loyalty to the running of the Chicago Marathon, a commitment to make the event happen. She attends Carey Pinkowski's annual kickoff dinner for aid station directors and workers who have been there from the beginning, including clubs like the Rainbow Runners and the Panteras, and friends like the Onines. She thus has a sense of personal loyalty and bonds of friendship that tie her to the race, and a pride in her city and region.

Pinkowski is central in the construction of this loyalty. Dean cited his assistance to the Arlington Trotters in putting on "the Stampede," providing marathon items for their raffle. More personally, she cited the tragic case of two prominent running activists (one an aid station director) whose daughter lay dying in intensive care. Pinkowski was there and later went to the funeral. Dean has no doubts that Pinkowski's solicitude was entirely genuine. "He becomes a friend and a supporter." She cites this as proof that Pinkowski is not just a race director, but also a true friend to those he works with.

Stuart Schulman, who has served as president of the Lincoln Park Pacers (a large running club centered around the Lake Shore in the affluent north side of Chicago), has been a runner for some thirty years. He qualifies himself as a regular runner rather than a competitive one.

Schulman manages Aid Station #5 for his club. As time has passed, the station has become an immense affair stretching for several blocks and staffed by an army of volunteers. Originally, when he used to run the marathon, Schulman would solicit volunteers for the aid station. Among his memories as a marathoner is running with a group disguised as a caterpillar. He arrived in about 4:30—slow going for him, but very entertaining for the spectators. Since Schulman has given up marathons, he handles the station personally. His recollections go back to before Pinkowski's arrival on the scene, when volunteers would meet at Flair House for briefings. Today, he handles a group of several hundred volunteers. By now, the job is routine, and he delegates ten club members to call twenty more asking each of them if they want to volunteer. There is a certain amount of paperwork involved for these contacts and seeing to it that they get their jackets and caps.

Schulman is, like a number of other directors, not interested in putting on a show or competing for a prize. He feels that you need a running club with a very strong sense of coherence to put on an effective show, and he feels that this coherence is less apparent in his club with the passage of time. Furthermore, many of his station's volunteers now come from schools, which means that they are effectively not club members and cannot be expected to have the esprit de corps that would produce a station spectacle. He estimates that there are about 225 people in the club, but he thinks it's become less social and less runner oriented—then again, he also wonders if he isn't just getting older. On the other hand, he does see older club members as more reliable. Once again, the day seems to be conceded to the Frontrunners. Schulman thinks it would require an individual with a strong personality or business interest (like David Zimmer of Fleet Feet) to put on a show.

Schulman finds the marathon morning rather stressful, but he gets through it. He is modest about the value of his commitment; he thinks that describing himself as being part of Chicago is perhaps too high-blown, but does feel that his club represents the local community's contribution to the race. Although Schulman views his commitment as low-key, he indicates the significance of personal bonds in running the marathon. Once again, it is his relationship with executive race director Pinkowski that increases his motivation to run the aid station. In this case, it is because of Schulman's particular gratitude to Pinkowski for his generous help with the autumn and spring 50Ks that Schulman sponsors along the lakefront. These races honor the memory of his friend and fellow runner, George Cheung, husband of Chinatown station director Celia Cheung. It's quite interesting to note that a runner who has retired from the marathon remains active in a volunteer role for the marathon while simultaneously trying to develop an even longer race.

Dave Zimmer is not actually a director of an aid station, but he runs what might be considered a major support station just south of Schulman's. Unlike most of the other station directors, his entry into this area is relatively recent (1996), and his association with running is more directly commercial. Zimmer is the owner of the highly successful Fleet Feet Sports that has now expanded to a second location on Chicago's north side and a third in Elmhurst, Illinois. He is an astute businessman who also sponsors a large running club. In short, his involvement with the marathon, though voluntary, has direct economic consequences and he is thus highly motivated to create a support station that will be noticed and, if possible, surpass the spectacle offered by Frontrunners. His station, like that of his rivals, cannot trade on ethnic nostalgia in the way that the Mexican and Chinese stations do. In many ways, this practice is a disadvantage because it fixes a community in an imagined past and inhibits the creation of more dramatic forms of self-representation. This is not Zimmer's problem. He has to figure out some kind of arresting display that can't be grounded in ethnicity. One could characterize his support station as a "yuppie" affair, but the dominant stratum of any given society is rarely inclined to self-parody. Instead Zimmer tries to provide humor from other sources. His solution is multiple Elvises, from the obese to the svelte. He also introduces many variations, including cowbells, to make his support station the loudest along the race route. Zimmer's efforts are highly entertaining and they help reinforce club loyalty, but they do not contribute to a specific neighborhood identity. This is hardly a fault; rather, it points to the dilemma of representing the upper-middle class and, to some extent, the depiction of nonethnic whites. Does one dress up the volunteers as stockbrokers? In this sense, the character of some neighborhoods is indicated by a lack of distinctive markers—or simply markers considered so normative that they escape denotation.[4]

Paul Oppenheim, who was president of the Oak Park Runners Club for over fifteen years, has also been in charge of organizing the club's aid station. Oppenheim has been running since 1979 and considers himself a competitive runner. That notwithstanding, he was quite removed from the marathon at its beginning. He felt no connections with it; in fact, he stated that it could have been "on Mars" for as much as it meant to him. Oppenheim did follow the marathon as it grew in fame. He saw Joan Benoit Samuelson when she broke the American women's record and former Chicago women's course record in 1985. He also attended the year that the marathon was reduced to a half-marathon. The watershed moment, the beginning of his own involvement with the marathon, was when Carey Pinkowski became part of the event. Although Beatrice had depended on volunteers from the corporation, Pinkowski reached out to the running community; as Oppenheim sees it, Pinkowski personally recruited the Oak Park Runners Club. Sharing the view of so many others, Oppenheim sees Pinkowski as the key figure in wider community involvement with the marathon.

Like Onines, Oppenheim has a specific appreciation for the location of his station. The first station was "Presidential Towers," located on the western edge of the city, convenient for his club members in next-door suburban Oak Park. His current designation, Aid Station #9, is also in the west Loop in the former Little Italy area at Taylor and Morgan streets—another site that allows his club members easy arrival and easy return. Although the Oak Park Runners Club is large, numbering over 100 members, it cannot support an aid station by itself. Oppenheim indicated that there is a lot of outside volunteering. A retired man he knows always recruits friends and family year after year to staff the aid station. This is typical of the marathon dynamic: people seem to just want to get involved.

Oppenheim states that it is not terribly difficult to do the recruiting under any circumstances. Each year, he brings three or four people with him to Pinkowski's coordinating dinner for aid station directors. He normally has a diagram of what tasks need to be accomplished on race day: table assembly, Gatorade preparation, crowd management, distribution of jackets and caps to volunteers—all these things as well as the recruitment can be delegated. He thinks that the jackets and caps, which many people find quite attractive, are a strong recruitment inducement for volunteers. Indeed, people wear them throughout much of the year.

It is interesting that Oppenheim has only run two marathons himself, and yet he is quite committed to supporting the aid station. For him, it is a matter of civic pride. He takes pleasure in being part of an event that has now assumed such extraordinary proportions. He thoroughly enjoys the experience, but he really doesn't feel particularly emotional about it. When asked if his club was interested in putting on a show, he, like Onines, deferred, believing that there was no point in competing against the Frontrunners. He also remarked that as a competitive runner, he doubted that he would really even notice the aid station if he was a participant. He felt that the show dimension of some of the aid stations was something that would appeal more to the back-of-the-pack runners who would not be interested in competition and were more concerned with taking in the sights.

In certain ways, Oppenheim is typical of a committed runner's involvement with the marathon. For many years, as president of the Oak Park Runners Club, he organized one of the finest 5Ks on the CARA circuit, the Race That's Good for Life. The race actually offered two races: a women's and men's competition. At one point, it even included spectacular entertainment, the Jesse White Tumblers, who performed in the local high school gym while the awards were being readied. The race and all that surrounded it bore the imprint of Oppenheim's thorough and minute attention to detail. Oppenheim has also competed for years on the CARA circuit.

Oppenheim acknowledged the powerful emotional appeal of the aid station. Some years ago, he had been able to interest a colleague in running. She became a water station volunteer. Thereafter, she was hooked—not as a volunteer, but as a runner. Indeed, station volunteering is often a transition to running the race. Oppenheim related his experience of an elite woman runner who had to drop out at his station. He asked her if she was all right. She said that she was and asked how to get to the finish line in the city center. He just pointed to the Sears Tower and told to go straight for it. This was as much his own link between the marathon and city, a way to show Chicago to visitors.

Clearly, with Dean, Onines, Schulman, and Oppenheim we see a long continuity of running-club and CARA officials committed to the support staff of the marathon. With the exception of Schulman, who lives in Chicago, we also see that they represent regional commitments, from the nearby suburbs of Oak Park to the distant suburbs whose residents make up the Alpine Runners. The marathon thus becomes not only a festival of civic unity but also one of regional solidarity. Its volunteers seem firmly bound by personal loyalty to Pinkowski and, for the most part, fired up by pride in the prestige of the region's marathon.

Bernardo Gomez de la casa, director of Aid Station #10, hails from San Luis Potosí; he started running in his native Mexico and has been running for most of his life. He describes himself as a competitive runner. In Chicago, he founded the team known as the Panteras, probably the first successful Mexican running team in the city. The team's name has an interesting story: Gomez de la casa's father was a glazier and wore a black mask at work. He was jokingly referred to as the "panther"; hence, "las Panteras." This first Mexican team led to the formation of several others, many of which were founded by former Panteras runners: the Aztecas, Saetas, Quetzlcoatl, and Casadores. Gomez de la casa was at the heart of Mexican running activism in Chicago. From the beginning, he approached team activity as something much broader than the individual runners. His idea was to involve the whole family. His own family (father, brother, and sons) all ran. Other family members from the team would staff water stations. Panteras thus went well beyond its immediate membership and had the necessary backup to assist in volunteer functions while running competitively. This ability to muster the community would translate well into the marathon aid station.

Gomez de la casa had been involved with the aid station for at least eight years at the time of the interview. He refers to Aid Station #10 as the Panteras aid station because it was originally staffed only by his team. But he had bigger ideas; namely, to involve the whole community. Now, the aid station has outgrown the team and involves the participation of many other groups and individuals from the area. His brother helped him bring the first band, and Gomez de la casa eventually brought in the mariachis, a frequent fixture of today's marathon. In fact, when interviewed in June of 2001, he was already hard at work with the bands and community groups in preparation for the upcoming October 7 marathon. He works to ensure the annual participation of the band from Benito Juarez High School as well as the folkloric dancers from Morton High School in neighboring Cicero, where he resides (Cicero is a community with a majority Latino population). His explanation for all of this: "I love the marathon." He does not do this work entirely alone; he also relies on four coordinators to recruit twenty-five workers each, but this still does not account for the more than

200 people who staff the station. He also hopes to see his station win the prize one of these days. As with the other directors cited, Gomez de la casa has close personal ties to Carey Pinkowski. He considers him a good friend and has visited Mexico with him on occasion.

Gomez de la casa has strong ambitions for his community and the Chicago Marathon. He wants the marathon to have the throngs of spectators that mark Boston's and New York's, and he is clearly bothered by any gaps along the route in his area. In 2001, he mentioned his sadness that Ashland Avenue between Taylor and Eighteenth streets was empty. Subsequently, marathon officials and sponsors like Starbucks came to the rescue with perks and incentives to draw people to the area. Executive race director Pinkowski noted that in 2004, there was a "great crowd" in that area. Despite its lower population density and with some help from the marathon and its sponsors, Gomez de la casa's goal of strong spectator support in his area became a reality within only three years.

At the time of the interview, he was concentrating on keeping up his team's regular volunteer activities (staffing other aid stations for races like the Shamrock Shuffle and the Main Course). A recent divorce (ironically, possibly a result of his strong focus on running at the expense of family activities) had reined in his ambitions. Curiously, when asked if he saw himself as the representative of the Mexican community in the marathon, he declined to view himself that way, despite his key role in affirming the Mexican presence in running. He views his participation as a much more personal commitment: his love for the marathon and his ambition to see it become number one. On the other hand, he realizes that his efforts have placed him in a central position and that the Mexican community comes to him for marathon support. The Mexican consulate contacts him to find out how many Mexicans are participating in the race. For 2001, he was trying to persuade the Eighteenth Street Chamber of Commerce to put up a banner declaring "Welcome to the Little Village" (the "Little Village" being "La Villita" of the Pilsen area, the core of Mexican life in Chicago). Without actually envisioning himself as the community spokesperson, he has become an active agent in promoting various demonstrations of Mexican presence in the city. Clearly, he wants his community to associate itself with the prestige of the marathon. His closing statement was his personal invitation to the entire Mexican community to participate in the marathon.

Celia Cheung, who directs Aid Station #12 (Chinatown), can lay claim to working the marathon aid stations from day one in 1977. Cheung, whose first love was dancing, never became a serious runner because of a knee injury. Her ties with distance running are, however, quite profound, long enduring, and very personal. Back in the 1970s, she and her husband George Cheung ran the Junk Restaurant in Chinatown. The restaurant served as the meeting place for serious long-distance runners from throughout the city, and their running club became the Junk Running Club. Despite the name, the club's members were ethnically diverse and mostly Caucasian. Her husband was quite a distance-running enthusiast, and he ran in the first Chicago Marathon, then known as the Mayor Daley Marathon, in 1977. At this point, Celia Cheung was already staffing the aid station then located along the lakefront. Although George passed away in 1994, Celia has continued her work as aid station director. A woman of strong will and generosity, one recognizes her devotion to her husband's memory, which, in part, shines through in her continued loyalty to the marathon and in other moving gestures, such as a commemorative plaque she had placed in Grant Park for him.

The Junk Running Club was itself a lively and festive group. In Chicago's one and only Masquerade Race, Celia Cheung arranged for friends from her dancing class to precede a float of a junk with signs announcing "Here comes the Junk!" The "ship" itself was complete with paddlers and people pushing it inside. It was followed by more dancers running with signs stating: "We missed the boat!" The float won an honorable mention. Despite the zaniness (or maybe because of it), the club's members showed a strong commitment to distance running. They took part in an annual Chinese New Year's Day ultramarathon, run entirely on the honor system and conducted in bitter-cold temperatures. Clearly, the Junk Running Club represented bedrock support for the Chicago Marathon from the onset. George Cheung was himself such an inspiring figure that the 50K race has been named in his honor by Stuart Schulman, also formerly associated with the Junk Running Club. Historical ties may thus run very deep between aid station directors who are linked by strong bonds of friendship and mutual respect.

Celia Cheung recalls the various transformations of the marathon, like how the first route infuriated the north side with the traffic jam it caused. She particularly recalls Carey Pinkowski's arrival when the marathon was having such difficulties finding sponsors, and she indicated that her husband had been especially useful to Pinkowski in introducing him to people throughout the city. She also remarked that an obviously moved Pinkowski attended Cheung's memorial service—alluding like so many others to the genuineness of the executive director's feelings for the people he has worked with; in this case, his strong sense of gratitude. Cheung cites the growth of the marathon as evidenced in the ever-expanding aid station instruction book, which has increased in size from a few pages to a hefty tome.

Today's Aid Station #12 is a rather complex undertaking, managed exclusively by Celia Cheung. The size of the station has grown from three or four tables to thirty. Cheung draws on several sources of volunteers: the local Chinese community, which provides the dragon dancers; the Joy Rehabilitation Suburban Center (not ethnically Chinese); the Rainbow Runners (an African American running group from the south side); a north side Boy Scout troop under the direction of Norb Talend; and various individuals and groups who ask for the Chinatown location. She personally contacts about 150 people and only retains those who prove steady and reliable and who understand readily what is needed. The location is an extremely popular one. At mile 19, it is easily reached by the El and is considered a safe and attractive rendezvous spot. Many spectators go there to cheer on their friends and family who, at this point in the race, will be confronting the famous "wall." Because of all the restaurants, it is considered a fabulous place to eat. Some runners are said to drop out at this convenient meeting place.

This is a large aid station with at least 300 volunteers that is situated closer to the end of the race. People are so anxious to greet and photograph the runners that they tend to mob them, and the police have to restrain the crowd. At this point, the first-aid function of the station becomes more important; hydration, of course, remains essential. Before the distribution of Power Gel and Gatorade, Cheung had resorted to distributing bananas (despite the danger of slipping) to provide runners with needed energy during the latter part of the race. Compassionate, she arranges to have the police bleed a fire hydrant and then leave it gently flowing for those runners who arrive after the official closing of the station, five or six hours into the race. The cleanup is a demanding process, especially getting all the Power Gel off the street.

The aid station did not originally represent the Chinese community;

in fact, like many communities throughout Chicago, that community was initially hostile to the marathon and the aid station. The race blocked attendance at the services of a local church, and it disrupted businesses. It was a social and financial loss. Attitudes have changed radically since then; now, the marathon is accepted and understood as a business enhancement for the numerous Asian restaurants clustered in the Chinatown area. Since the Beatrice sponsorship period, the Chinese community has contributed its dancers.

Cheung is understandably extremely proud of the station's role in the marathon. At one level, this means a great deal in terms of her husband's community—the contribution of a special club to distance running. It also meant originally a pride in the city of Chicago, bringing itself together through this race. At this point, given the international dimensions of the marathon, Cheung is very pleased that Chicago takes its place on the world stage through this race, and she is happy to be part of this effort.

Does she have any regrets? The only one she expressed is having never won the aid station prize, despite several efforts to do so. Her own theory on the then-seemingly never-ending streak of Frontrunner victories has two dimensions. First, she sees the rival club as quite active and committed to putting on an excellent show. Second, she feels that the runner/judges are fresher at the Frontrunners' aid station, which is only seven miles into the race. She surmises that, at mile 19, people are simply concentrating on finding the energy to finish. Other possibilities may be that the Chinatown aid station does not emphasize humor as does the Frontrunners. Comedy seems to have the power to energize. The Chinatown station, which is as beautiful as it is exotic, is unchanging—it always features the dragon dancers, and that may also be a reason for its inability to take the prize. Variety and humor are part of the essence of carnival, and they may be required for ultimate success. Whatever the reasons, Cheung accepts her rivals' victories with good humor, but would like to win the prize someday. One can only wish her well.

The Cheung experience once again reconfirms the level of commitment of aid station directors, the willingness of individuals to undertake rather difficult endeavors for no financial remuneration. In a way, it flies in the face of the notion of an all-for-profit society, and clearly suggests that volunteerism is alive and well in a great metropolis. It is also a testament to the social cohesiveness that running builds among diverse groups of people.

Bernard Lyles had worked for twelve years as of 2001 as the director of Aid Station #15, the Tri-Masters station. He is a veteran marathon runner with an impressive personal best of 2:54. Currently, he serves as president of the Tri-Masters Club, which emphasizes triathlon performance. This club is the direct successor to Rainbow Runners, for which Lyles also served as president. Like so many others, Carey Pinkowski reached out to him as a running club president to assist the marathon by taking charge of an aid station. Since he has assumed that responsibility, he has not run the marathon, despite his inclination to do so.

Lyles has several recruitment bases. First, there are veteran aid station workers, for whom the marathon is the highlight of the season. A second source is high school students. Since he also runs a youth program, the Tri-Masters Sports Initiative Program (www.Tri-Masters.org), this club provides good recruiting grounds. Currently, students who want to graduate from high school have to do some kind of social service—and aid station volunteering is considered a social service. Between the veteran workers and the students, Lyles is able to meet the marathon request of 300 volunteers. The number is particularly large at his station because volunteers show up in two waves, the first arriving at around 6:00 A.M. and the second at about 10:30 A.M. This exceptional demand reflects the special burden caused by the station's location at mile 23. So many people arrive five and six hours after the marathon has begun that the earlier workers are already exhausted.

The station definitely puts on a show: it has the Du Sable High School band and a disc jockey or musical group. A blues band has played there in the past. It seeks to provide some energy to runners near the very finish of the race. It is also meticulously organized to provide efficient hydration. Lyles regrets that his station hasn't yet won the aid station prize, and he stated that the volunteers tried on several occasions but have more or less given up. He gives the Frontrunners credit for putting in the work to win the annual prize, but would love to be able to win the prize purse to help his youth group.

The aid station itself provides inspiration to him and to his volunteers. People get motivated by watching the athletes, and many of the younger volunteers end up wanting to run. For Lyles, the personal commitment to his community obviously outweighs his own desire as an athlete to participate in the race, and he clearly derives great personal satisfaction in creating community involvement. He believes that running brings the city together. For his student volunteers, watching the marathon is a kind of personal inspiration: they see the Kenyans and other African runners not as exotic foreigners but as "black guys up front"—a welcome change from much of what they see in their society. The aid station thus simultaneously reinforces the unity of the city as a whole while providing particular examples for emulation by young African Americans.

Lyles also has a personal anecdote about his station—it seems to be the point at which many champions decide not to continue with the race. As a result, he has had a chance to meet many of the elite runners—though perhaps not at their happiest moments. On one occasion, he even directed Steve Jones toward the finish line—he was truly surprised at encountering him and asked why he hadn't already won the race. Clearly, mile 23 has its social advantages!

The Chicago Marathon enjoys exceptional grassroots support. It is sustained both by an umbrella running organization and the long-term commitment of its aid station directors, who are bound to it by deep ties of personal loyalty to its race director and to each other. What is so inspiring among the directors and the throngs that staff their aid stations is a generosity untainted by any ulterior motives for gain. The intensity and reliability of this support speak to firm foundations that ensure the continuing success of the marathon.

Major sponsors like Gatorade join forces with smaller community and civic donors.

PART III

Sponsorship
and General Assistance

Sponsors' support for the marathon is apparent on signs, water bottles, jackets, even the mylar blankets enveloping the finishers.

five

corporate and
small-business sponsorship

All marathons are heavily reliant on corporate backing. Because spectators pay no fees, television revenues can be relatively modest, and runners themselves finance only a small part of the actual cost of participation, race directors and owners must find other sources of income. In
the United States and abroad, marathons must have corporate sponsors willing to assume the substantial costs involved with these events.
There may often be more than one corporate sponsor, although there
is usually one "senior partner," either the event owner or the title owner that directs the marathon and recruits additional corporate support.
Generally speaking, in the United States, and most certainly in Illinois,
the law forbids these sponsors any direct profit from their endeavors,
which are defined as "not-for-profit." But corporations do not spon-

sor marathons on the basis of pure altruism. Some incentives beyond the love of running must fuel corporate participation. LaSalle Bank's sponsorship of the Chicago Marathon and its affiliated sponsors offer excellent case studies in the modalities and motivations for corporate involvement.

The Chicago Marathon, initially the Mayor Daley Marathon, underwent various changes in sponsorship throughout its history. Prior to LaSalle, the two most important sponsors were Beatrice Foods (1979) and Old Style (Heileman Brewing Company) (1988). Both had the necessary deep pockets to publicize the marathon and to provide prize money to attract world champions. Neither, however, was the actual owner of the marathon, which belonged to Lee Flaherty through his firm Flair Communications. The problem of each of these sponsors lay in their relatively limited commitment to the event. After a corporate shake-up, Beatrice pulled out of sponsorship to take over the Western Open golf tournament in 1987. The marathon lost an effective, highly respected sponsor. Old Style took over event sponsorship in 1988, and once again money was available to allow the marathon world-class status. This new stability was soon compromised by Old Style's withdrawal as title sponsor in 1991, which meant diminished purses for victors.

After a period of instability in the early 1990s, there would be a significant change in sponsorship and ownership. The first significant positive change took place in 1993, when Lee Flaherty decided to sell the race to Major Events, formed by Chris Devine and Tom Cooney. In early summer of 1994, then–race director Pinkowski was approached by intermediaries for LaSalle about the prospects of bank sponsorship. By mid-summer, LaSalle had become the title sponsor and actually purchased the full rights to the marathon in 1996. The institution would further demonstrate its commitment to Chicago running by purchasing the spring Shamrock Shuffle 8K in 2000 from the Chicago Area Runners Association.[1]

LaSalle's decision was not taken lightly. As Kim Woods, former senior vice president and director of internal communications at ABN AMRO (LaSalle's parent company), points out, LaSalle looks carefully into the strategic and tactical benefits of any prospective sponsorship.[2] Strategically, LaSalle seeks sponsorship opportunities that it feels reflect its values, which it characterizes as "integrity, teamwork, respect, and professionalism." It focuses on possibilities that reach a key demographic and that will improve brand awareness. The bank fully expects greater name recognition from any sponsorship activity. It also looks for internal marketing opportunities; that is, sponsorship that makes its employees proud to be part of the institution. Further, the bank seeks beneficiaries that will deliver tangible or intangible value greater than the cost.

Among the tactical benefits that the bank looks for are cross-promotions with local, national, and international partners. This serves as a form of additional publicity. LaSalle also appreciates the importance of client entertainment as an asset for its commercial bankers. Finally, it seeks access to VIPs in any sponsorship endeavor. LaSalle abundantly realizes all of these benefits in its sponsorship of the Chicago Marathon, as does its Dutch parent company, ABN AMRO, because its association with the Chicago Marathon grants it high visibility on the world stage.

LaSalle also takes into account other considerations in sponsorship decisions such as the duplication of effort, potential synergies or tie-ins with other bank sponsorships, the availability of value-added programs, the data possibilities that will lead to quality market research, and whether the bank will possess category exclusivity (as in sole or title sponsor). Further, LaSalle's sponsorship of the Chicago Marathon is part of a broad pattern of sponsorship, although it is probably the marathon that draws more attention to the bank than any other endeavor.

The marathon commitment notwithstanding, the bank's existing sponsorships are extensive. In 2003, it had completed its twenty-seventh year underwriting the LaSalle Bank Do-It-Yourself Messiah, which is comprised of a 100–piece volunteer orchestra, four professional soloists, and the audience's 3,000 voices merging in a performance of Handel's oratorio, *Messiah*. It was also the original sponsor of the Dame Myra Hess Memorial Concerts—another twenty-seven-year commitment as of 2003—a series of free-of-charge, live concerts to showcase talented new artists. They are broadcast live over WFMT-FM, Chicago's last remaining classical music channel, and around the world on the channel's web site. In 2003, the institution was in its second year of a three-year commitment to the LaSalle Bank Winter Wonderfest, a holiday-time spectacular on Navy Pier that includes sparkling lights, decorated trees, ice-skating, bungee jumps, rock-climbing walls, and so on. In 2003, the bank also sponsored the Chicago Field Museum's exhibition of "Eternal Egypt: Masterworks of Ancient Art from the British Museum." Other Chicago sponsorships include the Old Town School of Folk Music, the Grant Park Music Festival Summer Concert Series, Christmas Glory, and the Black Ensemble Theatre.

Given this background of diverse sponsorship, LaSalle's decision to assume the chief sponsor role and then later to buy the marathon was a logical outgrowth of the bank's civic commitment; it was also a savvy economic calculation, a well-though-out venture into soft advertising, and a major move in the bank's effort to position itself as the city's chief corporate citizen. In general, financial institutions, when they turn to sports, tend to sponsor golf tournaments, obviously because this sport usually draws upper-middle-class to upper-class viewers of a higher age demographic. Indeed, the decision in favor of the marathon was made after considering golf and other sports sponsorship opportunities, and not without carefully weighed judgment. Marathon demographics are quite attractive to financial institutions. Runners tend to be urban and professional but younger than the golf set, on average. As outlined in chapter 1, runners are people interested in long-range financial planning; they are individuals who take a deliberate rather than impulsive view of life. Delayed gratification is their modus vivendi. In so many ways, the marathon corresponds to their lifestyle: long, persistent training with an eye to the future; a willingness to patiently endure adversity with the aim of accomplishing a distant goal; and a highly individualized sense of performance and accomplishment, measured not so much in defeating others as in achieving what one has set out to do. LaSalle, by assuming race sponsorship, would be able to address this clientele directly. It presented its image throughout the city, thus moving from the abstraction of a financial institution into the highly visible reality of a mass happening. In fact, the bank even created a boldly designed and, in principle, "unchanging" logo that identified it with the Chicago Marathon year in and year out. In 2003, over the weekend of October 4–5, the logo was nonetheless modified with the inclusion of the green and gold shield and the endorsement of Netherlands-based parent company ABN AMRO. The original logo, despite these modifications, remained intact and thus retained a definite sense of continuity. LaSalle, through its marathon promotion and its ubiquitous logo, thus assumes the role of Chicago's most visible corporate citizen and reaches a class of people who are highly investment-conscious.

Event ownership by a corporate sponsor sets off the LaSalle Bank Chicago Marathon from its major counterparts in Boston and New York, which, though reliant on sponsorship, are owned by the Boston Athletic Club and the New York Road Runners Club, respectively. Asset management and insurance firm ING, for instance, is the primary sponsor and title owner of the New York City Marathon. In a sense, the Chicago Marathon illustrates one possibility in the evolution of corporate sponsorship in which a business assumes total control of an event. One may only speculate whether the drive to ever-increasing participation may, in part, be fueled by a model of corporate growth in which continuously swelling numbers are seen as an undisputable plus. It must be said, however, that LaSalle has a vital interest in ensuring the quality of the marathon, and that concern has most certainly tempered an unlimited growth model.

This newer model indicates that marathons may progressively escape the control of running associations and become the properties of given businesses. Although this may lead to indignation on the part of purists, the compelling issue remains the quality of the event. So far, corporate ownership seems to have contributed to the quality of the Chicago Marathon. "Quality" is a broadly defined notion: it includes a race that is extremely well organized, professional in every aspect, and open to anyone who chooses to register (reverting to the marathon's original theme as being the "people's marathon"); yet, it is a race offering exceptional and creative incentives to attract the world's swiftest runners. All of this is quite unimaginable without a sponsor with vast financial resources.

To justify its significant expenditures, LaSalle—and all sponsors, for that matter—must in some indirect, "not-for-profit" way realize some kind of corporate benefit. The most obvious justification of these expenditures is the "soft" advertising value of race ownership. By its highly visible role in the marathon, LaSalle hopes to enlist new clients. The bank presents itself as the corporate citizen most responsible for providing tens of thousands of Chicagoans the opportunity to run the race and hundreds of thousands more the option to watch this major urban event. It can tap into this source of civic pride and link itself to the promotion of the city of Chicago. Bank officials cannot measure how much business this identification of LaSalle with the marathon actually generates, but they can determine relatively accurately the advertising value of their sponsorship, which was estimated at seven million dollars—or nearly three times the cost of race sponsorship in 1998.

This advertising is qualified as soft because it never pitches for banking with LaSalle and never describes the bank as a financial institution. On the contrary, it limits itself to name identification, or "branding" as it is currently referred to in advertising. In many ways, this strategy meshes perfectly with modern advertising—particularly sports advertising—which is increasingly soft. One need only consider publicity for corporations like Cisco—which, prior to the dot-com bubble burst in 2000, chose to celebrate the world-transforming power of the Internet while only discreetly suggesting its own role as the underlying technical facilitator—to grasp how much style and image overshadow the hard sell. Corporations, even some of the most nefarious polluters, increasingly seek to be viewed as benign presences on the global as well as the local level. LaSalle's sponsorship of the marathon accomplishes this effectively on the local level. It fits perfectly into the new image-based society of wealthy urban professionals highly conscious of style and appearance, and, perhaps quite innocently, blends with new constructions of class distinction based on highly privileged young people very much swept up by their sense of self.[3]

LaSalle's highly successful involvement with the marathon led to other sports sponsorships. As previously discussed, it purchased the Shamrock Shuffle in 2000 from the Chicago Area Runners Association. This acquisition allowed it to "bookend" the racing season because the Shamrock opens the CARA circuit in the spring, and the marathon is the third-to-last race of over twenty circuit races and is the last of such races in Chicago. The aggregate of the marathon and Shamrock runners vastly exceeds the combined total of all those registered in other CARA circuit races. The two races can be fairly described as the alpha and omega of the city of Chicago's races.

Beyond foot racing, LaSalle moved into golf with a three-year title sponsorship (2002–2004) of the LaSalle Bank Open, which included four-day, live national cable-television coverage on the Golf Channel. The PGA tour has been extended through 2009. The bank uses a family-friendly admission pricing: kids and seniors free, adults pay $10 for a pass. Whereas LaSalle initially had chosen between the marathon and golf sponsorship, it is now in a position to sponsor both, thus covering two potentially strong client groups. LaSalle is also visible in the sponsorship of major league baseball (Chicago Cubs and Chicago White Sox), professional soccer (Chicago Fire), professional hockey (Chicago Wolves, Rockford Ice Hogs), and college athletics (Northwestern University and the University of Illinois at Chicago). LaSalle and its parent company, ABN AMRO, also underwrite events supported by the city of Chicago; the city's lesbian, gay, bisexual, and transgender (LGBT) community; near-suburban branch activities; and locally focused opportunities in Michigan and elsewhere in the Midwest outside Illinois.

Within the domain of corporate citizenship, LaSalle and its allies can lay claim to providing an enormous benefit to the city. Regional Economic Assessment Laboratory (REAL)[4] statistics indicated a nearly $70 million economic benefit for the Chicago area in 1999 and around $80 million in 2000. Based on ever-increasing marathon participation, LaSalle expected a $100 million benefit in 2001. With each passing year, revenues seem to increase. Thus, the bank can present itself as a true benefactor of the city, with the implicit message that Chicagoans should turn to it for their banking services.

Therefore, sponsorship that can lay claim to such broad social benefits is not so much a supplement to traditional advertising; it can be *the* most effective marketing strategy. It has been the fastest-growing trend in advertising over the past decade, and its appeal is particularly understandable in the context of the decreasing efficiency of measured media (e.g., advertising and sales promotions). Changing social priorities are emphasizing contribution to the community; that is, "giving something back." Consumers tend to accept a firm that benefits others in addition to itself. Banking and financial institutions find this mode of advertising particularly attractive; they are the second most active category in sponsorship, just behind packaged foods and beverages. In 1999, sports sponsorship passed $10 billion and accounts for the highest spending levels.

One corporation is hardly sufficient to sponsor a marathon. Title or key sponsors form coalitions to gather additional resources—essentially, they recruit other business to take over key events or provide essential equipment, supplies, and services. LaSalle, for example, has reached out to other corporations to broaden support for its marathon and to multiply the number of events accompanying the race. In so doing, the bank was able to provide additional economic stability and create greater opportunities for cross-promotion. LaSalle ABN AMRO's current most notable corporate partners are listed as official sponsors in the following order on the 2005 web site: New Balance, Dominick's Finer Foods, MasterCard, Volkswagen, American Airlines, Tylenol, Gatorade, Ice Mountain, and MarathonFoto.com.

One of the bank's first initiatives was to bring in its auditor, Ernst & Young, as a proprietary event program sponsor, namely the Ernst & Young Team Challenge. This relationship lasted until 2003, when changes in federal law ruled out this kind of client/sponsor relationship. The marathon—that is, LaSalle ABN AMRO—now handles the corporate challenge. Although this particular relationship has ended, its discussion is particularly helpful as an example of corporate synergy. The accounting firm accepted with enthusiasm and in 1999 sponsored a race that included 110 corporate teams and 124 teams in the open division. In 2003, its last year, there were 45 corporate teams and 145 teams in the open division. Then and currently, teams may range from three to five participants, and the top three competitors for each team are counted in an elaborate system that attributes value according the runners' performances by their sex and age category. It is not the absolute fastest who is necessarily the best contributor to the team's overall performance.[5] Team competition, detached from the limitations of age, appeals to a larger audience. Through its creative strategy, Ernst & Young was able to appeal both to corporate loyalty and to running clubs, thus adding a new dimension to the competition.

The enterprise was also able to improve marathon amenities. Ernst & Young set up a corporate tent to shelter both team divisions. It provided private changing areas and premarathon facilities that were much superior to the standard ones, including chairs and tables, fresh coffee and snacks, and, of course, water and sports drinks. It also provided far better postmarathon fare, again in the comfort of a private tent with its own facilities, and arranged for a team photo for each competitor. In short, Ernst & Young's association contributed to ritualizing and commemorating the marathon, thus furthering ongoing attendance and runner loyalty. Its collaboration with LaSalle meant a vast increase in material and personnel resources in managing the marathon. It was a symbiotic exercise in that both corporations derived prestige from their efforts and functioned as partners rather than competitors.

Once again, this allowed an enterprise whose function is highly abstract to identify itself with the race and thus create a concrete, visible presence for itself in the heart of an athletic event completely unrelated to its functions. Ernst & Young rapidly wove racing into its advertising with the slogan "From thought to finish." This discreet allusion to the marathon allowed for another soft sell, and it also linked investment to training—a delicate but critical identification clearly directed to urban professionals and their objectives.

Hence, two financial institutions used the marathon to target the same clientele. Ernst & Young, however, is not a local firm. Like LaSalle, whose own international implications derive from its parent institution, Ernst & Young has many international branches. It was thus able to use its overseas connections to bring in competitors from its office in Brussels, creating a sports-based form of corporate loyalty far beyond Chicago's boundaries. LaSalle does the same through the ABN AMRO running team. It also holds monthly lunchtime running clinics and employee fun runs, participates in CARA circuit races, and promotes volunteering. Indeed, this kind of intracorporate promotion may be as important as the soft advertising benefits for an enterprise because it facilitates the development of intangible emotional ties to a firm, making a position not just a job but also a dynamic and emotional form of self-realization played out even on an intercontinental scale. Employees discover that their firms offer them the world as their theater.

Marathon sponsors, most particularly LaSalle, also enjoy a heightened e-commerce visibility. By 2000, 88 percent of the registration was online. Even nonregistrants could consult the marathon's virtual training program (an idea that has now become a standard feature of big marathon web sites). The web site, of course, facilitates the purchase of marathon-related merchandise, once again promoting name recognition. E-post cards and screen savers are also available, all of which make LaSalle more visible. Regular e-mails are also directed to prospective participants. In short, the virtual world is fully exploited in getting out the name of the event owner.

Other businesses also saw the advantages of becoming a proprietary event program sponsor. American Airlines titles the Fun Run that precedes the actual marathon and Dominick's (a local food chain) sponsored the Youth Run, which was dropped in 2001 in favor of a year-round smart fitness program to promote healthy living among the youth demographic. These activities also provide an association with the marathon that continues throughout the entire year. American Airlines' Fun Run reinforces its other role as a product sponsor by providing reduced travel rates and serving as the official carrier of the Chicago Marathon. The Fun Run allows American to situate itself as the "prelude" event to the marathon and to challenge United Airlines, whose hub is in Chicago, as the city's most civically conscious air carrier.[6]

Other businesses were also recruited as product sponsors. These include firms such as New Balance, Ice Mountain, Gatorade, Nextel (in charge of wireless communication on race day), and Volkswagen (the pacer car). In the case of New Balance, Jim Tompkins, president and COO, made it a point to be at the kickoff press conference for the 2004 marathon to announce the extension of his firm's partnership with La-Salle and the marathon. He characterized the marathon as "one of the best run events in the world" and said it was "a perfect fit for New Balance." While he acknowledged the New Balance runners among the professionals, he saluted the 40,000 athletes who had been toiling for months "just to cross the finish line," whom he characterized as "heroes." Clearly, the president of New Balance understood the sales dimensions of inclusiveness, and his words speak to the extraordinary marketing opportunity the Chicago Marathon provides. In some sense, marketing imperatives demand that companies embrace a non-elitist and surely overinflated notion of the achievement of running a marathon. New Balance is, of course, an obvious presence at the marathon expo, where, beyond shoe sales, it provides services like timing bracelets and a sign-up sheet for the New Balance Three-Hour Club, a commemorative award for those runners who complete the marathon in three hours or less. By this, the company covers the entire range of runners, and, although it may exaggerate the achievement of some, it does offer a special inducement to the more accomplished athletes.

Nextel and Volkswagen are particularly interesting in that their connection as product sponsors is less obvious than most others. The new retro-styled Beetles that serve as pacer cars do, however, ensure continuous visibility for VW throughout the race. VW has noted extraordinary client interest during the marathon expo, where VW enthusiasts tend to drop by in great numbers. Nextel, which sponsors wireless communication at the Boston Marathon as well, filled a rather special niche. With the advent of the ChampionChip, Nextel provided worldwide web site information about the progress of runners throughout the race; hence, its services far surpassed the simple telephone links that formerly united race officials and addressed emergency problems. Nextel could make runners' times available as they passed specific distances throughout the race. For Boston, Chicago, and a host of other marathons, split times have become available at the 5K, 10K, 15K, 20K, half-marathon, 25K, 30K, 35K, 40K, and finish through the efforts of different providers. This means that friends and relatives who are thousands of miles away can now follow their runners in close to real time in all major marathons. With this, a service such as a wireless communication company that one would never directly associate with racing becomes as natural a product sponsor as a shoe company.

Whatever reservations runners may hold about this friendly but Big Brother–like surveillance, this kind of sponsorship will no doubt grow because it fosters a sense of intense, vicarious participation through virtual reality. Distance is no longer an absolute obstacle for those spectators intent on the performance of friends and family members rather than professionals. Traditional spectatorship meant either watching the race from specific spots or viewing it on television. With electronic monitoring of runners' progress, spectatorship has become infinitely more personalized; furthermore, this surveillance only reinforces the notion that everyone's race is significant. This personalization contributes to mass participation without concern for age and ability and without any need for teams. There is little doubt that creative sponsors will take this one step further: video on the web that will provide universal real-time viewing. At this point, the marathon will become the complete theater of individual self-realization. It will not only permit spectators views of their favorite runners, but it will also allow those people the complete narcissism of reviewing their own performances. Associating a sponsor's name with such capabilities is surely a branding bonanza.

The result of this creative fusion of the event sponsors and product sponsors is a vast synergy that not only permits the Chicago Marathon to flourish as a world-class event but actually expands it. Cluster events like a fun run, a health and fitness expo, and banquets surround the marathon, extending what is in reality a relatively brief competition into a happening that stretches over an entire weekend. As of 2001, the marathon was held on Columbus Day weekend, which allows many marathoners and their supporters the choice of staying over in Chicago for the Monday holiday. This strategy helps convert the marathon into a prolonged celebration during which the runners, having now completed their ordeal, are free to reward themselves with the pleasures to be found in such a major metropolis.

Just about all marathons make the event into a full weekend affair, but the Boston Marathon also exploits the idea of a prolonged, three-day weekend for its event. This weekend includes a pasta party ("Ronzoni Party") and a prerace fun run starting at Boston City Hall. Instead of on the weekend, however, Boston holds the race on Monday, Patriots Day—an April holiday celebrated only in Massachusetts and Maine, thus inconveniencing all participants coming from any other state. This is no reward for the runners who, already tired from their race, often must return home that Monday evening; nevertheless, the city reaps the economic benefits of a three-day weekend.

Indeed, the clustering of events is a general feature of most marathons. Officials from all the world's major races travel to targeted marathons, mingle at the races' VIP parties, and, most important, observe how their rivals organize the events surrounding their races. In a wired world, successful innovations are copied almost immediately. Given the financial pressures on almost all marathons, this kind of sponsorship interaction is essential.

––––––––––

While it is obviously key to understand the race owner's and title sponsor's roles in the marathon, it is also useful to look more closely at the role of event and product sponsors. Dominick's Finer Foods was heavily involved with the marathon from 1990 through 2005; it served as the marathon's "grocery store" until its sudden withdrawal from sponsorship in 2006.[7] Don Fitzgerald is former vice president of marketing for Dominick's, where he first began working in 1977.[8] Fitzgerald offered insight into the food chain's relationship to the marathon. He was not only professionally but also athletically involved with the marathon. Encouraged by Pinkowski, he became interested in running and broke the four-hour mark in 2003. Fitzgerald was thus more than a marketing executive who oversaw his firm's role in the marathon; he was an actual participant and understood the event as both a business opportunity and as a demanding sport. He noted that, in 2003, Dominick's relationship with the marathon was already more than twelve years old—it was back in 1990 with only about 8,000 runners in the race that

Dominick's marketers realized that the marathon could be a potential advantage. They were not slow to capitalize on it.

One of the most obvious advantages was location: there are Dominick's stores throughout Chicago—one in East Lakeview is actually directly along the course. Fitzgerald also noted the potential for cross-promotional opportunities. Dominick's received incremental funds from other products that shared in its marathon advertising. Dominick's also wanted to represent itself as part of the communities it served, and the marathon offered a truly unique opportunity for community identification. Initial involvement was relatively inexpensive, Fitzgerald noted, at only about $30,000. Given that the marathon is a massive revenue generator, Dominick's role as exclusive grocery sponsor was well suited to increase its sales

The key sponsorship for Dominick's meshed perfectly with the chain's other public missions that advanced its sales strategy and positioned Dominick's as a responsible corporate citizen. At the time of this writing, Dominick's missions addressed fitness, obesity, adult diabetes, and nutrition. The firm had a children's foundation whose specific goal was to combat childhood obesity, a severe problem given that 25 percent of children and teens in the Chicago area are considered obese. Dominick's was aiming at young children in the six- to twelve-year-old bracket. Dominick's youth program was elaborate—it included a Smart Fitness Youth Run, which were staggered runs for different age groups. It also had essay and shirt-design contests. In 2003, with the help of the Special Olympics, 100 Special Olympians ran up the finish chute.

The cost of marathon sponsorship for Dominick's was quite high. The annual fee was $150,000 plus an additional $25,000 in food products for the finish line. The firm also provided pizzas and lunches for the volunteers at the marathon expo. The use of a refrigerator truck for this purpose also added to the expenses. The total in 2003 was about $200,000. Dominick's also needed the support of food producers as copromoters to help defray cost and strengthen its marketing efforts. One of the great attractions of this copromotion was publicity in Dominick's advertising circulars; normally this amounted to about two million copies per week and included a special marathon section. These circulars were general and inevitably included foods that were from vendors not associated with marathon training, like Pepsi, Tombstone, Keebler, Frito-Lay, Anheuser-Busch, Salerno, and Dean's. Although many were national, some had more direct local connections. Dominick's relationship with LaSalle and the Chicago Marathon also had an additional advertising advantage: exclusive marketing rights for the Shamrock Shuffle, the next-largest race in the Chicago area, which had the same potential for copromotion by associated products.

Dominick's functioned in a manner similar to the Chicago Cubs and White Sox: it extended licensing and franchising to those who could not afford with their own resources to take advantage of this promotional opportunity. For example, Dominick's was the sponsor of the carbo-loading prerace dinner; despite the fact that other producers such as Barilla and Ragu donated hundreds of pounds of pasta and sauce, the dinner was known as the "*Dominick's* Pasta Dinner." Even though Dominick's name was branded on the dinner, these other producers were also recognized and their products were promoted at less cost than that of full sponsorship.

Dominick's strove continuously to expand these coalitions: in 2003, the firm was working with a local flower vendor to provide marathon bouquets. The firm had also come up with another way of leveraging the enormous street traffic during the marathon: "couponing." This had the advantage of allowing Dominick's to assess how couponing affects sales. During the marathon expo, Dominick's was very careful to check how many "eyeballs" their display attracted. In fact, its stand had a kind of wheel of fortune that people could spin to win. Such attractions allowed the firm to create a database from the reactions of expo visitors.

Dominick's knew quite well that the marathon provided excellent demographics for its client base. Most marathon runners were and still are between twenty-five and thirty-five years old; the average age is thirty-seven. Women comprise 42 percent of runners, and they tend to do most of the shopping, particularly if they have children. Dominick's is more of an upscale operation and marathon runners themselves are sufficiently affluent to figure in their client base: 36 percent of runners earn from $50,000 to $100,000 per year; 20 percent earn from $100,000 to $200,000 per year. Dominick's also extended its reach in the running community by offering publicity to CARA in the chain's weekly mailings and by providing food and drink to the running association's marathon tent. Clearly, Dominick's left no stone unturned. And this extended not only to running—the firm sponsored the White

Sox, the Blue Demons (DePaul University's basketball team), and the LPGA tour in the suburbs.

All things considered, Fitzgerald represented Dominick's as heavily invested in running because it understood the explosive growth of the Chicago Marathon and running in general. The firm considered the 40,000 runners to be an excellent market, an investment in growth that was focused on the common man and woman rather than on the elite athlete. Because of the marathon's inclusive nature, it offered a marketing opportunity that could not be achieved in other sports, where all the athletes were usually professionals.

Dominick's was and still remains concerned with developing local connections. In this sense, it valued its relationship with LaSalle because both firms were seen as Chicago institutions, even though both are now owned by outside corporations (Safeway owns Dominick's). Dominick's role as a local sponsor was clearly reinforced by its third-place listing among the top three sponsors in 2005 (LaSalle and New Balance preceded it). Executive race director Pinkowski was extremely careful to respect this listing and to characterize Dominick's as the marathon's official grocery store. The association with LaSalle and the marathon had also helped Dominick's launch into other domains, youth runs in particular, as the food chain was able to benefit from LaSalle's expertise in sponsorship. At the time, Dominick's was also featuring a program to educate children as smart shoppers. Clearly, the firm was using running sponsorship and the expertise it had gained from it to build an extensive and long-term customer base centered on loyalty to an institution that was seen as health-oriented and philanthropic. Dominick's hoped that this carefully crafted strategy would help defend it against cost-slashing competition. Clearly, however, the marathon and its principal sponsor/owner had radically influenced the advertising and image building of a significant local firm.

Gatorade is an official sponsor and a major presence in the Chicago Marathon. The firm, formerly owned by Quaker Oats, was purchased by Pepsi, a somewhat ironic twist but illustrative of the dynamics of contemporary capitalism, which can mean that products entirely at cross-purposes with one another can belong to the same enterprise.[9] Gatorade, nonetheless, holds fast to its integrity by maintaining the

Gatorade Sports Science Institute in Barrington, a distant Chicago sub-urb.[10] Indeed, its sales strategy is based on solid research, broad availability, consumer education (as it is convinced of the superiority of its products), and sports marketing opportunities like the marathon.

Gatorade is widely visible in the sports arena. Given its origin as an energy drink for football players, this is hardly surprising. From its humble days in Florida, it has expanded to cover the entire National Football League (NFL),[11] much of the NBA, major league baseball, and numerous conferences and bowls. It is highly prominent in major endurance events like the Boston, New York City, and Chicago marathons as well as the Ironman Triathlon. Internationally, it is the energy drink of Berlin Marathon aid stations. These races are ways of communicating the product's credibility. Chicago thus figures as part of a much larger pattern; its importance as a race makes it particularly valuable to Gatorade.

Whatever the race or sport, Gatorade, as a product sponsor, normally supplies the drink for free, but the beneficiaries must use Gatorade cups for all beverages. The company wants its name displayed prominently to all race participants and spectators. Marathon runners cannot miss Gatorade's presence at aid stations; television viewers and anyone in proximity to these stations will observe a sea of cups with the Gatorade logo on tables or strewn in the streets.

Sponsorship for the marathon really begins with the Shamrock Shuffle. At that point, Gatorade is already involved with all the training programs. On marathon day itself, Gatorade ships thousands of gallons in concentrated form that are mixed with Ice Mountain Water. Gatorade employees test all the aid stations for product quality, and they have a Gatorade volunteer for each station. Constant contact is maintained in the event that any difficulty should arise. Gatorade typifies a megafirm in action at the Chicago Marathon. The marathon is just one piece in a huge mosaic of marketing, but it is nonetheless treated with great seriousness and care because it is a colossal promotional opportunity.

Although runners are certainly ensured hydration through Gatorade's massive intervention, this service does not come without a cost. On a microlevel, runners cannot always visually ascertain where the water ends and the Gatorade begins as they approach the aid stations. All liquids are contained in identical cups bearing the Gatorade logo, and volunteers must shout out the hydration "frontiers" to runners who would probably rather not have to pay attention to this detail. This sponsor-imposed ubiquity is a relentless form of branding that obfuscates other product choices. The ubiquitous Gatorade cups suggest that there is only one legitimate choice for the athlete. Indeed, Gatorade holds a near visual monopoly over hydration at the marathon. In all fairness, however, this monopoly stems in part from the widespread conviction of the product's worth, which is constantly reinforced by ongoing research.

Dave Zimmer of Fleet Feet is one of the city's most dynamic running entrepreneurs.[12] In a few short years, his client base has exploded, and much of this has to do with savvy business strategy. He too is a marathon sponsor of sorts, but his firm's role, unlike giants like Gatorade, illustrates the interrelationship of a small, local business and its effects on the marathon. Fleet Feet is a national chain that is managed via franchise. Sally Edwards founded it in 1976 during the first running boom that took off with Shorter's Olympic victory and continued with the success of runners like Bill Rodgers. The chain in 2003 had some fifty franchises. Zimmer points out that 1984, the year of the first women's Olympic marathon, was particularly eventful for Fleet Feet, as this event marked the full inclusion of women in the running community. Currently, women, many directly influenced by the Olympic marathon and Title IX, now make up 56 percent of his franchise's business. It is thus no accident that Fleet Feet is a strong promoter of women's racing, which includes sponsorship of a women's-only race.

Zimmer sees 1995–96 as the beginning of the second running boom. It was in 1996 that his store opened in Chicago in a relatively small space, which it rapidly outgrew. Fleet Feet is now lodged in a 4,000-square-foot locale, next to a Starbucks and a cinema complex, on toney North Avenue in Chicago's Lincoln Park neighborhood. Zimmer opened a second store in the newly gentrified Lincoln Square neighborhood in 2001.

Zimmer, whose background is in banking with Citicorp, has a clear, concise business philosophy: determine Fleet Feet's sphere of influence. By this he means deciding precisely what people to talk to so that they in turn will talk about Fleet Feet to others. To achieve and broaden Fleet Feet's sphere of influence, Zimmer has strategies that are practiced inside and outside his stores. Within the stores, the typical marketing procedure for a first-time buyer is to videotape the runner on a treadmill to analyze the individual's gate and thus provide better counseling in shoe purchasing. This was an innovative tactic that attracted a lot of attention when his first store opened. Outside the store, Fleet Feet's forty-five employees also talk to marathon group leaders and to the participants in those groups. On a more convivial level, they have "married running and beer," as Goose Island (Beer) sponsors their running events and a party, thus capitalizing on the profoundly social aspect of the sport. Fleet Feet sponsors numerous races throughout the city and supports many charities. In 2003, the firm contributed $19,000 to the Ravenswood Neighborhood Food Pantry. Fleet Feet is now heavily identified with combating childhood obesity among the urban population because of the work that they do with the Fit Matters program at La Rabida Children's Hospital.

However, Zimmer had also conceived of a very simple but effective method of reaching the running community. Initially, Fleet Feet employees began distributing water (and often t-shirts and survey forms) by the North Avenue Beach House along the heavily trafficked lakefront jogging trail. They soon became a fixture for Lincoln Park and East Lakeview residents, home to the densest concentration of runners in Chicago—and some of the wealthiest. This was a very basic level of giving that established a clear presence.

Fleet Feet's programs are, of course, considerably more elaborate now. They handle more than 400 events throughout the year. Some typical examples are an appearance by local coach and CARA columnist Bill Leach to discuss core strength training and a presentation of yoga and Pilates for runners. In the beginning of the year, Fleet Feet offers training for Chicago runners who are "Boston Bound." Chicago Marathon official coach Hal Higdon comes to speak, and, of course, race director Carey Pinkowski comes to talk at the store. Fleet Feet also features teaching presentations on biomechanics and workshops on the basics of buying the proper footwear.

The Chicago Marathon is an especially critical part of the franchise's frequency marketing. Simply put, this means the more Fleet Feet logos people see, the more likely they are to keep its stores in mind. These visual impressions are made in several ways. During marathon training, which extends from April through October, Fleet Feet helps supply the lakefront hydration stations. This is the staff's largest effort—it requires 250,000 cups, 20,000 gallons of Gatorade and water, and thousands of hours of work. Fleet Feet's strategy is astute here. It understands how important water and Gatorade are to the runners training for the marathon, and its employees do everything in their power to be in front of the runners providing this service, which is also great marketing for them. Immediately prior to the marathon, as an additional promotional measure, Fleet Feet employees make sure that the goodie bags at the expo are stuffed with coupons to the stores redeemable for discounts and picture-frame refrigerator magnets. They also display eight-foot maps of the marathon indicating where to eat in their "Feed Your Feet" campaign, which promotes local restaurants. Fleet Feet also offers the "Orange Wave"; those runners who purchase their marathon shoes at the store are entitled to receive orange singlets (athletic jerseys), which not only advertise the firm but also entitle the runner to a free marathon photograph. Given the actual cost of professional photos, this is a strong inducement that ensures multiple impressions of the Chicago franchise. As mentioned in chapter 4, Fleet Feet also has a ten-mile rally station along the marathon route, whose volume, enhanced by 1,000 Nike-supplied cowbells, and entertainment, provided by Elvis impersonators, call attention to the sports store in a way that ensures notice by neighborhood residents. Marathon festivities are followed up by Fleet Feet's annual volunteer party for 300 people on Goose Island in November. These and other activities are intended to make Fleet Feet the center of the Chicago running community.

It is difficult to overemphasize the effect of the Chicago Marathon on Fleet Feet. It is an event that provides energy and constant organizational focus all year. The marathon also brings in a 60 percent increase in runners from outside the Chicago area, and some of this presence translates into additional sales. It affords a partnership relationship with Nike and a chance to offer special features at the expo, such as wrist bracelets with mile splits. The sales figures for the marathon dates are quite remarkable: in October 2001, Fleet Feet saw a 32.8 percent increase in sales; in October 2002, sales increased by 34.4 percent; and in October 2003, sales were up by 40.8 percent.

In short, the marathon is a bonanza for Fleet Feet and other local running stores, and for the moment, its impact continues to be felt. Inevitably, it has an imposing effect on sports marketing throughout the area. Sports stores like Fleet Feet enjoy a dual relationship with the marathon; it is clearly a source of profit, but these stores also promote the marathon and contribute to its success by providing support and many benefits for marathon runners. Although these contributions are hardly an expression of disinterested altruism, they nonetheless enhance the event.

The modern mass marathon has become a vehicle for many business interests, whose intervention sustains and expands the event and allows significant opportunities for branding, the soft advertising that is essential for the sponsor visibility needed to market products. This visibility affects large and small firms alike. In larger firms, sponsorship has the added advantage of promoting internal loyalty, a broader sense of belonging than that gained from simply being a wage earner. Sponsors, even though their parent firms are not local, also try to express civic spirit in serious contributions of time, money, and expertise to the city as well as the event. Although an underlying self-interest is the sine qua non in all sponsorship, it would be excessively simplistic to deny that sponsors—both as corporations and as distinct individuals within those corporations—have a genuine concern for broad civic issues. Indeed, the breadth of contributions from institutions like LaSalle suggests a deep commitment to the older traditions of corporate philanthropy and a strong sense of community.

For city officials, the marathon offers a chance to show off the city's assets—from the spacious Grant Park finishing area to the architectural highlights of the city's North Side.

six

city government and
sister agency support

Marathons, unlike many other races, are almost always associated with cities. The world's largest marathons—London, New York, Paris, Chicago, Berlin—are all run within the confines of the host cities. Suburban marathons (unless they actually conclude in a city and bear that city's name, as in the case of the Boston Marathon) are usually modest affairs, and rural marathons are even less frequent. Much of this is explained by the fact that the huge volunteer commitment needed to sustain a large marathon field is not available outside an urban setting, and spectator support requires a dense population with easy access to a lengthy course. Despite the extraordinary disruption these races cause, most major cities relish marathons because of the prestige and recognition such events confer. They are image builders that enable cities to compete with one another in the quest for tourist dollars. Marathons allow cities to send a message of affluence and celebration to the larger world beyond their limits. In many ways, a city without a major marathon is a city that has not arrived.[1]

Chicago's case is particularly instructive because only after a period of dramatic ups and downs in the 1980s and early 1990s did its marathon come together to the point that it can now vie for world supremacy in the number of participants. This stunning rise closely follows Chicago's dramatic recovery from a "rust belt" city whose future was in grave doubt to a revitalized metropolis capable of retaining an affluent citizenry and attracting a well-heeled body of tourists. The synergy that brought Chicago's marathon to life came principally from three sources: (1) the sports/running community; (2) the corporate community; and (3) the political community. As Chicago moved out of its economic doldrums, the success of its marathon became one of the indicators of renewed urban health, which was becoming apparent in the highly appreciated real estate values spurred by the widespread gentrification of many of its formerly depressed neighborhoods and the revived city center known as the Loop.

Whereas the roles of the corporate and sports communities constitute the subjects of other chapters, the political community's role is the principal focus of this chapter. Even Chicago's first marathon in 1977 enjoyed the support of then-Mayor Bilandic, but the race was a relatively minor affair by today's standards, though with a substantial field for the period. Then called the Mayor Daley Marathon (in honor of the deceased mayor and father of the current occupant of that office), the race underwent a name change with the backing of Mayor Jane Byrne, who had replaced Mayor Bilandic—the pompous "America's Marathon." Byrne's successor, Harold Washington, the first African American mayor of the city, also took a keen interest in the race. Executive race director Pinkowski remarked that, when he saw New York Mayor Rudi Giuliani inspecting the course for the first New York City Marathon after the September 11th tragedy, the memory of Harold Washington checking out Chicago's course came back to him. Clearly, the city's mayors have always shown a proprietary interest in Chicago's marathon. In fact, it was only Mayor Bilandic's intervention with park superintendent Ed Kelly that made Chicago's first marathon possible.

Although support from the top was always there, widespread political support was not; nor did city officials have a clear understanding of the marathon's potential. One alderman, Bert Natarus of the Forty-second Ward, championed the marathon, but others were less than enthusiastic. One alderman is rumored to have threatened to mow down runners with a tank if they moved north of a certain street in his ward! For many, the marathon was originally perceived to be a nuisance, a disruption of traffic, and a general irritant for their constituents. It meant that businesses lost revenues to an invasion of somewhat insane people who had nothing better to do than ruin a Sunday morning by pouring into city streets and, in some cases, keeping people from attending church services.

As related in chapter 3, it took the special intervention of alderman Kathy Osterman, then the director of the Mayor's Office of Special Events, to reach the mayor and obtain his endorsement. James "Skinny" Sheehan, her assistant at the time and later assistant director of McCormick Place, also helped Osterman. Sheehan, a former teacher, avid runner, and a marathon faithful, was able to articulate the economic and social importance of the marathon to city officials. This enhanced access to the city's inner circles of political power, and the city officials' heightened awareness of the marathon's value enabled Pinkowski to receive greater cooperation and even enthusiastic support from a political community that was not always universally enchanted with the marathon.

When current Mayor Richard M. Daley first took office in 1989, Chicago was still in the throes of turmoil following the death of its first and highly charismatic African American mayor, Harold Washington, and the unsteady period under his successor, Eugene Sawyer. Racial tension was still rather acute, and the fate of the city was very much in doubt. The larger questions were whether Chicago could overcome its racial polarization, whether it could function as a united community, and whether it could be perceived as an appealing place to live and work. The new mayor understood that Chicago had a serious image problem. It was viewed as a decaying, rust-belt city marred by racial tension, and its international image was particularly negative. All too many Chicagoans on their travels abroad would discover that any mention of their city would prompt allusions to Al Capone or parodies of gangsters firing tommy guns. Mayor Daley realized that a city that was associated with dreariness and crime could not go forward. He was aware that new associations were desperately needed. He instinctively grasped that appearance was critical to the city's survival, and that its identification with an attractive, welcoming environment would enable the city to prosper.

Gradually, as money became available, a massive renewal program began. Scoffed at by political foes for his hanging-flower-pot initiative, the mayor persisted in giving Chicago a greener, softer look. Key streets, including State Street downtown, were restructured. In the particular case of State Street (but typical of much of this initiative), the sidewalks, which had been previously quite broad, were narrowed to create a more pedestrian-friendly space.[2] The newly widened street was provided with a heavily planted divider/median along the length of the new Harold Washington Library, and the sidewalk received trees and planters. The subway entrances were retro-styled to add charm, and modern street lamps were replaced by 1920s-style lampposts. Discreet high-tech lighting was added to accent the architectural features of buildings on the street, creating depth and beauty at night. This general pattern, on a more modest scale, was implemented throughout the city, and the primary entry port for airborne tourists, O'Hare Airport, had its highway approach adorned by hanging plants.

As noted in chapter 4, the Daley administration was particularly sensitive to the city's neighborhoods. To valorize their distinctive characters, architectural markers that evoked specific features of a given community were erected: a gate representing the Puerto Rican flag, Greek columns, and rainbow pylons. The intent was to signal diversity as a strength—a cause for celebration, not conflict.[3]

The mayor also targeted the downtown Loop Lakefront for special attention. Like State Street, this area comprises the core of the city; it is, in fact, its showcase. The most dramatic modification accomplished was the creation of a museum campus at the south end of the Loop, which was achieved by rerouting Lake Shore Drive to allow park and pedestrian space to join the Field Museum to the Shedd Aquarium and the Adler Planetarium, creating a vast green belt extending from the heart of the city. Both the Adler Planetarium and the Shedd Aquarium experienced major architectural expansions during this time, further enlarging and modernizing their exhibit space with innovative additions. By 2004, a brand-new, highly avant-garde band shell designed by Frank Gehry in Millennium Park marked the northernmost boundary of the Loop green belt. These modifications emphasize the central area of Chicago from which its skyline is readily visible and affirm its renewal.

But this is not empty park space—it is designed for enjoyment by a mass public. Throughout the year, and most specifically in the spring, summer, and autumn, this park area becomes the locus of numerous urban festivals. It is the site of Taste of Chicago (the city's food extravaganza), the viewing point for the Fourth of July fireworks, the home of the Chicago Jazz Festival, and the harbor for Venetian Night (a regatta with fireworks), to name just a few of the major celebrations that occur here and draw hundreds of thousands or perhaps even a million spectators. The strategy is again clear: to make the downtown Lakefront into a place of largely free mass entertainment. This entertainment space is intended to draw not only city residents but also the population of greater Chicago; further, it serves as an attraction for visitors from across the nation and abroad. The function of these ongoing celebrations is to change the popular impression of the city from a dangerous and depressing place into one of vibrant life and activity. By and large, that policy seems to have worked.

It is thus no surprise that the Chicago Marathon also begins and ends in Grant Park. The space, which is large enough to host the tents of a major food fair, easily accommodates the numerous pavilions that house the various sponsors, teams, and service stations required by the marathon. One of the city's most spectacular ornaments, Buckingham Fountain, is, on this occasion, surrounded by alphabetical markers to make it serve as the postmarathon family reunite center, thus cleverly offering weary runners and anxious spectators another visual delight as they await family and friends. The actual finish with its grandstands looks south toward the museum campus and new upscale housing. This central positioning of a buckle race rather than a point-to-point contest ensures that the marathon's television broadcast will begin and end with sweeping aerial shots of the most dramatic views of the city center. The city is thus showcased with compelling images of skyscrapers and a lakefront harbor that may replace the long-held criminal associations of the Prohibition era.

Sports are already playing a significant role in transforming popular stereotypes of Chicago. The earlier success of the Chicago Bulls with Michael Jordan's incomparable playing had already in part contributed to a new image for Chicago. Younger people throughout the world recognized Jordan and realized that he played for the "Chicago" Bulls. The marathon does not rely on star power the way basketball does—Khannouchi is hardly a household name—but because it is an event that attracts international attention and is rooted in a specific place with its particular architectural and topographical attributes, it contributes by accretion over the years to a new perception of a renascent city. It serves as the great closing festival of the autumnal celebration along the lakefront, a mega-event whose panoply and color are witnessed here and abroad.

The Daley administration is, of course, acutely conscious of the particular utility of the marathon as just elaborated, and its support is concrete. David Kennedy, former director of sports from the Mayor's Office of Special Events (he moved to a new post in 2004), handled all arrangements and worked in tandem with executive race director Pinkowski to plan the course. Kennedy worked out of an office with a staff of sixty that coordinated all special events and acted as the liaison with all city services and events within the city limits. Since the marathon taps all of the city's resources, officials must know the exact date of the marathon by January 1st. Even the Bears must have an away game that weekend; this, of course, requires NFL approval. One of the most preoccupying concerns is last-minute construction; small companies are often issued permits to do work far too close to the race date. This entails last-minute course inspection and, at times, emergency measures to cope with problems caused by such repairs. The Park District provides the space for the marathon pavilions in Grant Park; Streets and Sanitation supplies cones and barricades, tows cars, and helps with the garbage cleanup; the Department of Transportation fixes all the potholes along the route and implements a traffic plan; and the Chicago Police close the streets and try to facilitate the traffic flow. The outlay of police officers, though not publicly announced, is the largest for any event held in the city.[4] Every street crossing requires about four officers and four vehicles. City services are provided at a greatly reduced rate, making the city a de facto sponsor of the Chicago Marathon. This sponsorship is not without a substantial payback. The economic impact estimates for the marathon weekend now exceed $100 million dollars, a sum that guarantees a handsome return on city investment.

The city government's supportive activities are reinforced by those of its sister agency, the Chicago Transport Authority (CTA), which promotes and facilitates the marathon.[5] This promotion is both long term and day specific. The CTA advertises the marathon and strengthens its existing services to make transportation more feasible on marathon day by adding more rail cars. Actual CTA planning for the marathon is a yearlong process. The first planning meeting for 2004 took place on October 16, 2003, just four days after the 2003 race. The CTA functions as major advertiser for the marathon. This advertising can be quite spectacular—it includes two "marathon bus wraps." These are buses wrapped with 3M material with a custom design provided by the Chicago Marathon. The wraps cover the bus exterior from front to back and prominently display the marathon's logo, its web site, and an inspirational message (e.g., "Redefine Your Limits"). The CTA also furnishes car-card interior advertising for many of the cars in its system and for bus interiors. These cards promote not only participation in the marathon but spectatorship as well (e.g., "Be One in a Million! Join the LaSalle Bank Chicago Marathon 26.2 Curb Crew"). The slogan obviously plays on the fact that one million people come out to watch the event. The ads, besides encouraging the population to use the CTA for the marathon, indicate that they can watch it on CBS, hear it on ESPN Radio 1000, read all about it in the *Chicago Tribune,* or follow it online on the marathon web site—in short, a cross-promotional extravaganza of options. As marathon time draws near, the CTA issues a customized fare card. In 2003, this showed a city street overflowing with runners as the elevated train line passed above. The caption read "Get There Before They Do," and it carried the marathon date and urged riders to take the CTA to the marathon. The CTA also has a booth at the marathon health and fitness expo. In 2003, CTA employees distributed 10,000 course/spectator maps, which designated viewing areas along the course and advised how to plan to see runners at particular locations.

The actual marathon and the period immediately preceding it place heavy demands on the CTA. Numerous meetings are held to plot transportation strategies; bus-service customer alerts are posted and distributed to warn of temporary reroutes. Thirty-nine bus routes are affected on marathon day, and some have more than one rerouting depending on which streets reopen as the marathon unfolds. Officials pass out downtown transit guides and information specialists are available to help out riders with potential difficulties. The CTA aims for careful coordination with the city and the event organizers. CTA officials introduce themselves to the police officers directing traffic to coordinate efforts. CTA supervisors are directly responsible for the buses; their careful planning ensures that buses are rarely trapped by the progress of the race. The Chicago Police Department arranges rolling closures, but at the beginning of the marathon almost all streets are closed to bus traffic. At the same time, the CTA uses the marathon as a golden opportunity to promote rail ridership, and herein lies the chief value of marathon promotion for the CTA.

The Regional Transportation Authority must achieve a 50 percent recovery ratio from system-generated revenues from their service boards, which include the CTA. Public funding for the CTA has been falling over the years. At the same time, federal funding has diminished despite costly federal mandates. Whenever the economy heads south, there is always talk about raising fares, a practice that often diminishes ridership. Any big capital project depends on ridership, and rider statistics are important for support in the form of local and federal grants. To build a new line or expand services on an established one, the CTA must be able to document current ridership and project new ridership expectations. The CTA must also provide para-transit for people with disabilities, which is very costly. In bids for expansion, the CTA must also provide estimates concerning revenues lost in traffic and the impact of pollution on the community caused by car traffic. But the clearest, most obvious argument for any kind of improvement or expansion remains ridership. Here, the role of the Chicago Marathon is particularly valuable. The CTA looks for peak event ridership statistics to present evidence of its real and potential utility. A look at the Chicago Marathon/Sox-Thirty-fifth Street Station on marathon day provides a dramatic illustration of the kind of spike a special event provides. If one compares peak A.M. and P.M. patronage on Thursday, October 7, 2004, to peak marathon day patronage on Sunday, October 10, 2004, at around noon, the difference is quite impressive. The Thursday peaks were more than 100 people entering each half-hour, whereas the marathon had about 400 people entering at noon. This kind of volume sends several important messages: it demonstrates the real utility of rail during a special event, signals its potential for greater utilization, and constitutes a form of advertising to those who familiarize themselves for the first time with the CTA on this occasion. Clearly, the advantageously priced advertising and fare card publicity the CTA offers the marathon are not forms of mindless altruism but an expression of symbiosis. The CTA promotes itself as it promotes the marathon.

It is not just the CTA that enjoys a marathon impact that continues beyond marathon weekend. The city as a whole benefits. Tourists who return to the city as a result of their race involvement obviously contribute to enhanced revenue. Although it is difficult to estimate how much the marathon experience influences the decision to reside or remain in the city, there is little doubt that it contributes to the sense of Chicago as a desirable place to be. It becomes another factor in making the city a site of self-realization for an affluent, younger professional elite. The marathon is thus a solid investment in continuing prosperity.

The city also is aware of the marathon as an international promotion tool. Chicago has embarked on ambitious Sister Cities programs, and one of its most prominent foreign sisters is Paris. The marathon, largely through the initiative of one talented individual, David Reithoffer, has been enormously successful in recruiting French runners. Reithoffer has worked with Paris contacts to build connections that radiate throughout all of France. Every April, he is a regular presence at the Paris Marathon, where he takes charge of the highly visible Chicago support area along the Seine in the well-heeled sixteenth arrondissement. He also staffs Chicago's stand at the Paris marathon expo, extolling the virtues of the event to French runners. As indicated in chapter 3, Reithoffer is president of Chicago's Groupe Professionnel Francophone; he is well connected politically and socially in Paris. Reithoffer does not restrict his recruitment efforts to the metropolis. He also travels regularly to the French cult race of Marvejols-Mendes. A little over a half-marathon in distance with two mountain ascents and descents, this is one of France's most grueling races. It attracts a pan-European field and is concluded with feasting and a particularly scandalous, near-naked late-night run. It is also a wonderful opportunity to publicize Chicago's marathon. Reithoffer does so with the assistance of Gérard Delort, accomplished French runner (see chapter 10) and an enthusiastic Chicago booster. Delort himself also publicizes Chicago at a popular French marathon, the Marathon de la Baie du Mont-Saint-

Michel, a June event whose course extends from Cancale in Brittany to the famed monastery in Normandy. Curiously, all this is unsalaried work, and indicates the kind of attraction the marathon exerts on otherwise busy professionals.[6]

Reithoffer's work has yielded results. In the early 1990s, there was only a handful of French runners in the Chicago Marathon; at the 2000 race, some 800 French nationals registered, making that nation number one in foreign entrants. In 2000, LaSalle Bank offered a splendid reception for all foreign guests in the inviting setting of the older neoclassical section of Union Station, which was gently backlit. Hors d'oeuvres and beverages (including wine and champagne) were served to foreign runners and their families by liveried waiters as they were serenaded by a chamber orchestra. This was an advertising and image extravaganza directed at bringing back a foreign clientele to Chicago and ensuring that the good word about the city would be spread when those visitors returned to their home countries. Given the popularity of U.S. coastal cities as tourist destinations over Chicago, this kind of promotion is obviously critical. It illustrates the merging of the city's and the primary corporate sponsor's goals, as both the city and the race owner presented images of worldly sophistication to visitors who may have had an entirely different notion of Chicago in mind.

––––––––––

The international dimension of the marathon, its current massive registration, and the ambitions of its planners to make it the world's largest marathon fit into the spirit of "gigantism" that has always marked Chicago. Indeed, the city's explosive growth from a tiny trading post at the beginning of the nineteenth century to America's second-largest city by the end of that century has left Chicago with a sense of collective ambition for massive undertakings that endures to this day. Current visitors to Chicago are assailed by a list of civic accomplishments that emphasize magnitude: the Sears Tower was the tallest building in the world from May 4, 1973, until February 13, 1996 (just under 23 years; it's still the tallest in the hemisphere); O'Hare was for a long time the largest airport in the United States; McCormick Place is the largest exhibition space in North America; the Harold Washington Library is the world's largest public library; and even the Deep Tunnel Project represents the world's most massive sewer drainage project. Chicagoans link significant accomplishment to the massive scale of their urban projects. Thus, it is hardly any wonder that the Chicago Marathon should eschew qualifying times and low registration caps like those imposed by the Boston Marathon (15,000 in 2000) or that it should refuse New York's lottery entrant system and mandatory registration through travel agencies for foreign runners. Instead, Chicago prefers its first-come, first-served system; it will keep its unrestricted registration for foreign runners, which avoids the imposition of costly hotel packages. The strategy has paid off well, as evidenced by registration that is now capped at 40,000. In fact, the marathon staff realizes that the race has reached its maximum capacity and thus achieved the very "gigantism" that characterizes Chicago's endeavors and fires its citizenry. At this point, the only means of enlarging the field would be some kind of adaptation such as starts in waves. If the number of registered no-shows can be lowered, the race may finally achieve parity with New York and, in this area at least, put an end to the "second city" label.

Whether second or first city, Chicago has now situated itself among the world's first tier of marathons. The city can bask in the glory of a goal that has been fully realized, and it can expect more huge crowds and probably more world records in the years to come. All this will bring attention to Chicago. The marathon's success locally reinforces civic pride, renders the city more attractive to suburbanites in the greater Chicago area, and ensures that the city will attract ever more tourists, national and international. The massive revenues brought in by the marathon and the recasting of a somewhat sordid city image provide both real and intangible benefits fully appreciated by the city's political community. In such a context, the city's de facto sponsorship is a gesture of lucid self-interest.

Elvis lives at the marathon thanks to Fleet Feet!

PART IV

Marathon Alliances

From aid station volunteers to charity fundraisers, the marathon fosters alliances inspired by enthusiasm and generosity.

seven

charities

Fundraising for charitable institutions is now part and parcel of all major U.S. marathons and many international marathons. Indeed, it is hard to think of any U.S. distance race, even of the most modest size, that lacks at least one charitable beneficiary. All marathons and smaller footraces with any significant fields not only select official beneficiaries but also actively encourage their runners to raise money for charity. As the Chicago Marathon's 2004 web site put it, "Consider being a part of the 2004 Charity Program and make your Marathon more meaningful."[1] Large races now ally themselves with a whole array of worthy causes and offer runners a vast selection of charities to choose from. One might say that fundraising has become so tied to running that it is practically an aspect of the sport itself. This new trend obviously strengthens the bond between charities and marathon running, and it offers an unusual opportunity for charities that must struggle in the ever-more competitive world of fundraising.

The Chicago Marathon has experienced recent explosive growth in its association with charities. In only three years, the number of associated charities grew from three to, by 2004, twenty-nine charitable causes. The marathon divides these charities into four categories: (1) official charities (e.g., American Cancer Society, Leukemia & Lymphoma Society [Team in Training, TNT], National AIDS Marathon Training Program); (2) charity partners (e.g., Alzheimer's Association, Cancer Research UK, Children's Memorial Hospital [Kids First], Opportunity Enterprises); (3) participating charities (e.g., American Liver Foundation, American Red Cross, Arthritis Foundation [Joints in Motion], Memorial Sloan Kettering Cancer Center [Fred's Team], Hope Worldwide, Inspiration Corporation, St. Coletta's, Spinal Cord Injury Association, St. Jude's [St. Jude Children's Research Hospital], Y-Me National Breast Cancer Organization); and (4) associated charities (e.g., American Lung Association, A-T Children's Project, Cornelia de Lange Syndrome Foundation, Cystic Fibrosis Foundation, Depression and Bipolar Support Alliance, Girls on the Run, Jane Addams Hull House Association [Jane's Place at Nettelhorst], Live! Foundation, Lungevity Foundation, Sargent Shriver National Center on Poverty Law, People's Resource Center, Scleroderma Foundation). Official charities must have 250 participants or more; charity partners must reach 100 or more; participating charities must recruit fifty or more participants; finally, associated charities have no minimum number of participants (Richards, "Charity Running," 3) According to Lisa Kaplan, former community relations and special programs director for the marathon, a charity must complete a request for proposal (RFP) to be included among marathon charities. The RFP asks ten questions to see if an organization is fit to handle the operation. For instance, does it have a staff person to handle its fundraising and marketing plan? The RFP seeks to determine what the organization has done in past charitable endeavors. The marathon tries to find out if runners have responded or given to charities in the past, even before they were part of the marathon. Generally, with smaller operations, the marathon tries to help them develop incentives and aid them in constructing a more elaborate fundraising plan. The marathon's attitude is more one of encouragement and inclusion in the evaluation of prospective marathon charities than of exclusion.

With the significant increase of charity participation, the money raised in the Chicago Marathon has increased dramatically: $3 million in 2002, $4.5 million in 2003, and a goal of $8 million for 2004 (Richards, "Charity Running," citing Lisa Kaplan, 1). Yet this figure, however impressive, pales when compared to the 2003 Flora London Marathon, which raised more than $56 million. Kaplan remarked that only 5 to 10 percent of Chicago's total field was comprised of charity runners, whereas 76 percent of London participants run for charity (Richards, "Charity Running," 2). Kaplan told this author that she felt that London had a longer history of charity involvement, while Chicago had started these efforts much later.[2] She added that London has a "Golden Bond" scheme that enables charities to secure guaranteed places in the race—something Chicago has not adopted.[3]

Even a cursory look at Flora London's 2004–5 web site makes it clear the path that Chicago must follow to reach similar fundraising success. A brief note from race director David Bedford designates the UK hospice movement as the marathon's official charity for 2005. Bedford remarks that "we are delighted to be supporting such an important cause and feel it truly reflects the ethos of the Flora London Marathon, which is all about reaching out to people and changing lives" (Flora London Marathon). The web site has several charity-related headings such as "how to raise funds," "charity listings" (four pages plus a supplemental alphabetized list of links), "fundraising tips" (twelve key points that include topics like choosing a sponsor and approaching donors), and "inspiring stories." Although individual sponsors handle this in Chicago, London is very proactive and tries, quite successfully, to direct runners in a forceful manner toward fundraising. The web site also informs runners that charities have a set number of reserved places (a practice currently in Chicago as well but less significant because of the open entry system) and that runners will have to raise from £750 to £2,000 to benefit from this privileged placing. Although the differences in the expectations of charitable sponsorship for Chicago and London are really not all that significant, the proactive emphasis of London distinguishes the two. Chicago's open registration, one of its most attractive features as a leading world marathon, ironically seems to diminish the motivation for fundraising among its runners.

Kaplan added that in terms of the United States, Chicago works with numbers similar to Boston. New York, on the other hand, does more community-based fundraising, such as concentration on certain boroughs, but that marathon also features international fundraising. Because all these major U.S. marathons have become increasingly more aggressive about fundraising and observe each other quite carefully, it is highly probable that their fundraising tactics will become more homogeneous.

Chicago has certain financial transparency requirements for charities. They must supply the raw (total) number of funds raised and the number of runners who sent in checks. Chicago does not, however, require charities to divulge the exact percentage of the revenues raised that actually go to the beneficiaries. This is a delicate matter because, depending on the nature of a given charity's services to its runners (e.g., the complexity of the training program, the extent of support staff to encourage the continued commitment of participants, the advertising costs of a given charity, etc.), the actual return to charity may be as low as 50 percent. This calls for some discussion.

Fundraising has become an increasingly more demanding business in and of itself. To solicit contributions from likely donors, charities use extensive mailing lists, they have phone campaigns, or they rely on employers to pressure employees to contribute to omnibus associations like the United Way and the Crusade of Mercy to fund a raft of worthy organizations that the employee can designate on an individual basis. In a country that has a long tradition of relying on private initiative and of stinginess with tax dollars to sustain general health care, charitable giving is seen as part of civic duty. Nevertheless, given the scarceness of resources, charities are always in search of new ways to raise money. The general public, especially in times of economic uncertainty, tends to resist the insistent calls for donations that are replicated from one worthy institution to the next. Irritated by thank-you notes that make renewed requests for funds in the same paragraph that they acknowledge a recent contribution, often exasperated by several funding "emergency" letters or calls that come throughout the course of the year from the same charities, bombarded by the "free" gifts (cards, address stickers, calendars, etc.) that are intended to guilt the recipient into giving, and overwhelmed by a plethora of requests from competing, genuinely worthy causes, potential donors often harden their hearts to the ceaseless demands of charities. Effectively appealing to their generosity in this context presents a constant and evolving challenge. Here, the marathon as the paramount extreme sport represents an incalculable opportunity—at least for the time being.

The unique and compelling value of the marathon lies in its status as an ordeal sport—in fact, *the* ordeal race in distance running.[4] One of the Chicago Marathon's three official charities, the AIDS Marathon, provides a dramatic example of the value of extreme sports in fundraising. The AIDS Marathon takes its inspiration from the several regional AIDS bike rides that extended over several days and hundreds of miles. These mass-scale fundraising events, which disappeared for a time in the face of criticism that their managers were making hefty personal profits, enjoyed unparalleled fundraising success. Much of the appeal of these rides lay in the protracted physical ordeal of the participants (sometimes HIV-positive themselves), who bonded through their own sufferings in a visceral way with the AIDS patients they sought to aid or, if ill themselves, affirmed their hope and commitment to struggle in the face of disease. The latter case is analogous to the situation of Fred Lebow, from whom "Fred's Team" takes its name; he ran a marathon, despite his cancer, in a final gesture of defiance against his illness. In any event, the AIDS rides outstripped by large margins all other AIDS funding initiatives (something that is also true of the AIDS Marathon), and their disappearance, whatever their faults, left a hole in funding that is yet to be filled.[5] AIDS charities are hardly the only charities that bank on the ordeal nature of running, particularly the marathon. Charities fighting cancer, stroke, heart disease, juvenile diabetes, arthritis, and so on all profit from the highly effective fundraising accomplished by runners soliciting pledges, most especially for the marathon. When runners sponsor specific individuals, most poignantly children, they elicit an enormous sympathy that opens many wallets and purses of otherwise oversolicited donors. No matter who the beneficiary may be, the fact that the fundraisers have engaged themselves in a prodigious test of will and endurance makes it difficult to refuse a donation. Charities cannot afford to disregard this irrational but powerful dynamic.

Many people seek out a charity because they want to do something for a particular individual. As the association between marathon running and fundraising continues to grow, it becomes more of an automatic response for many people to consider a charitable cause when running a marathon. Indeed, as previously indicated, marathons are doing their best to ensure such a response by extolling charitable causes on their web sites as well as by reserving precious guaranteed registration for those who will commit themselves to a charity. Charities further cement the relationship by offering training, usually in conjunction with the marathon, that is especially appealing to first-time runners. Charities become in themselves highly effective premier recruiters of neophyte runners, often from the most unlikely of quarters.

If the marathon is now a civic festival, it is inevitable that considerations other than those of sport intervene in the motives of those who compose the race's field. It can be argued that there exists a powerful drive to make the marathon a manifestation of social coherence, a locus of urban and regional altruism. In Chicago, the title sponsor and owner of the race, LaSalle Bank, has by its extensive program of corporate giving positioned itself as the city's premier corporate citizen. Running for charity is a way that individuals who race can participate in a parallel form of civic generosity. Because the race, like all major marathons, is far bigger than even the region, running for charity, like corporate sponsorship, assumes national and even international dimensions (like Cancer Research UK, which appears on Chicago's list of charitable beneficiaries). Charity fundraising ensures that the marathon is endowed with a noble purpose and that this great collective festival goes beyond the thirst for excellence that is sport and becomes an expression of human solidarity. The pain endured by its participants serves as a bridge that unites the community with the sufferings of the ill; it assumes the status of a heroic offering of self, a kind of secular sacrifice to needy and stricken humanity.

For case studies, it is highly useful to look at charity running from the perspective of two of the Chicago Marathon's three official charities because such institutions are critical in the recruitment of runners and the molding of their attitudes to the sport. The Leukemia & Lymphoma Society (Team in Training [TNT]) and the National AIDS Marathon present many common strategies that characterize charity fundraising while at the same time show certain differences that underscore the fact that such fundraising is not homogeneous. It is also helpful to get a glimpse of the practices of a charity partner, Children's Memorial Hospital, to compare the requirements for a less demanding category of sponsorship.

Debbie Lample, a campaign manager for Team in Training (TNT), states that locally, the team raised over $3 million in 2004. Nationally, TNT has brought in $600 million in donations since its inception. The monies raised through the LaSalle Bank Chicago Marathon are used locally to fund eleven researchers and to assist patients with expenses that are not covered by insurance. A small percentage of these resources may be redirected nationally. Lample stated that 75 percent of all monies raised go directly to the mission, which, besides research and assistance to financially hard-pressed patients, also includes education. To be a team member, a participant must raise $1,400 to run the Chicago Marathon. If Chicago runners wish to go further afield, they can participate in other events such as the Adidas Vancouver International Marathon/Half-Marathon, but then they must raise $4,900 to cover the additional expenses of transportation and hotel accommodations. Team members are paired with a local patient, but not one-on-one. Patient Honorees may be currently going through treatment or be in remission. In some instances, family members have continued their involvement after losing a loved one to a blood cancer. Patients themselves do not have to be children—anyone with a blood cancer qualifies as a Patient Honoree.

TNT reaches potential runners by direct mail, advertising in *Windy City Sports,* CTA car cards, and word of mouth. Because this is its eleventh year in Chicago, the organization has a solid core of former participants for word-of-mouth references. TNT assists runners in their fundraising in several ways. It provides each individual with a manual containing model fundraising letters and a list of over 100 fundraising ideas. TNT also pairs neophytes with a mentor, an alumnus of the program, who helps with that individual's campaign. They have a web site with personal pages that feature pictures and a training diary. The site is also equipped to accept online donations.

TNT does not have a particular runner profile. Its program includes just about anyone from the beginner to the more experienced runner. TNT has its own coaches who are certified through its national office; some come from a fitness background. The TNT coaching philosophy is to get the runners healthy to the starting line. Lample states that if TNT coaches can do that, there is over a 99 percent chance the runners will finish, which is their objective. As a measure of TNT's training success, Lample points out that in 2003, all of their half-ironman team finished in a race that had about a 20 percent dropout rate. TNT training is broader than marathon training; it includes walking, run-walking, running, triathlons, and century rides. The fall, with the approach of the LaSalle Bank Chicago Marathon, is the time when there are the largest training groups. For 2005, TNT had just under 400 people from the Illinois chapter in training. An additional 300 other runners from throughout the nation were expected to join them in the marathon.

Because TNT's offerings extend beyond the marathon, the organization tries to channel participants into appropriate events. For instance, coaches and recruiters tell people that they cannot walk the Chicago Marathon and inform them that the finish line officially closes in six and a half hours. In the case of those not physically able to meet these standards, coaches try to direct these individuals to other events they sponsor that are more appropriate to their abilities. For example, in 2004, they were encouraging female marathon walkers to plan on the Nike 26.2—a San Francisco women's marathon with an eight-hour finishing deadline intended to accommodate walkers.

Lample reported that reactions are very positive from program participants. She remarked on the satisfaction they experience as they move from being frightened and hesitant at the prospect of a three-mile run to comfortable and assured with twenty miles. She also noted that quite a few participants develop strong relationships with the Patient Honorees, some of whom are able to attend events like pizza outings, going to the zoo, and the race itself. Lample felt that just getting people out to exercise as program participants was a health benefit. She also expressed an optimistic view of prospects for the development of charity running in the LaSalle Bank Chicago Marathon. She felt that there was improved coordination between race officials and fundraisers.

The National AIDS Marathon training program also stands out as one of the more successful fundraising groups in the nation and can boast of raising some $45 million in the five-year period preceding 2003. Its local beneficiary, the AIDS Foundation of Chicago, distributes pledge contributions broadly to institutions meeting the needs of AIDS patients throughout the entire Chicagoland area. The AIDS Foundation of Chicago, however, does not directly involve itself in runner recruitment and training. These activities are handled by an outside, independent, for-profit organization, Walk the Talk Productions, whose local program director, Mike Dilbeck, and his staff of four focus exclusively on program participants. This obviously creates a special dynamic in recruiting, training, and running.

The AIDS Marathon training program does not seek out the seasoned runner, even though many seasoned runners join the program. Instead, many AIDS Marathon's runners are first-timers with no previous experience in the sport. Indeed, Dilbeck points out that the target runners are often people who typically do not consider themselves runners—most likely "couch potatoes" who have decided to run a marathon for a worthy cause. In this aspect, the recruitment strategy for charity runners is becoming more typical of the marathon itself; namely, marathon participants now often start from zero and go directly to running a marathon as their first race. This probably occurs because the marathon is endowed with a prestige unmatched by any other running events, and because the runners are seeking something special in their lives not available elsewhere. In any case, the profile of this kind of charity runner is that of a neophyte more focused on an ennobling cause than a superior time. This will be someone who views finishing as an accomplishment rather than an inevitability. The notions of an outstanding performance and excellence will not be serious concerns, perhaps not even considerations.

Recruitment, training, and eventual race participation represent an A-to-Z process that runs from January through October. The members of the AIDS Marathon staff function as mentors and fundraising coaches; their job is to support the participants. Recruitment is normally in progress through April (the Chicago Marathon normally occurs in early October), and the advertising targets a nonathletic as well as athletic pool. The organization does not advertise in magazines like *Runner's World* because 60 percent of their eventual participants are not runners. Instead, AIDS Marathon staff members focus on requests for information (RFIs). Rather than passing out pamphlets, they focus on point-of-purchase stands and "take one" brochures in the pockets of the stands. In 2003, they received thousands of RFIs, even though the Iraq war interrupted their publicity campaign.

The second dimension of their 2003 campaign was the placing of similar posters in train cars of the Chicago Transit Authority and on train platforms. This simple form of advertising is effective and relatively low cost. They also use print advertising, but only in free or low-cost newspapers like Chicago's *Red Eye*. Curiously, advertising in the gay press, though still ongoing, does not work particularly well. Their fourth strategy is the direct mailing of hundreds of thousands of pieces from specially generated mailing lists. Their lifeblood is truly the RFIs generated from all these forms of advertising. Again, this is hardly recruitment directed at the traditional running community. Fundraising managers must seek to expand their base, and, obviously, athletic considerations must take second place to critical mass.

Training begins in April, and participants follow a regimen that is designed especially for the nonrunner: the Jeff Galloway training program. Galloway is a well-known author of running books; his particular method of marathon training is widely disputed. It is, nevertheless, particularly well adapted to the needs of those who are beginners and whose race ambitions are very modest. One of the particular features of the Galloway program is its frequent walk breaks; for example, six minutes of running with one minute of walking until the run is completed. The walk break offers trainees a respite from the intimidating relentlessness of a long run and helps deter injury. Trainees are placed in pace groups of up to ten people. They bond and often become close friends. The pace groups are named for illustrious runners like Frank Shorter, the American Olympic marathon victor at Munich; however, the achievements of the likes of Shorter are in stark contrasts to the goals of the pace group. The Shorter group is a 10:30 per mile pace. Trainees are asked to run three times a week, with a long run on the weekend, which eventually reaches 26 miles—a distance rejected by some training manuals as potentially harmful, but embraced by Galloway and the AIDS Marathon as essential for confidence building. The ultimate goal of the program is to run the marathon injury-free, to enjoy it, and, above all, *to finish.*

To run for the AIDS Marathon and other charitable organizations, participants must, however, meet one formidable, nonathletic challenge: fundraising. For Chicago, the fundraising minimum is $1,400. If participants want to go further afield—to Dublin or Honolulu—they must raise $3,400 (for which they get airfare and hotel accommodations). Team participants receive full hands-on support, more than they could expect from the Chicago Area Runners Association, which itself handles charity runner training programs but emphasizes structured training more than personal attention.

Participants benefit from considerable help in the fundraising: they receive model letters and their own home page on the organization's web site. Donations can be made online. Participants learn how to give fundraising parties. They can even "sell" body parts—that is, they'll write a donor's name on a part of their body; the forehead, of course, is the most expensive site. Pictures of the runner at a given mile can be made available to a donor. Over the past five years, the AIDS Marathon has returned 57 percent of every dollar raised, which is within the national fundraising executive guidelines, according to Dilbeck. In 2003, because of war and recession, the split was about fifty-fifty. The intense support offered to runners in this AIDS Marathon training program inevitably cuts into the return to charity, but it is hard to see how, with so many first-time runners, such support costs could be easily reduced.

Clearly, every aspect of fundraising has been rationalized with great intelligence and meticulousness. This is a competitive market, AIDS is still a stigmatized disease, and attention is shifting to other afflictions such as breast cancer. What is striking, however, is the "genius" of U.S. capitalism in these endeavors. No detail is neglected, every option is exploited, and all efforts are channeled to achieve with the greatest efficiency carefully defined objectives. Cold reason and the generous warmth of altruism are fused to ensure fundraising success.

Children's Memorial Hospital calls its marathon team "Kids First." As a charity partner, it places considerably less fundraising demands on its team members. It asks only for a $30 nonrefundable participation fee (in 2004) and a $500 minimum fundraising goal. Participants must also pay the Chicago Marathon registration fee, unlike the AIDS Marathon and TNT team members. Their sole advantage here is that registration is guaranteed. Team members have the right to be part of the CARA marathon training program, which is available to all area runners, not simply team members. They receive a training singlet and Hal Higdon's *Marathon: The Ultimate Training Guide.*

Because Children's Memorial Hospital is a local institution, much of its recruitment strength comes from local recognition. It does not have the resources to recruit and retain team participants on the scale of TNT or the AIDS Marathon. It does have the advantage that runners may know individual children/patients, which is a highly personal way to make fundraising meaningful. Because recruitment is a much lower-cost operation without specific runner targets, Children's can direct 100 percent of all pledges raised to the hospital. There is obviously a direct advantage in local fundraising in its lower overhead and its community recognition. In the case of Children's, there is the particular appeal in that the beneficiaries are those who are afflicted in the earliest phases of life and whose plight is therefore almost always more touching than any other category.

With the enormous explosion of charitable options, potential fundraisers now have many considerations in selecting a beneficiary. They must consider not only the cause, but also the minimum fundraising requirements, the percentage of monies raised that actually goes to a cause, the assistance they will receive in fundraising, the availability of training for the marathon and support as the marathon actually takes place, and even their potential teammates as they embark on their project. Such generosity requires considerable reflection or, more simply, a passion to aid a particular cause or individual. Like the marathon itself, fundraising is now emerging as a highly personalized affair tailored to the individual goals of the participant.

––––––––––

Charity fundraising in marathon running has not gone without criticism. The presentation of the AIDS Marathon, in particular, reveals certain practices that have provoked resistance from some quarters, and this resistance has been articulated in one of the major U.S. magazines devoted to foot racing: *Running Times*. A September 2003 article by Roger Robinson and Jonathan Beverly that was ambivalent about and critical of the effects of charity giving on running elicited an unusual volume of heated correspondence from readers who either strongly favored or strongly opposed its position.[6] The authors had clearly touched a nerve. Given, as has been indicated, the immense role that such fundraising plays in racing, the intensity of the response was hardly surprising. Yet Robinson and Beverly were themselves reacting to ways in which charity running was, from their perspective, already distorting and even undermining the sport; namely, by its emphasis on finishing rather than performance and by its implied message that running is somehow not quite legitimate if done only for the sheer pleasure of it. In short, charity running was undermining athletic excellence.

Although there is certainly no disputing the nobility of the focus that charities bring to the marathon, there is little doubt that the transformation of the race into a fundraising event is a kind of postmodern decentering. Running can be viewed as a pretext rather than a goal. This development suggests that running is unique among sports in that it can be deemed insufficient as a reason unto itself, a curious and, for many, highly irritating paradox. This devaluation of competition is thus met with fierce resistance by bearers of older, more classically athletic values—to put it more bluntly, by people who value running, racing, and winning for their own sake.

Robinson and Beverly's article is well worth considering in detail as it points out some of the tensions evident between a more traditional, race-centered notion of running and the event status of running in part fostered by charity training. The authors state that in 2002, Americans raised more than $500 million for charity (Robinson and Beverly, 14), and they take a rather cautious view of USA Track and Field (USATF) CEO Craig Masback's statement that charitable giving "transforms a sport that is individual in nature into a phenomenon with a wide-reaching, positive effect on society" (Robinson and Beverly, 14). The authors ask for evidence that this transformation was "wholly to the benefit of running," and suggest that the sport and charities have a mutual obligation to debate the issue, especially given complaints from people who call running their sport. The authors point out how Khalid Khannouchi's 2002 London Marathon world-record performance and Paula Radcliffe's best women's-only time were overshadowed by the saturation coverage of a charity runner dressed in a deep-sea diving suit who took five days to complete the marathon. The coverage of Sean "P. Diddy" Combs's run at the New York City Marathon, which occurred after the publication of the article, is another example of a mediocre marathon performance done for charity (4:14:52)—this time by a celebrity—once again overshadowing athletic accomplishment. The authors state that charity running transforms the sport into "a means to an end" (Robinson and Beverly, 16) rather than something done for itself, and they quote Charles Sorley's "The Song of the Ungirt Runners," which proclaims, ". . . We run without a cause / . . . We run because we like it/ Through the broad bright land" (16). They also lament the demise of the Greek ideal of athletic excellence; that is, that humanity comes closest to the gods and best improves its condition through competition. They point out that charity running deemphasizes this competition.

The authors ponder why running rather than other sports seems to attract charitable endeavors, and they speculate that running is more charged with meaning that most other sports and allude to running in religious rites in ancient times as well as its symbolic uses in modern times (the Peace Marathon in the Czech town of Kosice founded in 1924 and the Run Free Marathon in Berlin in 1990 after the destruction of the wall; Robinson and Beverly, 19). They evoke the public acclaim afforded marathon finishers and refer to national AIDS Marathon literature emphasizing this.

The authors also supply counterarguments to their criticisms of charities and race directors. David Bedford, executive race director of the London Marathon and former 10,000–meter world-record holder, acknowledges that the marathon is more than about racing and states that London does give special entry to charity runners, but he remarks that they do the same for registered UK clubs (Robinson and Beverly, 19). For Bedford, it is a matter of balance. Susan Shay of Fred's Team points out charity running's role in the recruitment of runners, and she attributes her own commitment to running to her initial involvement with charity running (Robinson and Beverly, 20). TNT coach April Powers alludes to the positive media coverage brought in by charity running (Robinson and Beverly, 19). Powers states that charity organizations provide a more supportive atmosphere for first-time runners, who often view the clubs as too elitist (Robinson and Beverly, 20).[7] The authors, however, note the emphasis on completion rather than performance and question the continuing commitment of charity runners, who are often one-time marathoners; they point out that TNT records indicate that only 15 percent of their marathoners go on to a second race.[8] The authors remark that "charities may move on, like driftnet fishing fleets, if they think they have depleted our waters" (Robinson and Beverly, 20). Their conclusion is guarded and qualified toward running for charity. Defining running as "unique in its mixture of joyous freedom and significant competition," they state, "In so far as the alliance with charities enhances these unique strengths, we welcome it. But we value the strengths so much that we believe they must not be sold, however good the cause" (Robinson and Beverly, 21).

Although the Robinson and Beverly article makes a strong case, it is important to realize that many of the practices it describes are broader than charity running and that many charity runners are very committed to the sport. For a fair number of race participants, running to raise money and running to compete are not mutually exclusive categories. Mass participation in running the marathon devoid of any sense of athletic competition and focused solely on finishing, though significantly fueled by charity running, is a much broader phenomenon. It is a powerful, perhaps irresistible trend that defeats the attempts of even major marathons to impose reasonable finishing times. One need only refer to the success of John Bingham's "Penguin Chronicles" in *Runner's World* or to his book *No Need for Speed* to understand that well-developed, anti-competitive, and, shall we say, anti-athletic attitudes are part and parcel of the mass running phenomenon. Today, last-place finishers are often cheered rather than booed. The notion of a disgraceful performance that the ancients would have so well understood barely exists.

But it is also hard to imagine that competitive racing will ever be entirely eclipsed. Race directors still earnestly seek to recruit the fastest runners, to discover new talent, to garner world records (in the case of the flattest marathons), and to offer an elite field of near-superhuman ability. Even television, while including various human-interest stories, still focuses primarily on the actual race in the marathon. It is more accurate to say that racing has simply become sensitive toward expressing and encompassing the traditional sports value of competition and the more recent value of participation. The marathon in particular has evolved into a gigantic happening that includes professional competition, amateur competition, personal competition, and vast masses of casual runners—all members of a great civic procession. The marathon is thus an omnibus carrying a diversity of values and objectives, many of which have only the most tenuous connection with sport.

It is also essential to point out that the world's greatest charitable fundraiser among marathons, Flora London, has been the site of both men's and woman's world's records. More important, this excellence is not restricted to professional competition. A cursory glance at its 2004 age-group results indicates a very high level of performance. All of this confirms that it would be a mistake to see charity running and competitive running as essentially working at loggerheads. Great world marathons can be outstanding across the board, sacrificing neither athletic performance nor prodigious charitable giving.

Running may be the most postmodern of sports. If modernism implied clear hierarchies, whether intellectual or otherwise, postmodernism confuses our sense of primacy. The comic strip may be as valuable as a novel from the literary canon; pop culture is worth high culture. With running, the first-time, plodding, six-hour-plus marathoner (whether engaged in fundraising or just there for the thrill of it) who has literally power-walked the course may be more important in the "people's race" than the triumphant athlete who shatters a world record. For those who cherish and strive for high performance, this can only be profoundly discouraging, an abandonment of the quest for excellence for a misguided inclusiveness. Nonetheless, this does not invalidate the efforts of those charity runners and others who simply want to finish the course; it merely confirms that running comprises many separate—sometimes complementary, sometimes competing—objectives that exist concurrently throughout the race or event. Perhaps the appeal of racing lies in the option of all runners to ignore other objectives and to focus on their own, to define themselves as they please, and to savor their own triumphs, be they modest or glorious. The question for the future is whether social forces will erase the notion of foot racing as competition in favor of completion and in so doing alter the nature of the sport of running itself. To some extent, this has already happened, and this emphasis on completion works in favor of charitable fundraising.

2005 victors Felix Limo and Deena Kastor are joined by Norm Robbins of LaSalle Bank and Carey Pinkowski, the executive race director, for a media photo.

eight

the media

An event of the Chicago Marathon's magnitude requires intense media coverage, in part to satisfy the information needs of the general public and in part to promote the marathon's continued growth and to sustain its prestige. The marathon/LaSalle Bank staff are active players in creating and facilitating this media coverage, whether it be by creating their own e-network to communicate with the public, reaching out with press releases, facilitating articles in local newspapers, cooperating with radio coverage, or interfacing with local television. The journalists, TV broadcasters and engineers, and radio commentators in turn forward their own media agendas that spin off the marathon.

Elizabeth Kiser is the communications manager for the marathon.[1] She writes most of the marathon's direct communications with runners and spectators, and also proofs press releases as a support person. But Kiser is essentially a web communicator. She is not a trained technician. With a degree in public relations and previous work experience in a nonprofit, low-budget organization, she taught herself as a matter of survival the necessary web skills to flourish in an e-communications environment. Her function is to reach out to the largely younger demographic, which readily utilizes the web and makes up the greater part of the marathon runners. Communication is segmented: there are general messages to runners, others for the 26.2 curb crew (the more enthusiastic spectators), and other messages targeting debut marathoners. Kiser and her staff try to discover and speak to the specific needs of each group. Messages increase from monthly to weekly as the marathon draws closer. Successful promotion can often be confirmed by response volume; for example, if 150 pasta dinners were reserved shortly after e-publicity for that event.

Kiser outlines some of the other dimensions of e-communication such as maps, photographs, screen savers (very popular), and almost-live coverage for those who cannot be at the race. Such coverage is conceived as a supplement to television. CBS 2, which broadcasts the marathon live locally, has included a blog ("web log"; a hybrid daily log/diary/personal web page) on its web site for live, stream-of-thought commentary on race day. It also allows the marathon to use video clips and static information. Kiser notes that the running audience wants something fun, continuing the innovations in communication possibilities. In short, the marathon staff strives to use cutting-edge developments in the new technology that fascinate its target audience and enhance that audience's sense of contact and immediacy.

The person ultimately responsible for media communications for the marathon is Shawn Platt, first vice president and director of publications for LaSalle Bank. Platt handles all the publicity for LaSalle and the Standard Federal Bank in Michigan, and all sports marketing for these institutions. He deals with anything requiring publicity, be it checking accounts or the marathon. The latter represents about 15 percent of his time commitment. He also has a support staff and believes he could use one full-time person dedicated exclusively to the marathon. Platt's area-specific task centers on establishing what kind of information to distribute and how to do so. He must maintain extensive media relations.

One of the challenges for Platt's office is to find things that stimulate journalists to write articles about the marathon on a long-term basis. As an annual event that lasts only a few hours, it can easily slip from media attention throughout the rest of the year. Platt must resort to a series of strategies to keep interest going and to build up to the eventual race. One tactic is to call attention to the establishment of elite fields; for instance, the signing of a multiple-year contract with Khalid Khannouchi was enough to put the athlete on a morning television show. Platt's office followed a similar strategy with Evans Rutto and Jenny Spangler, thus calling attention to the previous year's male winner and a local female masters celebrity. Another topic that generates ongoing news is the opening and closing of registration. Because the latter occurs ever earlier, it becomes a way of getting attention during the late summer.

Platt sees special opportunities in the race itself. As an event of 40,000 runners, it also comprises 40,000 individual experiences. It lends itself to narrative—that is, human-interest stories—far more than other sporting events. Unfortunately, such stories are not sustainable throughout the year. Although there are sometimes yearlong training stories about runners, these tend to be one-time affairs. Repeating them could promote a notion of staleness. Originality fades once the concept has been established. It is not at all clear whether this will ever become a sustainable newspaper sports genre.

Platt maintains a database of key contacts. The main form of communication is the press release to twelve to fourteen contacts, often through one-on-one conversations. Although Platt will call journalists, he doesn't believe in exclusivity. He will ask people if they want to do an article on a given marathon subject. Platt's press contacts include journalists such as Philip Hersh, Marlen Garcia, and Lew Freedman at the *Tribune* and Larry Hamel at the *Sun-Times*. Platt communicates directly with former *Chicago Athlete* editor Bob Richards, who was hired by the marathon to write all its web columns. As Richards provides content for the editorial calendar, his materials serve as leverage with the media when marathon officials feel they aren't receiving adequate coverage.

Platt also relies on the marathon's practice of establishing media partners, as of this writing CBS and the *Chicago Tribune*. Both of these media derive specific benefits from the arrangement. CBS and the *Tri-*

bune may lay claim to be the official coverage of the marathon. In the case of the *Tribune,* the marathon benefits from the special "Chicago Marathon" section that follows the running of the race. It includes all times, articles on the victors, and sundry aspects of the event. It also sets off the race as enjoying a special status among sporting events and constitutes the biggest entitlement the marathon receives from the *Tribune.* The *Tribune*'s coverage has also become broader in Platt's view: since the marathon's twenty-fifth anniversary, the newspaper has begun to focus more on the cultural significance of the marathon, which reflects a deeper understanding of the larger implications of the emergence of a sport.

Platt feels that the marathon expands emotional connections through these partnerships. The *Tribune* allows individual runners to find themselves in its complete listing of finishers in the special marathon section (although the *Sun-Times* also lists all runners and times); CBS is helping the marathon staff produce a personalized DVD of each runner crossing the finish line—an irreplaceable moment of triumph that can be permanently archived for the runner and his or her family and friends. Here one sees the value of a marathon partner's expertise in fostering the appeal of this sport, which permits a kind of everyman's/-woman's apotheosis without regard to the actual quality of the performance—perpetual acclaim for the finishers in their moment of transcendence on the urban stage.

Platt understands that CBS's willingness to serve as a media partner is highly valuable in itself. The fact that one network will undertake a four-hour telecast on the marathon raises the stature of the event. It ensures that all other TV newscasters will not only want to cover the event, but will almost have to do so. CBS's telecast also reinforces the Chicago-area population's perception of the marathon as an event analogous to the Super Bowl: people gather for breakfast, premarathon, and postmarathon parties. It's a sporting event worthy of being televised, a unique event that marks a particular season.

Although the marathon also uses radio (ESPN) to broadcast the event, that medium gets the least amount of attention. For Platt, the reason for this is quite straightforward: ESPN listeners are not very enthusiastic about the marathon. Language difficulties are also a barrier on radio and serve as a filter. It is difficult to interview a champion like Evans Rutto, who is not entirely fluent in English. Other winners have

to rely on interpreters. Both print and TV are less daunted by these issues because in the first medium, the problem has been resolved prior
to printing and in the second, the athlete's visual presence, not words,
dominate the telecast.

Bob Richards currently works in the *Chicago Sun-Times* sports department as well as for the marathon. He writes articles for the marathon's
web site, the *Mile by Mile* newsletter for participants, the official program, and the results booklet. He is the former editor of the *Chicago
Athlete,* a monthly magazine that serves as an additional news source
besides the city's two major daily newspapers, the *Chicago Sun-Times*
and the *Chicago Tribune.* Richards thus represents a kind of transitional
figure: someone with a long history as an independent journalist prior
to becoming part of the marathon staff. He came to the *Chicago Athlete* with background in sports journalism that began in high school.
He received his degree in journalism from Southern Illinois University,
where he covered many sports events. For a time, he was the managing
editor of a local suburban newspaper, and then he became a sports journalist in Milwaukee. This became his niche and he did a lot of freelanc-
ing. In the late 1990s, the opportunity presented itself to become the
editor of the *Chicago Athlete.* He subsequently developed this journal
and complemented it with an electronic newsletter. Richards is an avid
and accomplished runner, and this personal knowledge of the sport informed his reporting for the *Chicago Athlete* and fuels his enthusiasm
for events like the Chicago Marathon.

The *Chicago Athlete,* founded in 1986 by Eliot Weinberg, covers running, cycling, triathlon, and Nordic skiing in the Chicago area. Despite this multiplicity of coverage, its primary focus is running, and the
premarathon issue is usually dedicated almost entirely to the Chicago
Marathon. The journal also provides a race calendar to the *Sun-Times.*
In general, Richards sees the *Chicago Athlete* as a source of more detailed
information for the committed runner. Commentators like Mike Prizzi
and Hal Higdon, the official Chicago Marathon coach, contribute regularly to this journal and thus ensure high-quality input for its readers.

The Chicago Marathon calls all of Richards's talents into play, especially for stories prior to the race, which often require radical last-
minute revisions. In 2003, Khalid Khannouchi's withdrawal from the

marathon due to injury and Paul Tergat's new world record in Berlin shortly before the running of the Chicago Marathon threw reporting into turmoil. Richards had to obtain an immediate reaction from Carey Pinkowski to the setting of the world record, and he had to reconstruct the sports preview, which was affected by the sudden folding of the Pittsburgh Marathon. Fortunately, Richards has developed over the years a deep knowledge of the marathon and excellent contacts, all of which he can bring to bear at a moment's notice when sudden revisions are required.

Richards states that covering the marathon is quite different from covering a stadium sport like a football game. For one thing, it is impossible to take in the entire 26.2–mile course in a single gaze. People are not necessarily handing out the information such reporting requires. A reporter who follows the lead man cannot comment on the lead woman or vice versa. A reporter has to stay in the pressroom rather than out on the course if he is to command an overview of all the simultaneously occurring events. Like most major marathons, Chicago supplies media guides with essential athlete information for journalists, who have to be sensitive to the sometimes profoundly different cultures of the runners. Khalid Khannouchi knelt and prayed to Mecca after his world-record victory in 1999. Diverse language skills are also essential for interviewing elite runners, especially given that world records are often set in Chicago.[2] Reporters are given access to these champions over the course of a day. Several are available at the same time, and it becomes critical to choose the correct runners and to pose the questions needed for a story line. Relationships can spring from these interviews, which in turn allow for rapid e-mail communication for up-to-the-minute reporting and privileged access to information—that is, scoops. In any event, Richards religiously attends the Thursday marathon kickoff press conferences and returns for more on Friday. His next step will be the marathon expo on Saturday, when the journal invites selected guests to a party. He is, as indicated, at the pressroom on race day Sunday, where he can watch the splits and the pace. He has to be inside when the race officials bring in all of the top runners after their urine specimens have been given—something that often takes a bit of time. Richards finds that interviews conducted at this juncture are particularly good because they are raw and from the heart. He also finds it rewarding to see that the professionals are also exhausted, which establishes a link between them and the rest of the mere mortals who finish spent and very much in their wake. In any event, after assembling all of this information, Richards then must look for a new angle to give his work freshness. Obviously, a world record solves the problem, but often a greater degree of creativity is required.

The actual processing for sports journalism, and the marathon in particular, as Richards sees it, occurs in a very short time frame, about twenty-four hours. Naturally, such a time frame is feasible only with the kind of background that Richards possesses. He states that most of the work is actually completed in three or four hours, after the decision is made for top billing of the day. The *Chicago Athlete* site will be the object of particular attention at the height of the marathon. Indeed, the site received some 250,000 hits in October 2003; in 2002, the server actually crashed after the marathon. Besides covering the overall champions, Richards also has to cover the masters and age-group champions. He will, of course, pay attention to local victors whose exploits are largely confined to age-group competitors, but Richards will also feature many human-interest stories that include interviews with first-time runners, charity runners, highly experienced competitors— in short, runners of diverse and varied talents. Richards is a runner-writer whose visceral understanding of the sport allows him a special vantage point and gives him sensitivity that permeates his interactions with professional runners and ensures optimal communication with his readers.

As Richards's experiences indicate, the Chicago Marathon media staff also provides critical reporting access, most importantly for print journalists, immediately before, during, and after the actual race. This access requires a more detailed presentation. In 2004, the official media format included four press conferences: an annual kickoff conference on the Thursday preceding the race (October 7), a returning champions conference (Friday, October 8), an elite American and wheelchair athletes conference (Saturday, October 9), and LaSalle Bank Chicago Marathon champions' awards breakfast at Tiffany's (Monday, October 11). Additionally, and most important, there was a press conference immediately following the marathon that included U.S. stars and the men's and women's first through third places. The press is particularly well treated at these affairs: a sumptuous luncheon is offered to all comers immediately following the kickoff conference. Prior to the marathon, as Richards remarked, various star athletes make themselves available for interviews with journalists, who are constantly supplied with food and, of course, equipped with computer workstations, all of which are used extensively throughout the race itself. Access is easy, open, and friendly; information is plentiful. The gathering includes the local, national, and international press; of course, reporters from the nation's chief running magazines are always present. It is a gathering of press celebrities as well as sports celebrities—in some cases, both are merged in the same person as with Amby Burfoot, former Boston Marathon champion and former editor-in-chief of *Runner's World.* It is clear that marathon officials try to create a positive atmosphere for journalists as they do their work.

The annual kickoff conference is clearly intended to dazzle. In 2004, it consisted of a hit parade of local potentates including no less than the mayor of Chicago himself, Richard M. Daley; Norman Bobins, president and CEO, LaSalle Bank Corporation; Jim Tompkins, president and COO, New Balance; Joe Ahern, president of CBS; Carey Pinkowski, executive race director; Khalid Khannouchi, four-time LaSalle Bank Chicago Marathon champion; and an elite athlete field. The kickoff is designed as a way to merge political, business, media, and athletic interests into one harmonious, celebratory, and well-integrated event. It is highly self-congratulatory. The 2004 conference was opened by the manager of the Hilton Chicago Hotel, the site of all press conferences except the postrace awards breakfast, who qualified the marathon overenthusiastically as the world's largest marathon and announced that he was himself running the race. Carey Pinkowski thanked the mayor and the city departments for their help in the marathon and described it as a "citywide celebration." Pinkowski introduced Norm Bobins, who noted that in the past ten years the marathon had moved from a field of 7,000 runners to its current 40,000, making it the third-largest marathon in the world. Bobins stated that he found it gratifying to see how the people of Chicago have embraced the marathon. He introduced Mayor Daley, who offered his compliments, and read a proclamation dedicating the coming days to the marathon. Thereafter, Pinkowski presented the athletes, an array of newcomers to Chicago like Dos Santos of Brazil. There were star speakers like Khalid Khannouchi whose cordiality and ebullience were infectious. Significantly for the journalists in attendance, he expressed his hopes for a new world record. Former champion Joyce Chepchumba also conveyed considerable warmth as she spoke of how she always felt at home in Chicago and how happy she was to be there. The star athletes added a touch of charisma to the general euphoria of the conference. The conference then moved back to business and media figures. Joe Ahern announced that CBS, media partner for the next four years, was thrilled to be part of what that network views as the biggest sporting event of the year in the city. Jim Tompkins announced the extension of New Balance's partnership and described the Chicago Marathon as one of the best-run marathons in the world. In short, the kickoff conference effectively established a highly upbeat atmosphere, insisted on the prestige of the marathon, and presented the image of a united community proud of its extraordinary race. There was nothing amateur about its careful orchestration.

Perhaps the most significant of the other press conferences was the postrace presentation. Once again, athletes appeared in the Hilton conference room and recounted their impressions of the race to a marathon-selected moderator and answered questions from journalists comfortably seated in rows facing the podium. The atmosphere was definitely not frenetic. Athletes were given plenty of time and encouragement to recount their stories. Unfortunately, the dominant theme of 2004 was dashed expectations: rising stars like Blake Russell and hometown American masters champion Jenny Spangler had disappointing experiences. No world record was expected of the women's field, but there had been high hopes for a new male record. Unfortunately, a contrary wind during the second half of the race took its toll on the male pack that had been on world-record pace—a subject that obviously interested journalists. Much time was spent on American disappointments and many attempts made to analyze why difficulties occurred and to learn the athletes' future plans in the light of their frustrated efforts. Nevertheless, all was far from glum. Evans Rutto won for the second time in a row after his world debut record in 2003; Constantina Tomescu-Dita, after suffering a defeat in the final stages of the race in 2003, this time held on to her early lead, which is the hallmark (and often the pitfall) of her running style. Most surprising was the fact that she had been quite ill on her arrival at Chicago. Her victory under such unlikely and adverse circumstances was good story line. In general, reporters try to tease out interesting stories, but questions were limited to a few journalists. Language barriers are often quite obvious in the process: Evans Rutto is not really comfortable in English; the third-place Japanese male runner, Toshinari Takaoka, could only speak through an interpreter; and for the woman's event interviews, the third-place and former champion Svetlana Zakharova used a Russian interpreter. These barriers temper to some extent inquiry from the U.S. media. Despite the difficulties posed by language barriers, what emerged was a carefully organized information session during which journalists had immediate access to the victors and to some of the hopefuls whose promise had not been realized. It was clearly a time to garner new information, develop story angles, and gain perspective for future articles on runners whose careers were beginning to take shape.

———————

Chicago's two largest newspapers, the *Chicago Tribune* and the *Chicago Sun-Times,* give the marathon detailed coverage, and that coverage includes not only the results on marathon day but long-term human-interest stories, editorials, and similarly themed material. Currently, the *Tribune* is the marathon's official newspaper partner. Nonetheless, both newspapers rival each other for thoroughness and variety of coverage. For instance, in 1999, shortly before the running of that year's race, *Sun-Times* reporter Larry Hamel wrote an analysis of the marathon's incredible growth in an attempt to examine who and what was responsible for this late-1990s phenomenon (Hamel, "Long Run to Greatness," 29). Hamel reported that, with a field that was expected to swell to 27,000, it would even be possible to imagine a race that would have 40,000 registrants—a prediction that was realized in 2003. One might remark that this prediction was not only accurate but also far-seeing in its vision.

Perhaps one of the most famous local journalistic accounts of the marathon was the long series of reports by *Tribune* reporter Eric Zorn, who chronicled his preparations for the marathon starting January 6, 1998, through his eventual completion of the event that October. Zorn became a kind of marathon "everyman"—or even a male Oprah! Presenting himself as someone turning forty, overweight, out of shape, and unable to keep his usual New Year's resolutions, he publicly declared his intent to train for and run the Chicago Marathon. The self-presentation was very much to the point. Like the popular running author John Bingham, the reporter understood that his own preoccupations were far closer to the great mass of runners who aspired just to finish the race, something that would be distinction enough. He also tapped into the middle-aged anxiety that propels so many people to prove to themselves that they can still do something extremely physically demanding. Writing for an increasingly obese population troubled by its sedentary habits, Zorn struck the perfect chord. Encouragement and advice were freely offered to the journalist. Zorn invited those interested in sharing their first attempt at the marathon to write and even train with him. Because the response was quite strong, he formed a group he named FOOLS (For Once in Our Lives Society). In his February 5, 1998, article, he discussed the opening of the spring racing season and CARA marathon training—participation in the latter had what seemed to Zorn already-daunting minimum mileage requirements (Zorn, "This Fool Trains"). Zorn also established a good-humored rivalry with a fellow FOOLS runner, suburban Press Publications columnist Jack Zimmerman, who was nearly thirteen years Zorn's senior and self-avowedly "fat" as opposed to "overweight."

Besides the comic rivalry and real solidarity, Zorn fixed on two messages he was getting from the general public: (1) anyone can run a marathon, and (2) if you do it, it will change your life. Again, he had hit on some of the prevalent assumptions about the marathon. It is true that healthy people well into their sixties can complete (let's not say "run") a marathon. This truism establishes the feasibility of an imagined impossibility, something one can do despite the intimidating message of Greek mythology. Yet, thanks precisely to this intimidating message, finishing the marathon inevitably offers confirmation that individuals' lives will be transformed by the realization of extraordinary powers of will and self-discipline they discover within themselves.

Zorn continued his columns, recounting the group performance at the Shamrock Shuffle that March and following its progress through the spring and summer, especially the Chicago Distance Classic, whose distance was a partial indicator of marathon readiness. He featured his corunners, often with individual portraits, described their fears of unforeseen but debilitating injuries, and complimented his rival Zimmerman, who went from being fat to merely overweight. Zorn tried to cover the gamut of experiences of a novice marathoner in training, including the moments of discouragement.

Zorn provided a spirited and detailed account of the actual run in his October 12, 1998, column (Zorn, "Fools Rush In"). One of his group's goals was to beat Oprah Winfrey's 1994 time at the Marine Corps Marathon (4:29:20, an average pace of 10:16 per mile). They failed, arriving in 4:31:53 (after a three-minute potty break), as their pace diminished in the later part of the race. Nonetheless, Zorn proclaimed his pleasure on running the marathon: "What a ride! The whole process, not just the race, turned out to be one of the most rewarding things I've done in years. I recommend it enthusiastically, evangelically, to those who are able. Start planning now for 1999" (Zorn, "Fools Rush In," 1). He also understood the marathon as a kind of moral lesson to be applied to life: "I'm too sore at this writing even to guess if I'll ever take up this particular challenge again; it is kind of a nutty stunt. But what I hope for me and for all of Sunday's FOOLS, registered and unregistered, is that we begin to apply the lessons the marathon experience taught us to other things—that what we have now done for once in our lives we will begin to do with the rest of our lives" (Zorn, "Fools Rush In," 1).

Zorn's columns were an enormous success. He won the CARA award for journalism given at the annual January banquet in 1999. The success was not at all surprising, as his columns had allowed for identification from the majority of marathon runners. His group's performance was marked by average to slower times, and so it did not exclude less able runners. It also tapped into motivations and emotions that are common to all runners, even the elite. In short, the columns provided an excellent example of how journalism can serve the marathon as a form of recruitment, in this case by what might be termed "experiential reporting."

Not all columns are so encouraging. Philip Hersh, one of the *Tribune*'s most distinguished sportswriters, took a far different view in his October 14, 2001, rebuke in "Sports Talk" to those who, in his opinion, had no right to claim they had "run" the marathon. Noting that a woman had called the *Tribune* to inquire why her time of 7:12:05 had not been included in the paper's list of finishers, Hersh asked, "Does getting from the beginning to end of a 26.2–mile course, by whatever means of body-generated locomotion in however long it takes, constitute finishing a marathon, which is a running event?" (Hersh, "Sorry, Marathon Means Running," 16).

Hersh decided to brave offending "many, especially those who have used the marathon as a self-help exercise" (16). He called for respecting the Chicago Marathon's official closing time (6:30:00 after the start) and went even further, affirming that covering the distance in more than five hours does not constitute running a marathon. He decried the emergent "touchy-feely approach toward marathon participation" (16). At the same time, Hersh acknowledged the power of this new trend toward inclusiveness, citing Amby Burfoot, editor of *Runner's World* and 2:22:17 Boston Marathon champion. He also noted LaSalle Bank chief administrative officer Mark Nystuen's commitment to larger fields without regard to Boston's qualifying times. But the new inclusiveness did not placate Hersh. He concluded: "So take Ndereba's time [her 2001 world record]. Double it. That's a 4:37 marathon, about 10 minutes 30 seconds per mile. Make it five hours. That's a little over 11 minutes per mile. That's jogging a marathon. For the sake of inclusiveness, we'll call it running a marathon. Running is what the race should be about" (Hersh, "Sorry, Marathon Means Running," 16).

It would be hard to imagine a starker contrast between the positions held by *Tribune* reporters Zorn and Hersh. Hersh, throughout most of the history of the marathon, has not hesitated to point out flaws, readily blasting television coverage and even suggesting an alternative marathon course. What the columns of both reporters suggest is that local journalism, besides unofficially recruiting for the marathon, has also contributed to the debate on the nature of the phenomenon; in Hersh's case, he has shown himself willing to present a more traditional, performance-based notion of running.

Hersh also represents the unpredictability of media partners. Just prior to the 2004 Chicago Marathon, he wrote a scathing piece on Khannouchi entitled "In the Long Run, He Puts U.S. 2nd" in which he accused Khannouchi of not being a man of his word and largely focused on money. Hersh told spectators, "when you see four-time winner Khalid Khannouchi approaching, turn your back on him"[3] (Hersh, "In the Long Run," 2). He compared Khannouchi unfavorably to runners like Joan Benoit Samuelson and Paula Radcliffe, who continued to race despite physical adversity, while he depicted Khannouchi as too willing to pull out of races. He concluded, "At the time to put up, Khalid Khannouchi always gave up." Partners or not, the print press allows its senior reporters (especially one like Hersh, who has covered so many Chicago Marathons) the liberty to offend—as well it should, even if their opinions are thoroughly contestable.

—————————

CBS local television covers the Chicago Marathon. The CBS media partnership began auspiciously in 2003, the year its marathon telecast won an Emmy for Outstanding Achievement in Sports Programming. Jay Foot and Tom Schnecke, CBS director of broadcast operations, are the executive producers.

The ultimate responsibility for conceptualizing CBS's telecast of the marathon falls on the shoulders of Jay Foot. As part of his telecast background, Foot already has to his credit the highly successful *190 North,* a show he conceived for ABC in Chicago. Foot observes that the first thing a producer must do in any telecast, whether a marathon or a football game, is "to get down to the spirit of the thing."[4] A producer must decide on the nature of the story he is trying to tell, the essence of the event. Foot believes that, in the case of the marathon, it's human achievement and overcoming odds that are the impressive universal human themes. For him, it becomes "an opportunity to tell good, upbeat stories." Foot also states that a producer must ask what the Chicago Marathon in particular is trying to do and what it is known for. For 2004, he zeroed in on the notion of speed, which the telecast used as its coverage theme. Foot cites the various streaks of light, accents, and highlights in the customized graphic TV design package to foster the notion of a speed-focused event, thus drawing viewer attention to the fact that world records are set in Chicago.

Foot thinks that thematically each year's telecast will stand alone and have a distinct look and feel. On the other hand, he feels they'll most certainly be related. He speaks of "a family of experiences here that have a common thread." What he learned from the 2003 marathon enabled him to zero in and select speed as the 2004 theme. Building on this growing experience, Foot's team decided to choose "Get Into It" as the 2005 theme, which promoted both speed and involvement.

Besides theme, there is also the issue of look, which can vary from year to year. In 2003, CBS tried orange and yellow as design colors. In

2004, planners shifted to combinations of greens and yellows, which they thought made for a better visual effect. This choice so pleased the planners that it was retained for 2005 with only minor tweaks (a bit more black, a bit more streamlined to free more screen space). Foot explains that he and his design team view the event as a kind of canvas or blank slate; the telecaster is painting a picture. This picture includes 40,000 people in the race, a million more people along the roads, and "a sea of humanity and signage everywhere." He notes that one sees lots of dabs of green and yellow in this picture. The telecast needs to complement that. Another color palette would cut against the grain because most of what CBS does is keyed over live pictures.

Although Foot acknowledges that there is an increasing focus on fitness through running, he characterizes Chicago as more of a football town. Additionally, he notes the population's predilection for basketball, baseball, and, in some cases, hockey. Chicago is a major prosports town, and those sports have a hundred-year head start over the marathon. Foot notes that the CBS team must work to broaden the appeal—coverage has to include community stories; it must humanize the event. Foot strives to find a balance. He felt that the 2004 telecast represented an increasing emphasis on pure sports coverage while maintaining sufficient human-interest content.

A big part of the sports story is highly dependent on data delivery. Foot is concerned with turning around information quickly—that is, getting the 10K split times on the air immediately, not when the runners have reached the 11K mark. At this point, the marathon has evolved from cell phone communication to a real-time data stream coming back and an IT component. Foot is convinced that from 2003 to 2004, the biggest telecast improvement has been in data delivery; prior to the 2005 race, he reported that the data stream was excellent and even more useful.

When asked about the particular difficulties involved with a marathon telecast as opposed to other sports, Foot quipped that in the Super Bowl, the players run onto the field and don't run out the other side of the stadium. With the marathon, CBS must follow the action live for twenty-six miles through congested urban streets. This is obviously a real challenge. He believes that this technical achievement, blended with creative content, is what impressed Emmy Award officials for the freshman telecast.

In terms of the actual telecast, Foot sees CBS's job as differentiating runners as soon as possible and weaving in the "citizen runner" story, particularly early on. It is still a challenge to try to pick that runner out of a haystack, even though technology is making the task less daunting. Improvements in the data stream through chip, mat,[5] and the IT component are all moving in this direction. Foot anticipates zeroing in on selected runners and rapidly reporting their times mile by mile and their progress from 5K to 10K. It will still remain a challenge to pick them out with cameras. In 2003, CBS dealt with the problem by making arrangements with a couple of citizen runners to find them. They let the runners know the location of the camera positions and encouraged them to stop by. But Foot points out that the runners have to stop in order to talk to CBS, which is a sacrifice. He does not want to interfere with anyone's goals and times. But to the degree that people are willing to slow down briefly and talk, CBS can present the progress of citizen runners along the course.

Prior to the 2005 marathon, Foot discussed the genuine innovations implicit in the coverage theme "Get Into It." A prime example of this theme would be the "running-reporter-cam"; in this case, CBS reporter Megan Mawicke was to ride along the race route in a motorcycle side-car and jump out to interview runners—something that proved very effective. Intended to add a third dimension to the race and involve reporting with speed, the "running-reporter-cam" represented a creative departure from static interviews with paused runners. The "Get Into It" theme also encouraged viewer as well as reporter involvement. Viewers were invited to send in text messages of support to friends and family, and these appeared below the screen at appropriate moments.

For Foot, the most compelling visual of the marathon is the start—at least for the Chicago Marathon. There are points in other marathons, such as Heartbreak Hill in Boston, that attract his attention. But he becomes lyrical about "that amber-coated Grant Park right in the middle of fall, and the leaves are on fire, . . . and there's a sea of humanity, and the heads are bobbing. That's a beautiful picture." Indeed, Chicago's massive broad start in the very heart of the city along the lakefront is an image that is engraved in many memories.

Foot also cites other points in the race, particularly in the neighborhoods. He remarks on the run through the Belmont area down Broadway—namely the prize-winning Frontrunners' aid station that

CBS features during its broadcast. He also appreciates the various ethnic community locations, such as Pilsen (Mexican/Mexican American neighborhood) and Chinatown. Unfortunately, from a TV standpoint, CBS is not on the air long enough for the bell curve (the great mass of runners) to get anywhere near Chinatown, though the 2005 broadcast did feature shots of its dragon. The bell curve is anywhere from mile 13 through 15 as CBS is leaving the air—Chinatown is at mile 21. To deal with this situation, Foot frontloads the course with reporters so that they have places to go once the elites have finished and they have thirty or forty minutes of air time remaining. This is the moment when they flip back to the citizen runner, and the interviewing can only be done before mile 15. Clearly, telecast time limitations have a powerful influence on the narrative and course coverage. Aid stations at the rear of the course have little hope of attracting much attention, and citizen runner stories don't include the finish-line experience.

When asked what CBS gains from its partnership with the marathon, Foot responded with great enthusiasm. "The association is fabulous! We are delighted to be able to work with these guys," he stated. Foot notes that CBS has many partnerships on many levels, yet none exceed the marathon planners in terms of collaboration, relationships, and contributing ideas and support.

The second benefit Foot notes is the tremendous value of association with the biggest live event in terms of people and economic impact in the city. He adds that it's not the only thing CBS does. It handles community parades, special programs, documentaries, one-time-only specials, and other live events. Foot sees this involvement as analogous to that of LaSalle—not just buying a table at a function, but actual involvement in major urban endeavors. Foot notes that truly successful stations have additional community outreach aspects to them, which send the message to viewers that they are not just there for "the shooting or the fire"; they're there for "the good news too." This is all part of outreach, and Foot insists that it's by no means entirely about revenue. As a publicly licensed broadcasting company, it is incumbent on CBS to serve the community. The corporation must prove this, and such programming can make a compelling case to the federal government that CBS is a good citizen and deserves its license. Thus, the marathon broadcast itself tends to take on a broader role of community service as well as that of a revenue-generating production.

Clearly, media coverage represents a particular challenge. An annual event that lasts only a few hours and is televised for no more than four, the marathon almost begs for neglect during the rest of the year. A new sport in a professional sports town, the marathon has to vie for media attention with already well-established sports if it is to build a mass audience. Yet the event's now-ritual position as the high point of the annual autumn festival, the stupendous crowds it draws, its extraordinary economic impact, and the attention it commands from the business, political, and running communities ensure that it must be covered—and in a protracted fashion.

Add to this is the rather extraordinary fact that so many members of the media themselves have been active or casual participants in running and/or the marathon itself. A younger Philip Hersh ran a marathon in an honorable time; Bob Richards, in his earlier journalistic career well before his transition to the marathon media staff, was and remains an avid runner and Boston Marathon veteran; Eric Zorn lived and chronicled the neophyte marathoner's experience in the press; Tom Schnecke ran the New York Marathon; Jay Foot, as a result of his telecast involvement, has become a runner, and he vicariously participated in the 2004 Chicago Marathon through the running experience of his daughter. In short, it would be hard to imagine a sport that directly involves media figures not only as observers but also as participants. Few if any reporters could play in major league baseball in Wrigley Field or at Soldier Field for the NFL, but some can and have run the Chicago Marathon. This creates a proprietary relationship for amateurs—and possibly a loyalty—that is hard to imagine in any other professional sport, an extra motivation to provide superlative coverage.

The relationship between television broadcasting and the marathon is also one that fosters identification with the event rather than distanced, critical coverage. This has nothing to do with any lack of intellectual acumen on the part of television producers; rather, they are involved in an essentially collaborative exercise. They are not observers and judges of the marathon, as is an independent reporter, but they are actively engaged in the transmission of the event through its broadcast and in its conservation in the production of a digital document. In essence, while they are quite capable of making a critical analysis of their production, they are nevertheless in a situation that makes them advocates of their own product rather than critics of the race.

Finally, the marathon staff's good will and efficiency—constant themes when talking with race volunteers—also spill over into media relations. The presence of Joe Ahern at the 2004 kickoff press conference and the observations of Jay Foot suggest positive working relationships. The marathon in many ways embraces a friendly, dynamic, and highly competent community—one whose magnetism has a direct impact on media relations.

High-spirited runners are the heart of any marathon.

PART V

The Runners

Inevitably, runners, the people who are at the very heart of the Chicago Marathon, compose a huge portion of this book. Rather than overwhelming the reader with one immense chapter, the discussion of runners has been separated into four chapters: professionals and near-professionals (exceptional amateurs), older runners, middle-aged and younger runners, and charity runners. There are subheadings within each chapter, and the categories themselves are to some extent overlapping and arbitrary. For example, nothing prevents a charity runner from being a young, aspiring professional or an elderly age-group champion.

There is no simple profile of a marathon runner. Once an all-male sport, women, especially younger women, are ever-more numerous and may one day constitute the majority of participants in a given marathon. The marathon spans almost all age categories, with the exception of the very young; it includes runners from their mid-teens through their eighties. The motivations for running a marathon are also highly variable—a sense of camaraderie, the desire to experience a great adventure, the need to prove one's will, the determination to triumph over age or illness, the wish to prevail as a champion, and the generous resolve to help others are some of the motives that compel runners to take part in this event. As marathoners, they undergo a certain socialization joining a cast of tens of thousands and even hundreds of thousands on a global scale; they become actors in a new urban rite that is rapidly replacing or happily coexisting with more ancient religious rites and carnival festivities that cemented urban unity and even regional unity in the past.

The vast majority of runners, however, will have to make deliberate choices as to how to train for a marathon. Some will do it alone, relying on articles, books, web sites, and advice from more experienced friends to plan their training. Many will have already been significantly involved and will view the marathon as a step upward in their racing ambitions. Others, whether already veterans of races at shorter distances or neophytes set on making the marathon their goal (and even more frequently their first race), will join training programs. As noted, the most popular training program in Chicago is the CARA program, which is offered under contract with the marathon authorities. Training sites are within and outside the city, and numerous pace groups are available. The programs last for several months and draw significant numbers.

All runners, whether training independently or with groups, will be exposed to certain exigencies of marathon training. They will face the inevitability of increasing their mileage to minimal weekly ranges in the forties for those contemplating a sub-4:00 marathon to distances that may exceed 100 miles for professionals. They will learn to divide this weekly training into long runs, intervals (short and long, for the speediest of runners), marathon pace runs, lactate-threshold runs, and ordinary, leisurely running on more relaxed days. This combination, especially the intervals, can be quite demanding, and less experienced, slower runners—or those who just have too many other things on their agenda—may well limit themselves to a weekly long run, some speed work, and leisurely running to ensure recovery and the attainment of weekly mileage requirements. Those truly driven runners who are more technically inclined (and who have the financial resources) will purchase equipment to monitor their heart rate to obtain optimal training results. The wise and the knowledgeable will taper over the two weeks preceding the marathon.

What should be clear, however, is that marathon training is anything but simple and spontaneous, whatever the level of the runner's ability. It is extremely time-consuming and, in many ways, organizes and imposes on the runner's leisure time and even work schedule. It requires a rather significant degree of dedication to complete such training successfully. If runners are training alone, they must interpret the different training programs, whose directives are not always transparent and require serious study—if only to make a comparative analysis of different options. Runners will in all likelihood study charts that attempt to predict their marathon times projected from shorter race times. The most serious of them will be constantly trying to increase their speed at shorter-distance races as an act of self-encouragement for their marathon run. The strenuousness of the training brings with it a certain risk of injury. Runners have to be aware of their physical condition throughout training in order to avoid frustrating all their efforts by a last-minute injury. In short, the stakes are very high, and, like human fate, all things can be undone by a trivial incident—whether it is a bad meal, a turn in the weather, or an unexpected and inexplicable injury.

Clearly, the volume and requirements of this kind of preparation often make group training a highly desirable option. But even if those who train in groups are a bit less self-disciplined than those who train rigorously alone—which may well not be the case—all runners who undertake marathon training have some distinctive traits that set them apart. To say they are self-disciplined is very much an understatement; they have a superabundance of drive and willpower. People who are willing to deal with the physical and intellectual rigors of training enjoy the challenge of obstacles under the scrutiny of the public eye—for it is the public that grants them the acclaim so many pursue. They often share a sense of community with those who have undertaken similar efforts, and they frequently delight in the exchange of anecdotes and advice about training and racing. They are, by dint of their efforts and organization, a cohesive, highly reliable group of people.

While some generalizations about marathoners may be compelling, it is far more gratifying and informative to allow runners to tell their own stories about their marathon experiences—and those of the Chicago Marathon in particular. The following testimonials are from numerous individuals who have run the Chicago Marathon or who have in some way been associated with it, as in the case of the understanding and patient spouse of a runner. These runners demonstrate dramatically different abilities and expectations. Some are professionals of world stature, others are highly gifted amateurs, many are strong but not outstanding runners, and others move at a relatively slow pace, although the strain it imposes may be no different from that felt by their speedier counterparts. Because this book views the marathon not simply as a race, but as an urban festival, a mega-event that celebrates the life and vitality of the city, the concern here is less the speed of the runner than the diversity of coverage.

Outstanding runners come from around the globe to compete in Chicago.
Here, Kenyans in the front—hardly an unfamiliar sight!

nine

professionals and
exceptional amateurs

Although this book does not focus primarily on professionals, it would be unimaginable not to have their perspective. The author had the opportunity to join the press corps interviewing elite runners prior to the running of the 2001 and 2004 Chicago Marathons. During interview sessions, some runners were guarded, while others were quite expressive. The atmosphere was charged with the tension of those who would struggle for ultimate victory—or at the very least, an honorable and distinguished performance that would garner them invitations to future races. Nonetheless, the broader humanity of the athletes often emerged in these interviews, especially in the context of the tragic events of September 11, 2001.

foreign professionals

In 2001, Kenyan Moses Tanui, who had placed second to Ben Kimondiu after failing to win the race on two previous attempts, remarked on his earlier disappointments. He felt ready for the race but didn't want to talk too much about it; he said that it would tell its story. Tanui expected a fast course with a first half of 1:03:00 flat. Although he wanted to run approximately 2:06:00, he preferred to approach the race itself rather than the time. Tanui also remarked that with Chicago's flat course, anything was possible. Tanui, however, keeps his own pace and tries to remain on the safe side. He feels that it is only in the last seven to ten kilometers that one has to do something. In fact, he then became more precise, stating that in a marathon one looks and listens up to the 35K mark, but after that, it's all business. Beyond that point, the runner must focus on the race. In this, Tanui echoed the theme of many professionals who are acutely aware that victory is most often won in the final distance when the body has already been pushed to its limits.

Tanui emerges as a rather amiable man. He prefers to be friendly with all athletes and views friendliness as essential in training. Despite the fact that the actual race is not an expression of amicability, he insists that it's a sport, not a fight. He also appreciates the qualities of other runners. He noted with appreciation the then-young and soon-to-be world champion Paul Tergat. Tanui saw himself as near the end of his career—no more than two years away, he speculated. He wanted to leave the sport while he was still strong. He expressed only modest economic ambitions: a nice house and maybe two cars in his native Kenya.

September 11th had left its mark on Tanui; he recalled seeing the events unfold on CNN. He first thought he was witnessing an accident until the second crash happened. He viewed this barbarism as an assault on everyone who loved peace, not just Americans. Tanui deplored the killing of the innocent, stating that the aggrieved should have gone to those with whom they took issue. His revulsion with brutality brought him back to his sense of solidarity in sport, which he viewed as "uniting." He decided to come to this post–September 11th race because he saw it as a unification of all races and cultures. "When you go to the line, you are one."

Fellow Kenyan Lornah Kiplagat, who was also a contender for first place but placed second after Catherine Ndereba running a world record time, also had many perspectives on racing. Kiplagat, as a professional, believes that just to place is important. In the previous year's race, she had wanted to run as fast as possible, but she was injured. She considered stopping four times. She was aiming at 2:20 and was in pain when Catherine Ndereba caught her. Kiplagat was running basically on one foot, and was in fear of derailing her career. For the 2001 race, she expressed the desire to run at her own pace and refused to accuse Ndereba of using her pace. Kiplagat suggested that her competitor might wish to stay behind the leader to see what might happen but refused to attack her strategy. Like Tanui, she showed a certain generosity toward the competition and an understanding of the exigencies of strategy.

Kiplagat had a personal connection to Chicago. She stayed with hosts from the suburban Alpine Runners; in fact, she had arrived there a week before the marathon. She prefers staying with families because it relieves race pressure. During her stay, Kiplagat also met with children from Cabrini Green, one of Chicago's housing projects. She was confident that, when the race actually took place, the Alpine Runners' aid station would give her plenty of moral support. She has had similar personal experiences in New England. Kiplagat seems concerned with personal ties, particularly in acts of kindness toward children.

Kiplagat was prescient in her belief that in the coming years, four to five women would break 2:20:00 (three had done so by 2004). She was happy that the barrier was broken (it had happened in Berlin just before the Chicago Marathon, only to be bettered by her competitor, Ndereba, in the 2001 race). She felt that for the upcoming race a different strategy was required and intended to take it easy at the beginning; however, she expected a good pace from the Ethiopian runners.

Clearly, professionals like Kiplagat do not conform in any way to an image of an arrogant, overbearing champion. Instead, even while completely focused on the effort required to compete, she expresses respect for competitors and demonstrates warmth to people in general. Kiplagat emerges as someone who values ties with other people, ones based on feelings and real exchange. Her comments suggest a genuinely benign human being.

Paul Tergat, although recognized as a serious contender at the time of this interview (personal record of 2:08:15), was not yet world champion, and he did not win the Chicago race. He answered some technical questions on running and kept the focus largely on the sport. For Tergat, the marathon showed him how strong he was mentally. He stressed that mileage was the most important thing in marathon training; it was essential to develop stamina. He did not feel at the time that he lacked long training and spoke of his good experience running in London. Tergat also expressed concerns about overtraining and undertraining; he viewed both as nightmares. He tries, like so many other professionals, to run his own race. At the time, two years before his world record, Tergat stated that he wanted to see how far he could go with the marathon and speculated that he might run for the next four years. Clearly, even professionals can only guess at their full potential.

Mohamed Ouaadi, with the seventh-best time prior to the race (personal record of 2:07:55), was in a position to set a world record. Ouaadi represented France in the Olympics, but he grew up in Morocco and had shown much of the promise of his illustrious compatriot Khannouchi. Originally he played soccer and some basketball, but good results in running (10K time of 28:48; half-marathon time of 1:02:29) led him to focus on foot racing. At the age of twenty-five, he moved to France to continue his studies and trains at altitude in that country. Prior to the race, he felt in the best shape ever. Ouaadi stated that the marathon was the race that truly suited him. He believes that some people do better with shorter distances, while others are destined to be marathoners. Ouaadi tries to run his own race and not to be concerned with people out in front. He views no less than three months of training as essential for any marathon. When in training, he tries to run fast with more and more miles. He felt that he might achieve a 2:06:00 in the race but was cautious about a 2:05:00 possibility. He stated that he did not like being in front, which hurt him racing in Japan. He prefers that runners share the lead during the race. For Ouaadi, the concentration begins not in the last few miles but immediately after the first half of the race. He had chosen Chicago for reasons of his own preparation and the time possibilities. On a more philosophical note, as a runner who is basically binational, he speculated that the notion of nationality would soon disappear. When one considers the frequent changes of citizenship evident among marathon runners, this seems quite reasonable. Nationality is becoming an exchangeable label as runners move to the countries where salaries and training conditions are optimal.

u.s. professionals

Peter de la Cerda was a young American hopeful for this race with a personal record of 2:16:18. Although he was not a serious contender for first, his remarks give some insight into talented U.S. professionals. De la Cerda is a committed teacher, with a special interest in American history, who can only substitute-teach in order to focus on his running. He is also a coach; he coaches children, something he loves, but he also heeds his wife's reminders that they are not elite runners and that he shouldn't push them too hard. De la Cerda enjoys sharing his racing experience with children, but he also values hearing their stories.

In actual racing, De la Cerda likes the presence of a crowd—it takes his mind off the race. He noted the different ethnic groups and neighborhoods in the Chicago race. De la Cerda states that starting at around 30 to 35K, runners just focus on the race. From mile 20 onward, he takes the race one mile at a time. He has always been a marathon runner; he knew right away that it was his forte. He was aiming for 2:12 in Chicago, a time not that far off from his Olympic trial time. For future races, he was contemplating New York, Boston, and Los Angeles. Los Angeles represented a personal commitment—he comes from that area and his grandparents have asked him to run it. De la Cerda is very upbeat and even spiritual about running. He describes it as a God-given gift and feels that he should do the best with it as is possible. Running gives him the opportunity to meet other people and visit other places—an opportunity that shouldn't be thrown away. He views running as a spiritual philosophy that is an extension of his life.

Blake Russell is a rising professional among U.S. women runners. Carey Pinkowski, whom she didn't know at the time, recruited her for the 2004 Chicago Marathon. Russell, who was initially not that keen on running in the fall, became really excited about the idea. Russell, who failed to qualify for the Olympics (she placed fourth with 2:30:32), felt that she had gone out too hard at the Olympic trials. Her plan for Chicago was to aim for a 1:11:00 or 1:12:00 at the half. Russell's career has taken her from Chapel Hill, North Carolina, where she did her masters in physical therapy; to Boston, to work with Joan Benoit Samuelson's former coach, Bob Sevene; and then to Monterey, California, where she continues to train with Sevene. Russell normally runs alone on some eighty miles of trails. She stated that she didn't start to run well until her senior year, probably because of undertraining. Now in her late twenties, she noted that for women of her generation, distance running was accepted as normal; there were no obstacles like those faced by Benoit Samuelson. Russell sees herself as running for the next five years.

Although she placed ninth in the 2004 marathon with a time of 2:32:04, she did not meet her time goals. Russell's half proved slower than she anticipated—1:13:30. Although she was disappointed, she felt that her time was decent. She didn't feel well from the start: her hamstrings were hurting, and she couldn't get the stride she wanted. Plus, there was a strong, contrary wind during the latter part of the race. Russell thought that she had pushed her training too fast, too soon, and planned to take a break from marathon running in the spring. Nevertheless, she emerged with a very creditable performance, and, as a young woman, has a real opportunity to improve in the years ahead.

Carl Rundell, whose remarks date from 2003,[1] had qualified for the Olympic trials the year prior to the Chicago Marathon. He was in town to encourage his teammates from the Hansons-Brooks Distance Project who hoped to do likewise in the Chicago Marathon. His was a particularly unusual case. At thirty-two, single, well educated, quite well paid, and living abroad, he decided to quit his job to train for the Olympic Marathon. Rundell realized that he could not train properly while working and, at a relatively late age for a runner, chose to leave his job to live his dream. In doing so, he opted, at least temporarily, for a modest standard of living, consciously rejecting ordinary social expectations. He joined the Distance Project, a group of elite runners determined to restore U.S. performances in marathon competition. The group lives in Spartan housing and focuses entirely on running. In the fall of 2003, there were fourteen men and five women in this group. All of the men were training to run 2:12:00 and were aiming at competition in 2008. Rundell talks about the need to surround oneself with people who are passionate and supportive. He directs his efforts at developing efficiency and endurance, not speed. He thinks of mile 20 as the beginning of the race, the moment when he kicks in—close to the distance indicated by Moses Tanui. Rundell believes that the marathon fuels a sense of accomplishment. To run, he states, you need to be very connected. For the marathon, you have to put all your energy and mind into the effort. Finishing requires mental, physical, and spiritual energy.

Rundell follows an intense training program, often with two daily runs: the morning run is extremely trying, whereas the second run is based on how the group feels. The goal of the recovery run is to increase the pace rather than speed, as earlier in the day. Each runner tries to "borrow" energy from the group. With no special equipment or scientific backup, their results have elicited national attention. Rundell is perhaps illustrative of the individual for whom running is a ruling passion and who has the ability to rise to exceptional levels of performance. In a lesser way, almost all marathoners share his enthusiasm, but he represents one of the more totally committed.

Luke Humphrey, who is also a member of the Hansons Brooks Distance Project, was to run his debut marathon in Chicago. A Michigan local, he already knew of the Hanson brothers and the group they had assembled; he started working with them in the second week of August preceding the 2004 marathon. Humphrey had dreamed of the marathon since his college days when he had moved to the longer distances. To prepare for the marathon, he had been training intensely, first with eighty- to eighty-five-mile weeks, and then to 115 to 125 miles per week. He trains on the hills in his area of Michigan and relies on his teammates to help him pull through. Humphrey's goal is the 2008 and 2012 Olympics (when he'll be thirty-one). He was hoping to run around 2:16:00; his longer-term goal is to get faster for the next ten years. He adjusted his marathon goal from 2:20 to 2:16 because of his recent workouts. Three weeks earlier, he had run a half-marathon in 1:06:15. He believes that he can someday match the Kenyans, and he looks to Frank Shorter for inspiration.

Humphrey ran a strong marathon in 2:18:49, placing seventeenth overall and faster than his original goal of 2:20. Given the adverse wind conditions, his estimate of 2:16 does not seem unrealistic. He has lots of time to prove himself and, perhaps, to catch up with the Kenyans.

near-professional amateurs

A member of the National Guard, a Kansas resident, and a top runner in his region, Curtis Rogers is at the very least a top amateur, whose times are close to professional. He started running in 1982 and has run continually ever since. His first marathon was in 1986; since 1990, he has run three to six marathons every year. He views himself as primarily a distance runner and doesn't think that the number of marathons he runs wears him out.

When asked if there was a special attraction for him in running the Chicago Marathon, he replied that he hadn't done it before and added that he was trying "to get all the big ones in." Duluth's "Grandma's" is, however, his favorite marathon. He likes its competition, its organization, and the room to run that it offers. On the other hand, he wasn't preoccupied about the crowds in Chicago because he had a seeded start. Indeed, at thirty-five years old in the 2001 Chicago Marathon, he ran a 2:35:17. He usually doesn't pay a lot of attention to the spectators, but he remarked that Chicago does have an especially large crowd and it was hard not to notice the people along the course. The 2001 race had especially good weather and there were many spectators out. He said that it kind of got him going—at least, in the way the crowd affected those he was running with. "You get in a group of guys, and they're all feeding off the crowd a little bit." Rogers felt that this made them all go a little faster. Chicago yielded, nevertheless, only an average time for him, and he couldn't explain why this was so. He said that he didn't know if he took out some of the miles too fast. He wasn't injured; he just didn't have "a real good race." Despite this disappointment, his assessment of Chicago remains fairly positive: he views the race as well organized and appreciates the fact that there was always someone to run with.

Rogers is a thoroughly dedicated runner. He describes it as "pretty much of a lifestyle" for him. "If I don't get my run in every day or at least every other day, you know, I feel like I'm missing something." His future marathon goal is to break 2:30 again before he hits forty. Among U.S. marathons, he also wants to run Honolulu's; on the international circuit, he would like to run Berlin's. The only international marathon he has run so far is Helsinki's, which he describes as a small marathon with some hills. He hasn't run London's nor thought about doing it.

Rogers runs for the National Guard and has been National Guard champion, and he would like to repeat this feat again before reaching forty. He hopes to remain among the top competitors and doesn't foresee any major changes unless he gets injured. He also benefits from Guard sponsorship as they pay his way to a number of races.

Roger's training regimen is quite strenuous. His minimum weekly mileage exceeds peak marathon training for most amateurs. He runs no less than seventy miles per week and no more than one hundred and five! His mileage fluctuates depending on where he is in his training cycle. Usually, six weeks before a marathon he is running ninety to one hundred miles a week. Before a marathon or during the winter, he runs seventy miles per week. Clearly, Rogers is at the extreme of those who run marathons. He is not fixated on any particular race; rather, he is focused on grand competitions and achieving personal bests of exceptional quality. Although Chicago's reputation as one of the major marathons clearly attracted him to the event, he makes a careful evaluation of the race that is not influenced by other factors like civic pride.

Pat McKenzie is—like Curtis Rogers—a very fast runner. At thirty-four, he completed the 2001 Chicago Marathon in 2:33:30. As of 2002, he had been running seriously for about ten years. He didn't do track and field or cross-country when he was younger; for him, running was just a way to stay in shape during young adulthood. He had run Chicago as his first marathon in 2:49 "plus some seconds" in 1993 before his 2001 accomplishment. He "had fun, enjoyed it." His times kept getting a little bit better, and so he stuck with it. He thinks that he is well up in his age group—and he is, of course, quite correct. At the time of this interview, he had run nine Chicago Marathons and three Boston Marathons. He does no more than two marathons per year. McKenzie feels that two per year is the maximum that most people can run well, including himself.

He described the completion of a marathon as something that mentally feels great, despite the physically draining aspect of the experience. He has a particularly keen appreciation of Chicago: "Number one, Chicago is a great course. It's a flat course. So much to see, running through all the different neighborhoods and through the center of downtown." McKenzie is very aware of his environment. He feels that once he establishes his pace after the first three or four miles, he doesn't have to be really conscious of it—until mile 22 or 23, when a runner has to hone in, focus a little more. This automatic pilot obviously gives him the opportunity to view the surroundings.

The nearness of Chicago—he lives in Indianapolis—was an attraction for McKenzie, and, being the closest marathon, it was the initial reason he went to Chicago. He also appreciated the Chicago Marathon's scheduling; living in the north, it is far easier for him to train for a fall marathon than a spring one.

McKenzie was not disappointed with his choice. After completing the Chicago Marathon in 2001, he thought, "Wow, this neat. All in all, it was fun. . . . There was a lot to see. And there are a lot of runners around you too. So you're not alone." Like Rogers, who also comes from a less densely populated area, he appreciates being able to run with other fast runners. While many marathon runners never encounter this situation, rapid runners, especially in smaller events, often find themselves alone or nearly alone as they run. For a variety of reasons, this can be discouraging. There is the danger of getting lost and straying from the course, thus throwing the whole event away.[2] Most discouraging, however, is the lack of stimulation from a fast-moving pack and thus less motivation to realize an excellent time.

When participating in the Chicago Marathon, McKenzie goes to the expo, and he'll mill around there. He doesn't attend the prerace party because he likes to avoid the crowd when he's not running. He also doesn't like standing in line. After the race, he typically cannot linger long, although he thinks it's a great thing if you can do it. He loves the Chicago Marathon's organization and says that it's one of the reasons he keeps coming back. Even though the crowd has gotten much larger in the past four or five years, he notes that there isn't much pushing and shoving. People are respectful, and he appreciates the marathon's wide start. McKenzie begins his race right behind the professionals. Because he realized his personal record at Chicago in 2001 (and his second-best time of 2:37 at Boston in 2002), he hopes to be running the Chicago Marathon for many years to come.

Unsurprisingly, running plays a major role in McKenzie's life. He races with top runners locally but doesn't train with them. His weekly schedule includes six days of training. He doesn't cross-train much due to time factors. He serves as a running coach for his students and also runs with them, but he estimates that he does three-quarters of his running on his own. Coaching often cuts into running: giving students the attention they require takes its toll on his own training schedule. McKenzie has opted for a strategy of increased speed work rather than increasing his mileage as a means to further improvement. His weekly average is still high for most marathon runners but relatively moderate for people in his category. He does quite a few sixty-mile weeks, and maybe one or two in the seventies, if time allows. But he compensates by doing more mile repeats, tempo running, and even some four hundreds. In short, McKenzie, like most runners, has job obligations and a life outside competition—all of these factors limit the time and thus the mileage he can devote to training. Nonetheless, his training schedule would comprise a substantial chunk of anyone's life. It is illustrative of the tremendous dedication that marathon training requires and the demands it makes on any committed individual.

McKenzie believes that marathon running is healthy and thinks that it only becomes harmful if an individual tries to do too many—for instance, if he tried to do twelve a year. He feels that if he is comfortable mentally with the marathon, then it's okay. He is convinced that if he ever became obsessed with the marathon, then it would become unhealthy. (Of course, people who don't run marathons or don't approve of them regard all marathon running as obsessive! Not too many decades ago, almost any marathon runner would have been dismissed as an eccentric.) McKenzie asserts that if you do all those miles, you have to enjoy it.

Whenever McKenzie finishes a marathon, he feels elated. He refers to this runner's high as a "strong emotion, strong feeling of satisfaction." He also thinks there is a "runner's low." "You train for so long for something like that, and then it's done. And it's like, okay, now what?" If you catch a cold on marathon day, it can be disappointing, which is why, in McKenzie's view, you have to set your sights on another one. His general reflection on the marathon seizes its paradoxical nature: "The running . . . can be such a lonely sport. What really makes a marathon is the people along the way. The sights, the sounds. It's kind of a contradiction." He also feels that the marathon gives off a certain positive feeling, even if it is a competition. "There's nobody really against anybody. It's not an offense or defense type of thing." In that observation, he sums up the relatively nonaggressive nature of running, which is perhaps one of the contributing reasons for its success as a mass sport.

McKenzie believes that it takes a special kind of person to run a marathon. "You have to be disciplined to do all that. You have to be willing to learn about yourself, to push yourself, learn about your body, how your body reacts to so many different things with running. I mean how it reacts to heat, how it reacts to cold, how it reacts to what you eat." You also have to learn how to run marathons. McKenzie said he took off far too fast in his first couple of marathons. He says he didn't know what he was doing training-wise and racing-wise when he began. He feels that you learn pacing by doing. "It's amazing what the body does once it gets into a kind of rhythm. It kind of locks in." He adds that in the marathon, he takes energy from the crowds—which is not the case in a 5K.

Clearly, McKenzie is not only an excellent runner but also a thoughtful one. One could say that he has brought an intellectual perspective to the sport through his own experiences. His perceptions have sharpened over the years, and this sharpening of observations has led to heightened performance.

As the running population ages, older runners have become a familiar—and often successful—sight.

ten

older runners

Even while the body slows down with age, some runners continue to perform well into their sixties with results that far surpass most younger runners. They can also continue to race against themselves thanks to statistics developed by Dr. Ray C. Fair, a professor of economics at Yale and marathon runner.[1] Fair, a distinguished researcher famed for a largely accurate formula to predict winners of presidential elections, used the rich array of available racing statistics and his mastery of regression analysis to develop age-graded tables that allow older runners to see what their times would be for someone at peak running age. Such tables are now widely used by race officials, running organizations, and running publications in performance assessment. This tool certainly piques the interest of more competitive runners in the older age groups, but it is also fair to say that many older runners take part in the marathon for the simple pleasure of the event. Again, there is no single approach to a marathon that remains open to all comers as Chicago's does.

Dorothy Tanner is a unique runner. Hailing from Australia, Tanner had been a member of the Chicago Area Runners Association for over five years in 2002. She consistently dominated her age group, placing first by impressive margins. At age sixty, she had already broken nearly every Illinois age-group record and continued to break them (even though they were mostly her own!) prior to her return to her native land. Tanner was a proud member of Frontrunners, Chicago's chapter of an international gay and lesbian running club. Petite, extremely polite, and soft-spoken, she has considerable personal charisma. She is widely admired throughout the gay community for her work with people with AIDS and widely respected throughout the running community for her allegiance to CARA and her unfailing participation in circuit races. The local sports magazine, *Chicago Athlete,* saluted her with two articles in its fall 2002 edition, bidding farewell to a truly exceptional senior athlete.

Tanner has run all her life, but started running competitively in Antigua in 1990, when she entered a 10K race at a friend's behest. At the time, she was working as a chef on a yacht and had had to reduce her age by ten years to be considered employable. She decided to be up front about her birth date for competitive running, which she began at forty-nine. She realized that she could not represent Antigua with a false birth date. Because of this race, she became Antigua's female long-distance runner throughout the Caribbean.

Tanner did not become a marathoner immediately. After a visit to Chicago in 1993, she decided to run the marathon in the Gay Games being held in New York City in 1994. She had trained casually with her twin sister, a champion marathon runner in their native Australia, but she trained more seriously on her return to Antigua. Her experience at the Gay Games was a positive one. She took first in her age group in the marathon and the 10K; her marathon time was somewhere between 3:30 and 3:40. Tanner has run much faster subsequently.

Tanner discovered the expression "hitting the wall" during her participation in the Gay Games. Around the twentieth mile, she experienced the sensation of running backwards. Perplexed, she asked another finisher if he could explain what had happened to her. He replied that she had "hit the wall" and that there was nothing she could do about it. Typically, Tanner's reaction was anything but resigned. She resolved to solve the problem, and learned about carbo-loading and supplements to overcome lactic acid buildup. She never hit the wall again.

Despite her excellence in marathon running (she has broken the Illinois marathon age records for F55 and F60—3:20:45 and 3:42:41, respectively), she does not keep a careful count of all her competitions. She estimated that she had run about seven marathons as of April 2002—she would shortly thereafter win her division at Grandma's Marathon in Duluth. Tanner's choice of the Chicago Marathon is really an expression of where she lives. Although she has run marathons in New York, Boston, and Duluth, she does not like to travel to marathons or to stay in hotels or other accommodations away from her own home. In fact, she viewed Grandma's as challenging precisely because of the displacement. She likes the Chicago course and remembers fondly her first race in 1996, which was new for her and not that crowded. Now she views the race as too crowded, and especially as "far too noisy with the spectators." She concedes that most people seem to enjoy the racket, but she prefers tranquility. In fact, even in her choice of marathons, she is far less concerned with the fame of a specific venue than with the environment. Although she liked Boston, she doubted that she would ever run it again because of the crowds. Tanner is one of those runners who draw energy from within, a champion relatively indifferent to fanfare and festival, someone who fixes her efforts on the accomplishment rather than interaction with the crowd. She would clearly prefer a Chicago Marathon of 5,000 to one of 30,000.

Jo Dunbar is a very different sort of runner than Dorothy Tanner. She is not an age-group champion, but she is, nonetheless, extremely devoted to the Chicago Marathon. She has been running continually since 1982 and first ran the marathon in 1986. The original impetus came from a friend who had run the Chicago Marathon in 1984 and 1985—support for the argument that marathoners do make "converts." At the time, there was no formal training; there were no CARA groups to help out aspiring runners. Dunbar sought help from *Runner's World* and followed some of the magazine's advice. For moral support, she ran the first half of the marathon with a friend. She recalls that at the time there were only about 2,000 runners and that not many of them were women (somewhat over a hundred), and her recollections reflect a time when the marathon was just becoming a mass phenomenon. She compared this figure with the previous year's marathon in 2001, when she cited a number of about 15,000. Clearly, on a personal basis, Dunbar has witnessed the explosion of marathon participation.

The marathon is associated with certain traditions for Dunbar. The first time she ran the race, it was her birthday and she was determined to have a party after the race. In fact, she told herself this as a way of ensuring she would finish. At the time, the race ended in Lincoln Park, which meant that she could walk home. And so she started the practice, now a tradition, of having a bunch of people over after the race. In 2001, she was suffering with a hamstring injury as she ran and wasn't sure she would finish, but she did. She did not, however, go to any other party than her own, although she stated that one of these years she wants to go to the big party thrown for all runners. This party, however, is not a part of her personal tradition. It seems likely that many people, especially Chicago residents, prefer their own, more intimate celebrations to the postmarathon bash.

The evening before the race, Dunbar goes to Pat's Pizza (formerly on Sheffield Avenue and now further south on Lincoln) rather than to the official marathon banquet. This remains her personal tradition, rather than an institutionally determined practice. She eats pasta, not pizza, and takes one glass of wine. Like many marathoners, she is not averse to a drink. Her husband, who does not run, rides his bike along the race course and meets her at mile 7 and mile 16. He is an example of the family support that many runners benefit from. Dunbar in turn picks up some Sam Adams beer for him after the race and is usually ready to fall asleep after that.

Dunbar has suffered only a few injuries over the years but, like almost any long-term runner, she has not been injury-free. The 2001 marathon resulted in a pulled hamstring and a huge blister. In 1997, she was running down North Avenue and suddenly found that her leg was killing her. She nonetheless had to run home or be late for work. She ended up in physical therapy at the Rehab Institute and was satisfied with the results of her therapy: "They fixed me up great though, because I ran a good marathon the following year." Like so many runners, she can rebound from adversity and appreciates her recovery.

Dunbar usually runs alone. If she happens to meet someone on the path who is a friend of hers, she will run with that person. She does meet one woman friend and a man who lives down the block who runs at her pace. But she does not run with a training group or special program. She is away a lot on the weekends and doesn't feel that it is fair to commit herself, when she knows she is not going to be around. She started running because her job was so exasperating that she would take out her frustrations on the running path.[2] Now that she has a different, more satisfying job, she adds that she is not doing as well as she used to. (One might be tempted to say that job satisfaction can be bad for running!)

Dunbar thinks that running a marathon is healthy. She is convinced that you know if your body can handle it or not. She states that running slowly can make a big difference in a participant's postrace condition. If she runs slowly, she can usually run two or three miles two days after the marathon. She admits to hitting the wall. Unlike Tanner, she sees this phenomenon increasing with age. It now happens at eighteen miles instead of twenty. But Dunbar has the experience to cope with this situation. She alternates between walking and running and hopes that the race will be over soon. When she finishes a marathon, she has feelings of elation and "joy that I've crossed the finish line." Occasionally, she is disappointed by the time she sees on the race clock. Generally, however, she is in relatively good shape when she finishes and is happy about it. Dunbar also believes that the tenacity needed to train for and finish a marathon says something special: people who do this can probably do anything they set their minds to. Clearly, the expression "empowering experience" is entirely appropriate in this context.

Dunbar chose to run the Chicago Marathon because she lives in Chicago; the marathon goes by her home and thus represents a particular connection with a special place. During the first years of the race, her friend and that friend's husband also lived on the marathon course and were out to encourage her along the way. She still has a few friends who live along the course and come out to cheer her on, "which makes all the difference in the world." She had only run one other marathon as of 2002, the Detroit Marathon in 1993 in the pouring rain. She ran Chicago only two weeks after that! The reason she ran Detroit was because she was frustrated by the course of the Chicago Marathon at the time: up and down Lakeshore Drive, which she characterized as horrible and depressing. She had obtained an entry form for the Detroit Marathon, which was to be held over the Columbus Day weekend. She thought,

"Let's go to Detroit." As soon as she had signed up for that marathon and paid the hotel, the newspaper announced that LaSalle Bank had just bought the marathon and that it had changed the course, the primary reason she had decided to go to Detroit. And so she ran both. Dunbar remarked that she would like to run the Walt Disney World Marathon. She has a time-share down there, but because of her job, she can't take off at that time of year. At this point, she has a decided fondness for Chicago.

Dunbar appreciates the fact that world records are broken in Chicago, but sometimes she wishes that the race had only 5,000 runners again. Her favorite story about the transformation of the marathon concerns the turn off Ashland Avenue onto Eighteenth Street. She could see a particular house in the distance, and she would always ask herself, "Can I ever get to that house?" Now it is so crowded with runners at Eighteenth Street that she can no longer see the house. Despite her wish, though, Dunbar doesn't really mind the number of runners. She is not bothered by the huge field at the start now that all runners, except the elite, utilize ChampionChips. She is bothered by people who try to get up as far as they can at the start—something she admits to doing herself—but who then block the street by running five or six runners across (something she does not do), thereby bringing faster runners to a halt. She can't get around these slow-moving groups. Indeed, this is a classic frustration of mid- to back-of-the-pack runners. ChampionChips cannot compensate for the delays they encounter once the race is engaged, for it is not just at the start that runners must face pedestrian traffic jams. She does appreciate the crowds of spectators: "I think it's wonderful that people are out there." She remarked that if she wasn't running, she would be out there working one of the water stops. She does work at the marathon expo every year—usually at packet pickup. In 2001, she went at lunchtime and helped stuff the packets. Dunbar feels a great deal of pride about the Chicago Marathon, which she considers well organized, and believes that LaSalle Bank has done a wonderful job. Her own commitment as a regular runner and volunteer is a direct expression of this pride.

Unsurprisingly, all of Dunbar's personal records have been at Chicago. She would very much like to break 4:30 again, but she doesn't expect to see that. She registered for the 2002 marathon, but thought that it would probably be her last year because she was just getting so much slower.[3] "It's a waste," she stated and then revised, "Not a waste; it's fun, but . . . maybe I should be out there giving water." In fact, after arthroscopic knee surgery in January 2005, she decided to volunteer for the Lincoln Park Pacers' aid station for that year's marathon. Clearly, Dunbar incarnates the close association between runners and volunteers in her generous willingness to change roles. She expresses the spirit of cooperation that is so essential to the continuation of the modern mass marathon.

Dunbar's only strong reservation is one that flows naturally from the great success of the Chicago Marathon. As a participant from more meager times, she has a different perspective on this success. She acknowledges that race director Carey Pinkowski has done a wonderful job getting elite runners into the race, but she thinks he needs somebody on his staff more in tune with the everyday runners. On the other hand, she immediately qualifies that the marathon staff must be reaching out to everyday runners given the numbers of participants they're getting, although she does not personally experience this outreach. Although she insists on her appreciation of Pinkowski's excellent job in making Chicago a world-class marathon, she experiences a natural sense of diminished personal importance compared to the days when it was a relatively small affair and each runner counted far more in the survival of the marathon. In one sense, Dunbar's situation illustrates the dilemma of any marathon that has undergone a dramatic increase in participation. As the numbers grow, the individual runner is inevitably diminished, especially those whose commitment has lasted through the years.

Richard Gonzalez started running at about age forty-eight; prior to that, he had been a master swimmer. At the time, he was a professor at the University of Rhode Island, and he decided to improve his upper-body strength to become a better swimmer. When he joined a health spa for that purpose, he was put on a track. That launched his running career. He later moved to the University of Illinois in Chicago, where he ran his first marathon in 1989. His wife was so afraid he was going to die that she hired a taxi and followed him all over Chicago. That marathon was only his second run. He had completed a ten-mile run in Downers Grove (a Chicago suburb) before that and did reasonably well. He then bought Galloway's book on marathon running and took it from there without any formal coaching. During his first run, he really hit the wall and wondered if he could run any more marathons. But then he started doing marathons on a more regular basis. He returned to Chicago the following year and ran the marathon. After that, he didn't return to the Chicago Marathon for five or six years. But in spring 2002, he had run the last five consecutive Chicago Marathons for a total of seven; the 2002 marathon was his eighth. He regularly qualifies for Boston and ran his best marathon in 3:47 at about age sixty-six. Now in his seventies, he usually completes his marathons between 4:00 and 4:20. His last at the time of the interview was 4:20 at Big Sur.

Gonzalez spends much of the year in training and running marathons. He left Chicago in 1990 and moved to New Orleans, where the climate initially hampered his training. It's hotter and more humid in summer, but he has gotten sufficiently used to it to be able to train. As part of his training, Gonzalez runs two mile races, 5Ks, an occasional 10K, and an occasional half-marathon, but remains wary of injury in these lesser events. He says that sometimes you put a little bit too much effort into a 5K, and you pull something. Consequently, he does just one a month to keep up to speed. He thinks of himself as being better at the longer distance, but he also wins his age group in the 5Ks and 10Ks.

Gonzalez's training/racing schedule is highly unusual. He tries to run about one marathon a month throughout the year with the exception of the summer! So far, despite this draconian schedule, he has avoided all major injury and suffered only the usual pulled muscles. His most recent injury was a hamstring, which took nearly a year and a half for full recovery. It wasn't severe enough to stop him from running, but it bothered him. He had a hernia operation in January 2002 but was running again after about a month. Apparently, he has never heard of the more lengthy recovery time needed by older runners!

When asked why he runs so many marathons a year, Gonzalez provided an unusual answer: he doesn't like to do the long runs that are part of marathon training. If he does one marathon a month, he can largely disregard long runs. Because he does a ten- or twelve-mile run every other week, he does not have to go out and run twenty miles. He has a lifetime goal of 100 marathons. The 2002 Chicago Marathon was his seventy-sixth.

Gonzalez can be described as a marathon tourist. He has traveled a lot and run in different countries. Since he is a professor, he can sometimes get a conference invitation that corresponds closely to a marathon date, and thus deduct the travel from his income tax. His travels are as extraordinary as his running. He has been to Antarctica twice, and he has done marathons in New Zealand and in Europe. He has done nearly all the Scandinavian countries. His 2002 August marathon destination was Iceland. Gonzalez has run London's marathon four times and Paris's marathon a couple of times. Some of his other European marathons include Rome, Venice, Rotterdam, Stockholm, and Helsinki. Nevertheless, the Chicago Marathon continues to have a special appeal to Gonzalez because it was his first. Chicago was also his hometown of sorts for six years, while he was a professor there. He gets a chance to visit with his daughter every time he goes to Chicago, where she teaches.

Gonzalez is a competitive runner, and he usually wins his age group when he runs. He had just done so in the Big Sur Marathon at the time of the interview, but he added modestly that "it's not a big feat, because, when you're seventy, there are only about ten or twelve people in your age group." While that is true, it also downplays the fact that only a few people can still manage to run a marathon at Gonzalez's age. There is a kind of championship in the very presence of a seventy-year-old at a marathon. When asked whether completing a marathon gives him a feeling of rejuvenation, he replied ambiguously, "Yeah, maybe." He also responds well to crowds until twenty miles. Then, he adds candidly, "I sort of wish the thing would finish." Hardly an unfamiliar sentiment among marathoners! Gonzalez was happy with his 4:20 Big Sur run, especially because it is a fairly hilly course. As to favorite marathons, he likes those in big cities. He named Chicago's, New York's, and London's. He was born in New York, so he likes doing that one. He has run it eleven years in a row and states that he doesn't know how he has been able to get into it so consistently. He thinks that sooner or later they're going to turn him down.[4] He also likes marathons in different countries, as previously noted. He is not, however, particularly interested in running all fifty states. He prefers to repeat marathons. "Every year I sort of do the same ones." He does the Disney, New Orleans, Pensacola, New York, and Chicago marathons, along with London's or one in Scandinavia. His wife doesn't worry about him anymore. In fact, she enjoys coming along when he goes to Europe. He planned on the Singapore Marathon for December 2002 as his first Asian marathon. Then only one continent would remain: Africa. He was looking into Kenya but wasn't sure about it.

Gonzalez's case is an extraordinary one. He shows remarkable endurance for any age—his régime of about twelve marathons per year would be daunting for runners in their twenties. He exemplifies the growing trend in marathon tourism as he travels across the country and across the world in search of new challenges. In a sense, he illustrates how such a demanding sport as marathon running can become a ruling passion and still be successfully integrated into an already rich and full life. Gonzalez is obviously more likely to be admired than emulated.

A final note: Richard Gonzalez and his wife Lena were driven from their home in New Orleans in 2005 by hurricane Katrina. While awaiting permission to return home in Jackson, Mississippi, Gonzalez trained for the Chicago Marathon, which he ran on October 10 in 5:14:43 at age seventy-three.

visiting french seniors

The mayor of Paris's ninth arrondissement,[5] Jacques Bravo, at age sixty is a slender, active man who makes marathon running a part of his life.[6] Although Bravo participated in sports from adolescence onward, his involvement with marathon running came somewhat later in life under rather unusual circumstances. In the early 1980s, he suffered an accident that left him with a severely crushed leg. The gravity of the injury was such that it seemed doubtful that he would be able to walk normally ever again and it was unclear whether he would ever regain full sensation in the injured limb. Fortunately, Bravo had a highly competent and sensitive surgeon who encouraged him to go jogging on the beach. Bravo followed this seemingly impossible advice. Slowly, laboriously, he was able to regain feeling and movement. In a sense, the determination and will manifested in these first painful and protracted efforts on the sand were the prelude to his first marathon; Bravo's unshakeable persistence made his recovery into a refusal to accept invalid status and was a genuine act of self-affirmation. Within four years, Bravo found himself ready to run the New York Marathon, a definitive statement of his full recovery. He repeated this feat a second time with his son Gilles, whom he surprised in New York City with the news they were both registered for that marathon. Bravo has run twenty-one marathons since then, including Chicago twice, in 1996 and 1999. He is a strong booster of running cooperation between sister cities Paris and Chicago, and he is obviously a most welcome guest in Chicago as elsewhere.

One might easily assume that a man as busy as Bravo, who has serious political responsibilities and a heavy administrative load, would have little leisure for the lengthy and arduous training needed to run a marathon. Nonetheless, he finds the time because of what could be termed his philosophical convictions about the nature and utility of running. Bravo believes in the contact with nature and with the rhythm of life that running provides. He sees running as an integral part of human existence, something that has its own place alongside work and other social functions. Bravo also values the contact with others that is so much a part of running. His travels abroad to participate in marathons allow him to meet numerous people and to appreciate the diversity of the world. In many ways, he embodies the ever-growing international dimension of distance running, which now crosses most frontiers and has become a new form of bonding between people of diverse nationalities and cultures. Bravo emerges as a strong advocate of marathon running as a form of "global" socialization in the positive use of the term.

Bravo is also a connoisseur of French marathons. Naturally, he is most familiar with Paris' role in that domain, but he can speak with humor and enthusiasm about the famed Marathon du Médoc, whose wine-tasting appeal is renowned throughout France.[7] He achieved perhaps his slowest time during this marathon when he, like his "competitors," stopped to sample the different wines offered by the various vintners whose estates border the course. In short, Bravo is keenly aware of the difference between a "fun" marathon such as Médoc and those marathons that place central emphasis on time—an emphasis he does not really share.

Although Bravo has achieved quite respectable sub-4:00 times in his fifties (despite recurrent stress from his injury), he is less concerned with his times than with savoring the completion of each marathon. In New York, he told his son Gilles to slow down at the finish in order to observe and enjoy the culmination of their efforts. Bravo prefers to embrace the totality of the race rather than see it as a mere sum of hours, minutes, and seconds. This may, perhaps, have a linguistic dimension to it, for the term for "finish" in French is *l'arrivée,* literally "the arrival," which connotes more the notion of reaching one's destination than the termination of an ordeal, as the English equivalent might suggest. Whatever the influence of language, Bravo's approach to the end of the marathon remains a deeply personal approach, a kind of subtle epicureanism that understands the experience as a multidimensional form of enjoyment and achievement.

From a broader perspective, Bravo represents the upward mobility of the marathon, whose participants throughout much of the postindustrial world are frequently drawn from the ranks of the upper middle class and the wealthy, themselves usually residents of the vast urban agglomerations that host these races. Bravo is certainly a dramatic example of this tendency, given his high political office and obvious intellectual sophistication. Not unlike many Americans, he is a striking example of single-generation social advancement: his father was an Italian immigrant to France. A member of the first generation born in an adopted country, he preserves great affection for Italy and Italian mores, but he has also moved into a position of high prestige in his own society. To a certain extent, his association with the Paris Marathon and so many other international marathons is also indicative of successful social integration. This said, however, Bravo's own unique individual perceptions, which are so precise and personal, clearly differentiate him from any general pattern.

Gérard Delort is a distinguished French runner in his fifties and an avid promoter of many races, including the French classic Marvejols-Mendes and the Chicago Marathon, which he has run many times. At races throughout France, Delort encourages French runners to run Chicago's marathon and works with David Reithoffer[8] to facilitate their participation. His participation in the Chicago Marathon is in many ways a celebration of his commitment to international ties, ties that he continues to promote despite the difficult times in Franco-American relations that accompanied the second Gulf War.

Delort describes his first marathon as very hard; he evokes a "human tide" moved by the same goal: to arrive 10,000–15,000 strong "on the same sailboat." The 1956 Olympics inspired him as a child, when he saw a Frenchman win the marathon. Thirty years later, he ran his first marathon in 4:08—a disappointing debut for someone who would become a sub-3:00 marathoner. He had to walk after twenty kilometers because he hadn't done the necessary training. Since that time, he has run many marathons. Delort has a particular fondness for foreign marathons, and, besides Chicago, he also knows London's, New York's, and Boston's well. He particularly relishes memories of the New York Marathon, especially the start on the Verrazano Narrows Bridge with the sight of Manhattan in the foreground and the extraordinary public present at this event. Delort frequently runs both the Chicago and New York marathons back-to-back, even though these marathons are usually only about two weeks apart. This indicates his rather playful attitude toward marathon running. Delort is quite fast enough to contend for a top place in his age group, but instead he prefers the spectacle and the pleasure of participation. He frequently carries the American flag throughout the entire route of the Chicago Marathon, whose organization he keenly appreciates. Even encumbered with a flag, he finishes in between three and three and a half hours.

Delort does not, however, make light of the marathon. For him it has the sense of a challenge. He recalls that the name itself evokes the ancient battle of Marathon. Like so many others, he sees running the marathon as an empowering accomplishment: "Quand tu as fait un marathon, tu peux tout faire" ("When you've done a marathon, you can do anything"). He does, however, feel that the marathon is a healthy activity, so long as one doesn't have some physical impediment such as bone or weight problems. He states that even trotting ("trottiner") is fine. He would like to be "trotting" at ninety and beyond. But the marathon remains an event that demands preparation for him.

Delort would consider a 50K, but that's his absolute limit; he is not at all tempted by the 100K. He says you have to have the 100K in your head to want to do it. Even the marathon he finds a bit long. Had he started running younger, he thinks he would have been a miler. At the time, however, work kept him from running. In high school there were races and cycling, but he didn't really begin the marathon until he felt a need to do something else. That was at thirty-seven years old. Delort experienced the feeling of staying young. Indeed, this sense of rejuvenation is a phenomenon that accompanies the marathon experience for many runners. In Delort's case, it was shortly prior to reaching middle age, a time when people often feel the need to prove that they remain vital and dynamic. While his first marathon was frustrating, later results provided him with abundant proof of rejuvenation.

Marathons give thousands of runners the reward of accomplishment—though few have a real chance for place medals.

eleven

middle-aged and younger runners

The runners discussed in this section are not those who excel in their age groups like the near-professionals in Chapter 9. For these individuals, the race is more of an event than a test. They nonetheless derive considerable exhilaration from it, even though they are less driven by the clock. Among these runners, however, one was quite concerned about time, and he provides an excellent example of the use of technology in training and racing. This chapter, however, begins with his wife, who is not a runner, but who had particularly perceptive observations about the whole phenomenon.

Kathy Forcier is the wife of runner Gary Forcier. At her suggestion, she was interviewed because she afforded a unique perspective of the nonrunning member of a couple. She seemed to be a particularly empathetic person with a sense of humor. Forcier is a walker. She and her husband were originally walkers in their neighborhood, and he became involved in marathoning that way. She thinks there are many things you have to be aware of when you are married to someone so passionate about the marathon. "You have to be patient, understanding, allow them to have the time that they need to pursue their interest and be interested." Forcier indicates that sometimes you're not really interested "but you have to pretend that you're really thrilled about the amount of time it took to get somewhere." Sometimes you just have to say, "Gee, that's great." Most marathoners would be lucky to have such wry tolerance and encouragement.

Forcier thinks that the marathon is a good thing for her husband. She is supportive of him, indicating that despite his demanding schedule, he always finds time to be a part of their family. She notes his stressful job, and she states that "when he does run, he feels so much better; his mood is just wonderful, although he's a pretty mild-mannered man anyway." She feels that he just seems healthier with running, that he looks on life from a younger viewpoint. Overall, she is convinced that running is very good for him. She is hoping that her husband will take their six-year-old son on some runs with him. Their boy is very interested in running and will already go on a track. She thinks it would be great for their son even at his young age to start.

Although Forcier supports her husband morally, she does not feel any compunction to watch marathons. She went to Disneyland with the intention of cheering her husband on during its marathon. When some friends had inquired whether she would come to see him, she replied enthusiastically in the affirmative; however, it started pouring rain, and she never left the hotel room. She hasn't gone to Chicago to watch the marathon, but her neighbors have, and they have all reported back to her that they saw her husband. It always seems that there's someone or something that she has to take care of at home that keeps her from being at the marathon.

Initially, she did worry about her husband's running. Apparently, a woman her husband had met informed him that her spouse had died during the course of an ironman competition. The deceased spouse was a very fit thirty-six-year-old who had run several marathons. He apparently died of a heart attack. She brought up this incident to her husband, who responded by investigating in depth—even more so than she might have wished— his medical condition, which was excellent. She didn't worry much after that. She always tells him to know his limits, remember his age, and not to push himself. She tells him that he doesn't need to prove anything to anyone. She added that her husband has had several different interests that were potentially more dangerous than running: initially, he was a private pilot, and then he became interested in Harley-Davidsons. Running is his latest involvement and the one she is least worried about.

Forcier sees her husband as a much more fit person now. She thinks that this fitness has filtered down to her family in terms of eating in a healthy way and maintaining a healthy lifestyle. They have a sixteen-year-old daughter who is athletic and who will occasionally accompany her father running. She's on a traveling soccer team.

Forcier does not feel left out with all her family being involved in athletics. She was a swimmer when she was younger, and she also biked. She knows that those are things she can pursue again if she wants to. She has her own interests and is content with the situation. She doesn't feel any competitiveness.

Marathons really don't excite Forcier, despite her support for her spouse. Her neighbor across the street is the one who gets excited. She is always interested in hearing about the results and loves the pictures. Forcier qualifies, however, that "one of these days, I plan to get down there." Her lack of enthusiasm does not extend to all sports. She likes the action of basketball, but doubts whether she could enjoy standing around for a couple of hours watching a race. She would love to accompany her husband to marathons in California and Europe, and has suggested marathons in Italy as a way to get her husband to go there.[1] Forcier suggested interviewing another marathoner's spouse to discuss the various adjustments needed to allow a runner to pursue his passion. She suggested that adaptations for some people might be a source of conflict. In any event, Forcier seems to be a philosophical and amiable individual. She doesn't need to share her husband's enthusiasm for the marathon to support him.

Gary Forcier, Kathy's husband, is a physician and avid runner who came fairly late to the sport at age forty-seven. Before that he biked and did triathlons. He would commute to work thirty-five miles a day on his bike. Initially, he never enjoyed running; he considered it a waste of time as compared to moving on a bike. He was a committed swimmer who finished in the top 10 to 15 percent in his age groups in the triathlons he entered. He became interested in the marathon not through actual practice, but through Jeff Galloway's book—interested in the challenge of the race, that is. Forcier's involvement thus began as a form of intellectual curiosity concerning a potentially successful application of a widely utilized though controversial training program.

Forcier's approach to running is cerebral and methodical. At the time of the interview, he had been using a heart rate monitor for about the past two-and-a-half to three years. He had done a lot of reading on the subject: he owned about six or seven books on running and on triathlons. Forcier tries to be scientific about sports. He feels that the scientific approach contributes to significant improvement and cites a recent personal record in a 10K, which he attributes to this approach.

As a physician, Forcier belongs to the American Medical Athletic Association. He has researched a couple of articles on heart attacks and the risk of heart attack, but he doesn't really worry about getting one during a marathon. He says, "It's maybe a 1 percent thing." He has contemplated doing an ultrafast CT scan—a heart scan. He had a pulmonary function test and a stressed EKG test. He has no heart disease in his family, and his cholesterol couldn't get any better. He did participate in a heart study in conjunction with the Chicago Marathon in 2001, which included several echocardiograms. Clearly, Forcier brings a level of medical reflection and commitment to the marathon far beyond that of the layperson. He seems to be as methodical about investigating its hazards as he is about training.

In the actual marathon, Forcier monitors his pulse; he won't run without the heart rate monitor, which he uses to adjust his pace. It slows him down, as he tends to go out too fast. He is confident in this technology and states that he has gotten comfortable with it in training. He even bought a spare monitor just in case. He has a fancy one, which he can hook to his bike; it includes cadence and heart rate monitors, and all this information can be downloaded. He thinks only a small percentage of people use the monitors when they are running. The elite runners don't, in his opinion. Forcier himself illustrates a rather passionate minority that enjoys measurement and monitoring, and generally approaches running in a disciplined, highly technical fashion. His enthusiasm for relying on carefully accumulated knowledge and his participation in larger test projects speak strongly to his commitment to science even in sports endeavors. Recreation and research merge in his approach to the marathon.

Forcier sees himself as the kind of person who gets very intense with activities, but he can later put them aside and can go on to something else, alluding to his Harley motorcycle, two prior triathlons, and twenty-five years with a commercial pilot license. He thinks that he will probably always run; however, the Boston Marathon will be his reassessment period. In fact, it is Boston and not Chicago that represents the pinnacle of marathon running for him; it's "just the mystique, the challenge, something you have to attain." The fact that there are qualifying times, which Forcier hadn't met at the time of the interview, makes it important for him. He stated, however, that he was going to qualify for it in October 2002. Although he was twenty-eight minutes from the required time, he felt it was achievable.[2]

Forcier's attraction to the Chicago Marathon is based largely on the fact that it's local and it's flat. As to Chicago's human diversity, Forcier isn't really that interested in the neighborhoods or the crowds. In fact, he finds the marathon sometimes "too noisy and too distracting." "Except for maybe Chinatown, I didn't even know where I was running." He was focusing on his pace and heart rate; Forcier is very much the cocooned runner, one who largely disassociates himself from the aspect of collective celebration to focus on personal achievement. He remarked that if he had been in Nebraska instead of Chicago, it probably wouldn't have made any difference. But he also remarked that there were times when there were no spectators and that that was kind of a drag too. Spectators are needed, "but not the eight deep and screaming and all that stuff." And so Chicago retains a limited appeal for him, and it certainly does not command a strong loyalty beyond the fact that it is the most convenient site for marathon participation.

Forcier's case illustrates that, like Dorothy Tanner in chapter 10, the roar of the crowds is not necessarily a positive feature, no matter what marathon publicity may assert. Unlike Tanner, however, Forcier demonstrates the ineluctable narrowing of focus that technology imposes on a marathon. All serious runners, professionals in particular, must be acutely aware of the passage of time and their changing physical capabilities throughout the race. The technically inclined are, however, almost welded to their heart monitors. The instinct that may guide a professional is set aside for the readings of an instrument. Ironically, it may be instinct rather than software that elicits a superior performance.

Michael Campbell was thirty-five and registered for the 2002 race at the time of this interview. The 2001 Chicago Marathon was his first, which he characterizes "one of the greatest things I've ever done." Prior to this marathon, he had never even run a race before or considered himself a runner. A friend talked him into doing it, and he trained using the Hal Higdon program. He says, "It was such an amazing experience."

Campbell lived in Naperville at the time of the interview; his friend came from Boston to run the marathon with him. He went through the whole training program, but he couldn't say he did it rigorously—business travel forced him to miss training sessions, not an uncommon situation for many who choose to follow a program. Campbell added that he learned a lot from the experience, and he thought he "had some gas left" when he finished the marathon. He was anxious the day he started the marathon and said he was determined to finish it, even if "I had to crawl." He felt that when you set your sights on finishing, it takes the pressure off "because there is no option of quitting."

He felt "exhilaration," not exhaustion, on finishing, the adrenalin was pumping; it was an amazing experience. Despite the intensity of the experience, he didn't think he was hooked on marathoning—at the time, he was planning to do the 2002 Chicago Marathon, but not Boston's because he wasn't sure that he wanted to run throughout the winter. He doesn't train during winter because running when it's zero degrees out is just "insane." Although dedicated runners might disagree, this is hardly an unreasonable position—indeed, it may be a widespread one for those living in harsher, northern climates.

Running isn't competition for Campbell; it's struggling against himself. He is not cocooned when he races; rather, he sees everybody and he reacts to the crowds: "They really make a huge difference." He wants to surpass his previous time (4:26) in the next Chicago Marathon. He feels he really could have done 4:15 or 4:10, but he ran in a group of friends and one of the men was struggling. He figured he wasn't going to break any world speed record and decided that he would do it with the group and set his goal that way. Obviously, solidarity rather than maximum performance was more important for him.

Campbell finds Chicago's an attractive marathon because it is one of the "easier ones"—that is, it's flat. Like many other northerners, he appreciates being able to train in the spring and summer months, and he likes the fact that the marathon is in the fall. He found the temperature (about 55 degrees) perfect for the 2001 Chicago Marathon. He thought that all the factors were there.

He has civic pride in the Chicago Marathon. He appreciated going through all the different neighborhoods and seeing all the different people cheering him on; he enjoyed the music that people were blaring out the windows. He liked the bands; the music really pumped him up.

He did feel a sense of accomplishment in running the marathon, but, quite modestly, he also stated that if he could do it, a lot of other people could too. He is quite proud of his achievement, and, when interviewed, he was trying to recruit people for the 2002 marathon. He thought that the people whom he recruited would also share a sense of accomplishment—just to finish was the goal. In a sense, Campbell is a marathon proselytizer. Completion of the event has given him the urge to recruit others; he seems motivated by the desire to share a peak experience. His enthusiasm, like that of so many others with no special time goals, is a contributing factor to the continuing growth of the marathon. The personal elation he alludes to is an emotion that is widely shared among marathoners, particularly those who have completed their first race. It also is most likely the impetus behind so many advocates of the marathon.

Rex and Tracy Jones were both thirty-six years old in 2001 when they filled out a questionnaire on marathon running. Rex had been running for more than twenty years and Tracy for approximately ten. They both had started running marathons about ten years prior to this. Running plays a fairly significant role in their lives. Generally, they run four to seven miles a day and, when training for a marathon, complete a distance run of ten to twenty-five miles on Saturdays. They run because it provides them "wonderful quality time together." It also allows them to keep up with their three teenage children, who are all very athletic. They believe they have achieved something special through marathon running and are convinced that it is healthy. They chose the Chicago Marathon mostly for convenience: Rex was in the Air Force and he had just been stationed in the area. The Chicago Marathon was one of the closest. Other than that, the Chicago Marathon had no special personal importance to him, nor did its prestige count. They were only mildly impressed that there were world champions in the same race; Rex commented, "I suppose seeing the additional coverage on television was a little exciting." They both liked the effect of the crowd at Chicago. Their first few marathons had only limited spectators, but the large crowd in Chicago made the event a bit more enjoyable, and Rex thought that his wife and he had probably run better with all the excitement and enthusiasm generated by the spectators. Although they found starting in such a large field initially a little annoying, they don't compete against anyone except themselves and generally accomplish their goals, and this kept things in perspective. They run as a couple, not with any pace group or set of friends. At the end of the marathon, they experience an adrenaline rush and enjoy a great sense of accomplishment. They do not, however, attend any of the official postrace festivities. They also found the Chicago Marathon well organized. In fact, their response was "surprisingly *yes*." Perhaps people who are not natives of the area have a different idea than the locals, who expect good organization. Although they had achieved no personal records in Chicago, they felt it would be the place to set one; they thought it was one of the flattest courses they had ever run and that it was clearly marked. Rex stated that he would come back to run in the Chicago Marathon because it is well organized and has a great course, and he appreciated running through the city and "seeing much of what Chicago has to offer."

A charity fundraiser sends a message of energy and
exuberance.

twelve

charity runners

There are now so many people who run marathons for charities that they can be grouped in a separate category. But as the individual profiles reveal, these runners are as diverse as any group, and they span the gamut of running ability. They could be grouped into many categories, including age and time. Obviously, many charity runners are simply regular marathon runners who, at the behest of friends, decide to take part in this special kind of fundraising that characterizes the marathon. Though their times vary widely, their commitment remains deep. The first profile, Jane Ducham's, represents an almost heroic narrative. It demonstrates how runners with even modest times can display admirable tenacity in the face of constant pain.

Jane Ducham entered her first marathon with the goal of raising money for Children's Memorial Hospital. This was her first major experience in soliciting donations. Previously, she had served mostly in a support role rather than as the principal actor; for example, helping with drives for nieces' and nephews' schools and writing letters for the American Cancer Society.

Ducham was not new to running. She had at different times of her life run to stay in shape or for recreation, but had never undertaken a commitment on the scale of a marathon; running was more or less a way of exercising. Ducham had just started running on her own in the November before her marathon—about a year before the event—and was getting up to a solid mileage basis. Her sister-in-law had run two marathons for the leukemia group, which was her inspiration for doing fundraising. Ducham has a niece who was diagnosed with juvenile diabetes several years ago. She had done the Ron Santo Walk in LaGrange Park a couple of years ago, so, with her niece in mind, she decided that she would like to help with a cause to which she was more connected. It was her impression that the American Diabetic Association did not have a team for that year's marathon, and the Juvenile Diabetes Association definitely did not: they had a walk instead. She then searched on the Internet for an appropriate charitable cause. Ducham found that Children's Memorial Hospital had a relatively low fundraising minimum to participate—$500, she thought. Because she is in suburban LaGrange Park with her children and not in downtown Chicago, doing fundraisers at bars and other such places, where she believed it would be much easier to raise large sums of money, was out of the question. Therefore, she decided to go with Children's. She felt that even if she couldn't find people to participate, she could probably "scrounge that up" herself and meet her minimum fundraising goal. Another feature she liked about Children's is that you can earmark your funds for a specific cause within the hospital, so she could direct her funds to their research on juvenile diabetes. She liked being able to pinpoint the disease that was affecting her niece, who is also her goddaughter; it was something she could do specifically for her.

Ducham discussed her intentions with her then thirteen-year-old niece and explained to her that she wanted to send out fundraising letters talking specifically about her to people. Her niece consented, and Ducham was set.

Ducham found fundraising very easy. She just pulled out her Christmas card list and drafted a letter telling people what she was doing. She provided a narration of how her niece's life had to change, and how her niece inspired Ducham to make some changes of her own. The letter included a form with the message that anything a donor could do would be appreciated. She was surprised that the people she thought would contribute didn't, and the people she expected not to, actually did.

Ducham realized that, although her running was going well, she would need a group structure to help her train for the marathon; in fact, she considered it crucial to build up the mileage in the right way. She also liked the fact that Children's Memorial teams up with CARA and that their philosophy is: "First-time marathoners, you get to the starting line uninjured. Then your goal is to finish." Ducham found those goals reasonable. She had the example of her sister-in-law who had done the same thing, and she had never been a runner. About April, Ducham decided to commit and signed up with Children's Memorial and then CARA. The other thing that "fell in her lap" was that for the first time ever, CARA had a training group that was literally in her backyard (she lives close to the forest preserve, where the training took place). The group met for long runs in the preserve, meaning that she didn't have a long drive every Saturday for training. Under the circumstances, she decided that it was meant to be.

Originally, Ducham viewed herself as an exclusively solo runner. She felt that she didn't want the whole-group interaction; she wanted to have her solitude. During the week, she would get out just to run by herself, but the group experience turned out very well for her. She was happy with her training, which she found successful and injury-free—it was everything CARA had promised, and she followed every rule regarding diet, rest, and hydration. Despite her positive experience in training, her actual marathon proved disappointing. The day of the marathon, she recalls, there was a big temperature drop. A couple of her fellow trainees car-pooled to the race. They got into the starting area easily, but with the lowered temperature, they knew that they would have to stretch even more. However, at the start, they were all crammed "like in a cattle car." Under the circumstances, they couldn't stretch. They couldn't all run together, so she ended up pairing with one of the women in her pace group. Actually, they were initially three, at least for the first three miles; their group leader, who had recently discovered that she was pregnant, dropped out at mile 3. At about mile 2, she felt something funny in her knee. She thought that maybe it some-times takes three or four miles to get into it, and so she just shrugged off the discomfort. To complicate matters, there were "run/walkers" in her area of the course, and, on a number of occasions, someone directly in front of her would completely stop to walk. And so she found her-self weaving from side to side, which is discouraged in training with injunctions like "don't play tennis, don't play football." Ducham kept saying to herself "run a bit slower, run a bit faster, work it out," while trying to negotiate this stop-and-go situation. At about mile 9, she said to her running partner, "This isn't going away; there's something defi-nitely wrong." At mile 13, she thought she wasn't going to finish. With hydration in mind, Ducham and her partner walked to every water sta-tion and consumed fluids on the order of two waters and a Gatorade at each stop. Their desire to be well hydrated created a new problem and had them looking for every potty stop along the course. With her knee in pain, standing in line in the cold only made the situation worse. At mile 13, concerned as to what to do, Ducham told herself that she was forty and she didn't know if she would have the time to dedicate herself to running another marathon, given her small children. She also thought about her fundraising—she had far exceeded the $500 mark, having raised nearly $2,000. With all these considerations, she thought, "I can't quit; one way or the other, I've got to keep going on this thing." And so, at about the halfway point, she started run-walk-ing—something she hadn't had to do all summer. She had finished the eighteen-mile training run without walking, so she found her situation disappointing. Then, at about mile 15, Ducham and her running part-ner got separated at a water station, and Ducham just let her go. She knew that her partner would not leave her if she told her how bad her knee was, and she didn't want to ruin her day.

Ducham's husband and her sister-in-law had set meeting points along the course (mile 4, mile 9, etc.). They were at every previously agreed-on stop. The first one was a "thumbs up." At the second, she smiled but let them know there was a problem. At the third one, she asked if they would still be at mile 21. When they affirmed their inten-tion, she asked them to meet her there with Motrin. When she arrived, she popped a couple tablets, and then her sister-in-law jumped in with her. At this juncture, Ducham had fallen so far behind that the race officials were letting "anybody help anybody." She was back with the stragglers. Her sister-in-law was able to stay with her nearly to the finish chutes. By then, the medicine had kicked in and she was able to finish without limping, so she was able to run the final 0.2 miles of the race the way she had always pictured it. When she crossed the finish line, it was enough for her to have gotten that last little bit in. Then her husband couldn't find her and things were shutting down (although there were still some 2,000 people behind her). She had expected about a 4:30 time and finished instead in nearly 6:00. There were still enough medals left, but she felt "it was like the party had gone on already."

Ducham is now hesitant about running another marathon. She is afraid to try because she fears another day like her first marathon. She also worries about going through all the training, and asks herself, "What if I get halfway through the training and something goes wrong?" Nevertheless, it was a big accomplishment for Ducham. Her husband had all the neighbors come over; he stretched a huge banner across the front of the house, stating "See Jane run." She found everyone supportive and helpful, but in the back of her mind she remained a bit disappointed with her own results.

Ducham's experience touches on many common themes among marathon runners: the danger of good advice from training programs going awry (she feels that she took the CARA hydration advice too far; she had trained in heat and humidity, which made generous fluid intake essential, whereas during the actual race she needed less fluids given the colder temperatures); the time demands of training that rule out a second race for so many people; the need felt by people approaching middle age to prove themselves in some exceptional physical endeavor; and the exceptional support offered by their families as active spectators who hail runners at multiple viewing points, provide medication to ease their pain, and even jump into the latter part of the race to accompany their exhausted relatives nearly to the finish. Ducham herself illustrates that particular generosity of charity runners who will often push themselves to injury to finish even when they know they have no real obligation to do so to obtain pledged funds for their beneficiaries. She also illustrates that charity in itself is increasingly the initial motivation for undertaking the marathon. The desire to help a specific individual or group has become one of the chief motors of marathon recruitment.

Mike Long, who has also experienced his share of injuries, ran for

St. Jude's Children's Hospital in 2002.[1] The race was his first fundraising experience. He selected St. Jude's because he had seen something about it in *Runner's World.* At the same time, he had been following fairly closely the progress of his friend's grandson at that hospital. He decided that fundraising for this boy sounded like a perfect fit; he even wore the boy's picture on his singlet during the marathon. Although Long did not actually begin fundraising until fairly late, he made "a pretty nice haul." Asked if he found pledge solicitation difficult, Long responded that he experienced no problem. His wife was really surprised at how unbothered he was about it. He simply said, "Hey, it's for something that I really strongly believe in, and I don't give a darn." He has a four-year-old son who was born very prematurely; children are very special to him, so this was another incentive.

At the time Long made his decision to run Chicago's marathon, he had been running for about seven years. Had it not been for injuries, he believes he would have done so three years earlier. Even in 2002, he almost didn't make it. That year, he had been heavily involved in running, as he puts it, "a ton of races," which included a couple of half-marathons, a bunch of 5Ks and 10Ks, and ten-milers. About a week prior to the Chicago Marathon, when he was in the best shape of his life, he suddenly developed sciatica. He went to his orthopedic doctor and said, "I don't care what you have to do, just do something, because I'm gonna do this." The doctor gave him a shot of hydrocortisone and off he went. Long's resolution to continue despite infirmity reflects the determination typical of many marathoners, which is perhaps even more common in those who are running for a charitable cause.

From the onset, Long had specifically wanted to run the Chicago Marathon. His rationale was that you never know when it could be your last one, and he figured that if he was going to do it, he was going "to do a big one." Starting in a huge field of runners didn't bother him. However, during the marathon—Long didn't realize it until afterward—he sustained a stress fracture in his tibia. He nonetheless described the race enthusiastically as "almost like you were just in a sea of people; it just pulled you; it was amazing. And then all these hundreds of thousands of people standing along the route to cheer you on—it was incredible."

Long did have a time goal, but he missed it by only about three minutes: he was aiming for a sub-4:00 run, and he finished in 4:03. He felt that had he been able to run the Chicago Marathon two weeks earlier than its actual date, when he was in excellent shape, he would have been in a fabulous position to do really well. Events seemed to have proven him right: with far less preparation but injury-free, he completed the 2003 Chicago Marathon in a chip time of 3:54:00.

Despite the minor disappointment of the 2002 marathon, Long was nonetheless pleased with his results. He had not run one step the whole week prior to the marathon, and when he was actually standing at the starting line, he didn't even know if he was going to be able to run one block or twenty-six miles. But because he had invested so much effort and money into the marathon, he was determined to do it, even if he had to walk. Although he didn't have to finish to ensure that the pledges he had obtained would be honored, he nonetheless felt obligated to do so, especially as most of the donors had been quite generous. This sense of obligation to finish, already strong in most amateur marathoners, seems to be heightened among fundraisers.[2]

Like so many runners, Long was moved to tears at the end of the 2002 Chicago Marathon. The first time is often an extraordinary emotional experience. He socialized before and after the marathon, attending a gathering for the St. Jude's runners the night before and the marathon party the evening following the race. He characterized the latter as "a blast." He jokingly remarked that he had run just for the beer. He enjoyed being on Navy Pier, where he got to shake Paula Radcliffe's hand just after she had broken the women's world record. He also met the men's world record holder at the time, Khalid Khannouchi.

Much of Long's experience coincided almost perfectly with marathon planners' expectations. He loved the crowds during the race and basked in the celebratory atmosphere of the postmarathon party. He viewed Chicago, quite correctly, as one of the world's most prestigious marathons. He achieved a thoroughly respectable time and did even better on his second attempt. The race was clearly an emotional high point. On the other hand, what links him to charity runners is perhaps his extraordinary tenacity. Like Ducham, his own suffering had to take second place to his commitment, to the sense of obligation (purely self-imposed) to those who had pledged funds. The physical damage he did to himself, as with Ducham, should not have been necessary. Although noncharity amateur runners also push themselves to injury, it would seem that charity runners have even greater motivation to do so. In the interest of the well-being of these altruists, marathon officials must try even harder than they already do to persuade people to think more of their physical well-being. Clearly those who maintain that the marathon is a healthy endeavor need to reconsider its physical cost. Of course, this willingness to inflict injury on oneself, especially for a noble cause, is what creates for some the "heroic" dimension of the marathon.

Some people approach fundraising more casually and vary their beneficiaries according to the circumstances. Marta Glazier was twenty-seven at the time she answered the marathon questionnaire and had been running for nine years. She ran her first marathon in New York in 1998. She does not train regularly and usually runs alone for scheduling reasons, but for Chicago she trained with "Joints in Motion," which she liked very much. She felt she had achieved something special in running Chicago's marathon: "I had an overwhelming rush of adrenaline that I would like to replicate." She has a qualified judgment on the health of marathon running; she feels that it is healthy in some ways, but "ultimately . . . the toll it takes on your body is not healthy. Injuries are nearly inevitable."

Glazier chose to run the Chicago Marathon because she was living in Chicago at the time. For many reasons, it was fantastic experience for her. She speculated that it might have been partly because she was in graduate school at the University of Chicago, "which will hold a dear place in my heart." The prestige of the marathon did not influence her: she hadn't even thought of it before reading the questionnaire. She felt that the presence of world champions in the race made it exciting but didn't change much about her experience. She appreciated the crowds of spectators, but didn't enjoy starting in such a huge field of runners. She had to weave in and out of people throughout the entire course, which she found a bit frustrating. She felt that Chicago's was even more crowded than New York's. This difficulty in negotiating the course was the only complaint she voiced about the race. She wasn't sure of the effect this had on her time; she was trying to break four hours and finished in 4:03. Glazier ran much of the race alone except at one point when she chanced upon some people she knew and ran with them for about a mile. At mile 18, however, a close friend joined her and ran with her to the finish. The end of the marathon brought her "extreme excitement and adrenaline rush." She did not attend any official postrace festivities but went to her own. She would come back to Chicago because she has friends there.

This was not Glazier's first fundraising experience. She selected the Arthritis Foundation because a friend convinced her; her run did not sponsor a particular individual. She said that she would participate in this kind of activity again because she likes being able to contribute. Glazier clearly cares about helping others, but she does not dramatize her contribution. It just seems to fit in with her running.

Melissa Schulz, who hails from New York City, had run seven marathons prior to Chicago's in 2002, which was her first "official" fundraising marathon. She described becoming part of the effort as getting in "by default" because an extra team member was needed. She made a donation, but did not do the huge fundraising that is typically associated with Fred's Team.[3] A friend from New York, whom she had persuaded to run in the Chicago Marathon, wanted to do the race with Fred's Team and got her to sign up. It was too late for her to ask people to pledge when she got in. In the past, she had done other fundraising runs in New York such as the Revlon Walk for Women. She says that soliciting funds is a little bit difficult. With family, however, it's easy because she feels so comfortable and because her family donates to many of the charities with which she is associated. She thinks that the biggest problem is the concern that people are going to feel bad and feel "guilted" into saying "yes," or that they're worried about the repercussions of their friendship if they don't donate. She gets around that by saying, "You don't have to give anything—think about it." She is careful to avoid pressuring them. Because of her late entry, she did not sponsor a specific individual.

Schulz started running with the Chase Corporate Challenge when she was in high school. After graduating from college, from 1992 through 1995, she ran that race annually. In 1995, she realized she wanted much more than a single annual race. Schulz joined the New York Road Runners Club, trained in Central Park, and, by the following year, she had run her first New York City Marathon, a clear indication of the passion running had inspired in her. She has subsequently run Chicago's and Stockholm's marathons, and, of course, New York's several times. She chose Chicago because she had it on her list of marathons, because she likes the idea of a flat marathon, and because New York is so hilly. She also wanted to go to a different city and, in Chicago's case, she had friends who had done it and loved it, and she likes the city. She fully expected to enjoy herself. The prestige of the Chicago Marathon doesn't count for her; she thinks "Boston," when she thinks prestige, because you don't have to qualify for Chicago. Chicago for her was more laid back and was more all-around fun. She wanted a fast course. The fact that there are world champions in the same race doesn't make that much difference to her. She remarked that it wasn't likely she'd be "bumping into them at an 8:30 pace."

Schulz has always loved spectators and hamming it up for them, but she remarked, "the older I get, the less important that is to me." Actually, there was a point in the Chicago Marathon at which the crowds were so loud that she found it difficult to bear the noise. She felt like asking: "Can't I have some peace and quiet?" She termed this "shocking" because one of the reasons she used to do marathons was because she loved having that crowd support. It was as if she needed the attention, and now she no longer requires it.

Schulz was not bothered by the size of the Chicago starting field, although she thinks that logistically it can be tough. She was able to profit from the wide start and to get up relatively close to the front. Her first mile was at 8:35 to 8:40, quite close to her overall pace of about 8:37. She definitely met her goal in Chicago with a 3:46. She didn't get boxed in after the start because she was so close to the front that she did a nice pace for her first three miles—she thinks about an 8:30 pace despite the first mile. She felt great at the finish. She cried because it was a personal record for her. It also made her think that she could qualify for Boston, that she would be able to get in next year. She had wanted to run Chicago under 3:54 and she had done a 3:46. For her, it was "outstanding." She had no idea how fast of a course it was. "When they said fast, they mean fast!"

Schulz's experience had a powerful emotional dimension that went beyond her personal accomplishments. Her friends also achieved personal records at the race. Even more important, however, was the presence of her four-month pregnant sister, who came to the marathon to watch her race. In New York, her sister cheers her on at three meeting points. In Chicago, her sister was able to meet her for a surprise fourth time—quite a feat in a sea of 30,000 runners. This was spectacular for Schulz, who thought of her yet-unborn niece and imagined that from this experience the child would be a runner. Schulz described the 2002 Chicago Marathon as the "happiest day of the year" for her.

Schulz's elation is characteristic of her marathon running. She feels energized upon finishing. She has run five New York Marathons, and she jogged home after most of them. With each marathon, she felt like she could run more, with the exception of one year when she got hypothermia. Other than that, all of the other marathons were "just fabulous." After Stockholm's, she went jogging the next day. She thinks that the trick is to get a massage right afterward. She has done that for the past couple of marathons and feels that it makes all the difference in the world.

In Chicago, she went to the expo and enjoyed it. She has never gone to any of the postmarathon festivities; she flew out later that afternoon. In New York, she has her family or her boyfriend over afterward. She always has a small group of people at her place after a marathon, and after about two hours, her guests say that she needs to rest. Then she takes a bath or does something really pleasant like just lie on the couch, watch TV, and eat some tofu. Like so many runners, Schulz has her own postmarathon rituals, rituals that have little to do with the organized festivities offered by the marathons themselves.

Schulz would definitely consider doing charity running again. She was touched by the atmosphere in the hospitality tent; she thought it was "just so nice" to have food and drink and be surrounded by friendly people. At this point, she almost feels as if she owes Fred's Team because she didn't raise a lot of money. She'd like to do it again, and really do it right by collecting pledges in earnest. She would prefer to have an individual beneficiary, a special person she was helping out. She thinks that if she had been touched by a person in her family or a friend who had a serious illness, she would have been glad to raise money to support the fight against the person's illness or to encourage the person who was ill. Schulz has in a way come to fundraising by happenstance, although she feels that she was always a charity runner, if that means wanting to make a statement or donate to a special cause afterward. Her Chicago running experience and the supportive atmosphere of Fred's Team have only reinforced her commitment.

general observations on runners as a whole

From professional to fundraiser, from competitive amateur to leisurely jogger, or some combination thereof, it should be obvious that marathoners represent an extraordinary range of affinities and differences. Professionals can hardly be dismissed as "jocks." They often reveal themselves as thoughtful and caring people, able to take a broad overview of their profession and the world. Besides their extraordinary ability and intensive training, what differentiates them from most amateurs is their extremely sharp focus on the last six or so miles of the race. They know that all their discipline and training must be used to take them through this taxing and brutal final stretch. Although this focus is certainly evident among gifted amateurs, it tends to elicit less commentary from the greater mass of runners.

The much-touted elation produced by crowds would seem less than universal. Although most runners are energized by the enthusiasm of spectators, a significant minority finds the clamor distracting, even irritating; an obstacle to the peace and concentration required to focus on pace. Such runners cocoon themselves rather than connect with the surrounding masses. Attitudes change over time and even during the course of the race. The most inward of runners may feel the need for human support, while the most gregarious may need a break from constant acclaim.

The attraction of Chicago's marathon varies according to the runner. Some definitely want to be part of a world-class marathon, whereas others choose Chicago because of its proximity and convenience. Still others hope its flat course will provide them with a personal record. Some combine all these motives and more. Although marathon officials often see the presence of world champions in the same race as a lure, most nonprofessional runners do not even consider this aspect of the marathon. Their preoccupation is with their own experience and perhaps that of their running companions. This attitude tends to confirm the notion that the marathon is all about individual performance on the urban stage. In more practical terms, the amateur runners' indifference to the presence of professionals also attests to the fact that all but the swiftest among them never even get a glimpse of the professionals during the race.

Concerns about actual performance and achieving personal records, while more common among faster runners, manifest themselves across all ability levels, but they do not necessarily affect all runners. Some are quite happy just to complete the marathon, whether alone or with their friends. Others judge themselves harshly if they do not reach their objectives but experience great elation if they do. In fact, intense emotion, regardless of the level of performance, seems to be a widespread, almost constant reaction, especially in the case of a first marathon or a personal record. Men and women freely admit that they have cried upon finishing the race. The marathon offers an exceptional outlet for the positive feeling that accompanies a sense of self-realization.

Even as the marathon moves toward a gigantic procession, ever more an event than a race, the values of an athletic contest still endure, and runners of even modest ability exhibit an often touching courage and tenacity in the face of physical adversity. The marathon invites the individual runner to enact a spectacle of prowess that is accessible to the most as well as the least athletically gifted. Imbued with a classical heritage that evokes the ultimate sacrifice, the marathon still brings a heroic dimension to ordinary life and allows the individual runner a sense of otherwise unparalleled physical accomplishment and soaring emotion.

A sight for sore eyes (and legs): the finish line.

conclusion

The marathon is now a prominent feature of modern international sports life, and the Chicago Marathon stands out as one of its most dramatic success stories. Having survived two sponsor desertions, the race is now assured the financial attention it requires thanks to its sponsor and owner, LaSalle Bank. Given current beliefs about the healthiness of running, it is hard to see any impending decline for Chicago's marathon or marathoning in general, especially because its participants are often drawn from the more privileged segments of world society—something that ensures the race a strong advocacy. The marathon has clearly gone far beyond the dimensions of a sport and, although retaining competition, has also become a key urban ritual and, as such, an event coveted and promoted by civic authorities and wealthy sponsors.

The marathon serves as a kind of omnibus for diverse, even contradic-
tory values that range from racing to mere participation; it thrives from
this diversity, which has allowed it to expand to accommodate small
armies of runners. The marathon has imbedded itself in the mass consciousness of the residents of many cities throughout the world; it has
become part of the rhythm of urban life, a special marker for a given
season. It has largely replaced the carnivals and religious processions
of old. Like them, it attracts masses of actors and even greater numbers
of spectators. Because so many people who run marathons are not athletes in any sense of the word, expectations are continuously decreasing and "enablers" who grant permission for nonathletic performances
are prospering, and will most likely continue to do so. This seems inevitable, as completing a marathon has become proof of mental and moral
fitness, as much a demonstration of self-worth as an athletic contest. As
long as people, particularly those of higher status, see the marathon as
an act of self-validation, the ranks of marathon runners will continue
to swell. The race itself will reaffirm civic cohesion and vaunt the virtues of the cities that sponsor it.

The Chicago example is instructive because it illustrates just how
distinct groups within a community converge to stage an event of extraordinary complexity, an event that promotes many different interests and fosters civic harmony. The generosity of individual volunteers
speaks to a need for altruistic behavior among the citizenry and to
Chicagoans' genuine pride in the event. The marathon also suggests a
more subtle role for business sponsorship: while businesses must think
in terms of the bottom line, marathon involvement does not supply
clear measures of economic benefits to a business. Greater outreach
in branding is obvious, but the sales impact of enhanced name recognition is not necessarily in direct proportion to the numbers of those
who become aware of sponsors through their marathon commitments.
Larger, more generous forces would seem to be in play. But even without them, the current understanding of advertising as branding ensures
that sponsors will see in the mass marathon an unparalleled advertising opportunity.

The Chicago marathon also indicates the complexities of media involvement, particularly the issue of building and sustaining interest
in one-episode annual events. It provides a lesson in the interaction
between marathon officials and media outlets, and it indicates media-

specific strategies, particularly in the case of the press and television. Although the press remains independent, mutual interest may tend to stifle critical commentary. Television broadcasting, in the case of the media partner, is by its very nature collaborative, a relationship that largely rules out any public criticism and moves toward event advocacy.

The marathon also creates a special role for fundraising, the association of charitable endeavors with ordeal sports—a particularly fecund one, as statistics would indicate. This association only further underlines that the marathon has become a value-charged event. The puritan righteousness so characteristic of the early epochs of American society has, to an extent, migrated to health-related issues. Participation in the marathon as a charity fundraiser elevates the event to a pilgrimage or a sacred quest, and the actual fundraising eclipses performance concerns for some runners. In Guttmann's classic book *From Ritual to Record,* the author traces sport, before it even bore such a name, from "cultic" practice to a secular focus on record.[1] Some charity runners appear to be reverting to a more religious approach in which sport addresses the disharmony of disease and offers a symbolic remedy. Holding the forces of evil in abeyance through completion of an event has for some become far more important than the secular notion of time and, specifically, a record.[2] In any event, as an extreme sport, the marathon exerts far greater appeal to potential donors than more traditional forms of charitable solicitation. As long as this remains the case, the marathon will exert an irresistible appeal to fundraising associations.

Throughout the world, most marathons share many of the characteristics of the Chicago Marathon. They interact with one another, learning from the others' failures and copying, almost instantly, all the successful tactics and technical innovations in the sport. Because this is largely an open, mass-participation sport that invites worldwide tourism, a certain homogeneity in handling marathons and in treating their participants becomes inescapable. As a form of global behavior, marathons must per force share a growing uniformity in staging if they are to facilitate greater participation. Chicago's success will inevitably make it a model in approaching this extraordinary event.

Spectator support is so appreciated by many runners.

notes

chapter one: the marathon from myth to actuality

1. The English translations of the runner's name vary. Browning and other authors prefer "Pheidippides," but the Loeb Classical Library edition currently cited uses "Phidippides." The relevant passage begins: "... the generals sent as a herald to Sparta Phidippides, an Athenian, and one, moreover, that was a runner of long distances and made that his calling" [Herodotus, vol. 3, 257 (vol. 6, 105)].

2. For further discussion, see also Kleanthis Paleologus, "Marathon Man, the Historical Evidence," *Olympic Review* 261 (July 1989): n 261, 326–28.

3. See John Kieran and Arthur Daley, *The Story of the Olympic Games,* rev. ed., Philadelphia: J. B. Lippincott, 1961, 18; Jeff Galloway, *Marathon: You Can Do It!,*

Bolinas, Calif.: Shelter Publications, 2001, 19; and the episode "Marathon" in the History Channel's *Decisive Battles* series.

4. For some web-based examples of awareness of historical sources, see Ian Kemp, "The Great Marathon Myth," http://www.coolrunning.co.nz/articles/2002a007.htmd, (accessed October 20, 2004); see also the "Pheidippides" entry in Wikipedia, http://en.wikipedia.org/wiki/Pheidippides (accessed October 20, 2004).

5. For a discussion of this phenomenon, see Eric Hobsbawn and Terence Ranger, "Introduction: Inventing Traditions," in *The Invention of Tradition,* ed. Eric Hobsbawn and Terence Ranger, 1–14 (Cambridge: Cambridge University Press, 1983, 1988), and "Mass-Producing Traditions: Europe, 1870–1914," in Hobsbawn and Ranger, *Invention of Tradition,* 263–307.

6. Mandell supplies the exact distance for the first marathon: "Loues [alternative spelling for *Louis*] ran twenty-four miles, 1,500 yards, a little less than twenty-five miles"; Richard D. Mandell, *The First Modern Olympics* (Berkeley: University of California Press, 1976), 157. Bryant simply refers to "the 25-mile journey to Athens"; John Bryant, *The London Marathon: The History of the Greatest Race on Earth* (London: Hutchinson, 2005), 26.

7. Unfortunately, there is also reason to suspect that the champion Louis and the runner-up rode on horseback for part of the way; Bryant, *London Marathon,* 27–35.

8. Cooper cites Litsky's 1983 *New York Times*'s article that revealed that almost 90 percent of the New York Road Runners Club (NYRRC) were college graduates with an average income of $40,000—a solid salary at the time; Pamela Cooper, *The American Marathon* (Syracuse, N.Y.: Syracuse University Press, 1998), 142.

9. This new inclusiveness has its antecedents in medieval variants of football, which, although highly competitive, could involve whole villages—young and old, men and women—in occasionally fatal mêlées that lasted from dawn to dusk in a carnival-like atmosphere that sometimes scandalized moralists; Mandell, *Sport,* 155.

10. Mexican Americans are the only economically disadvantaged minority that participates in significant numbers, and this may be due to the enthusiasm inspired by the participation of Mexicans themselves. According to Elizabeth Kiser, communications manager of the LaSalle Bank Chicago Marathon, there were 912 runners from Mexico in the 2005 race.

11. John Bingham and Jenny Hadfield, *Marathoning for Mortals* (Emmaus, Penn.: Rodale, 2003); Jeff Galloway, *Marathon: You Can Do It!* (Bolinas, Calif.: Shelter Publications, 2001).

12. Boston may be the exception that proves the rule, as most of its desirabil-

ity comes not just from the fact that it is the oldest marathon but rather that, with the exception of the men's and women's U.S. Olympic marathon trials, it is the only North American marathon that imposes time standards. Were this to become a general practice, most marathons would experience a sharp plunge in participants.

13. Austin's 2005 Freescale Marathon (formerly known as the Motorola Marathon) openly advertises itself as "walker friendly": "the Freescale Marathon has something for everybody. So, whether the name of your game is qualifying for the Boston Marathon or *taking a leisurely walk to an eight-hour finish*—or, if you simply want to enjoy great music and easy running in a cool city—the Freescale Marathon is the name to remember" (Freescale Marathon advertisement, 38; author's italics). Walking a marathon has now become so commonplace that *Runner's World* had a feature article about the experience written by a credible (3:05) marathon runner who deliberately walked the P. F. Chang's Rock 'n' Roll Arizona Marathon (Phoenix) to evaluate the experience. The author gave a very favorable account of walking the race; John Hanc, "Walking the Walk," *Runner's World* (October 2004): 107.

14. For a particularly subtle analysis of class in the marathon and many other aspects of the event, see Helmuth Berking and Sighard Neckel, "Urban Marathon: The Staging of Individuality as an Urban Event," trans. Mark Ritter, *Theory, Culture and Society* 10, no. 4 (1993): 63–78. See also Vincent Serravallo, "Class and Gender in Recreational Marathon Running," *Race, Gender and Class* 7, no. 2 (April 30, 2000): 96–121, who makes a careful analysis of socioprofessional distinctions within class that determine who runs marathons.

15. Although Chicago and other marathons are open to teenage competitors, most coaches tell their runners quite pointedly that they should not run marathons until they have reached their twenties. The late-adolescent, not yet fully developed body is still viewed as prone to age-related injury from the marathon.

16. Ironically, Monroe was a "closet runner" who actually enjoyed running but confined herself to nocturnal, secretive runs to keep in shape. A woman jogger in the 1950s would hardly have been viewed as feminine.

17. Males frequently exhibit far less enthusiasm for group training and often prefer to train with one or two friends. Some men simply don't want to take part in a group activity until they are satisfied that they have reached an appropriate level of ability. Women may favor groups in part as a security measure, but this is surely not a satisfactory explanation for the far greater popularity of training groups among women. The group dimension must in some way reflect differing patterns of female and male socialization.

18. See the discussion in chapter 8, pp. 152–54.

19. The half-marathon does not really meet the same naming criterion because, defined not of and in itself but only in relationship to the marathon, it is relegated to a subordinate status; it "borrows" another race's name to define itself.

chapter two: a brief history of the chicago marathon

1. Sandy Treadwell makes it clear that not everyone found this name alluring, referring to it as the "immodestly named America's Marathon/Chicago"; Sandy Treadwell, *The World of Marathons* (New York: Stewart, Tabori & Chang, 1982), 62.

2. At the time, LaSalle used the plural, "Banks," in its company name.

3. Although death has been debated in other sports, especially in dangerous ones like boxing and mountain climbing, a runner's demise always seems particularly scandalous. Despite the myth of Pheidippides, running is generally viewed as a health-promoting activity. Runners are expected to be healthy and to enjoy longevity. The sudden collapse and demise of Jim Fixx, author of *The Complete Book of Running,* was particularly shocking in that regard. Fixx was in his fifties, and his premature passing seemed to discredit the health benefits attributed to running.

chapter three: the race director

1. This is not merely confined to the United States. Berlin's Horst Milder is a prime continental example of this development. On the other hand, the French example is somewhat different. Joël Lainé, the current race director of the Paris Marathon, followed a civil service path that led to his position. In 1989, he served as "adjoint au maire de Paris chargé de jeunesse et de sport" (deputy mayor for youth and sport) to Jacques Chirac, then mayor of Paris and now president of the French Republic. He actually took charge of the marathon in late 1998, when the marathon was placed under the administration of the Athlétisme Organisation (AO) at the mayor's wish.

2. Fred Lebow's autobiography, *Inside the World of Big-Time Marathoning,* is the story of someone evolving into the position of race director for the mass marathon he was in the process of shaping; Fred Lebow, with Richard Woodley, *Inside the World of Big-Time Marathoning* (New York: Rawson, 1984).

3. Interview in August 2001.

4. Actually, Pinkowski may have made a mistake on the age of the London Marathon. Chicago's first edition of the marathon, then the Mayor Daley Marathon, was in 1977; according to Bryant, the first London edition of the marathon was in 1981; John Bryant, *The London Marathon: The History of the Greatest Race on Earth* (London: Hutchinson, 2005), 5.

5. Pinkowski's exclusion of Paris and Berlin from his list is certainly contest-

able. Berlin has been the site of a brief woman's world record and the current men's world record (Paul Tergat, interview in October 2001). The finishers' fields in each of these marathons are relatively comparable to Chicago's.

6. It is interesting to note how midwesterners believe that they are more cooperative and caring than people in other regions of the country. Certainly, New Yorkers and Bostonians are quite fervent and caring about their marathons, but somehow there remains a persistent mythology about stronger personal ties and greater social commitment in the country's heartland. The basis of this unsubstantiated belief certainly calls for investigation.

chapter four: grassroots support

1. David Patt served as CARA's CEO for fifteen years, from 1990 until April 2005. His remarks were made in October 2003.

2. Fred Lebow recounts how he dealt with neighborhood toughs who told him they didn't want the marathon coming through their turf. He "recruited" them to "protect" the marathon as it passed through their area by offering them the white windbreakers that served as course marshal jackets; Fred Lebow, with Richard Woodley, *Inside the World of Big Time Marathoning* (New York: Rawson, 1984), 84–85.

3. The Frontrunners' unbroken winning streak came to an end in 2005 after the writing of this chapter. In 2005, their aid station received the second-place prize in a new award system that was based on web site voting that was open to any runner, volunteer, or spectator who cared to vote.

4. Of course, much has been written on how "whiteness"—as much an aspect of diversity as any other grouping—escapes characterization and even awareness of its nonuniversal status by the larger population, which views it as the norm.

chapter five: corporate and small-business sponsorship

1. In April 2001, the Shamrock Shuffle became the largest 8K in the world with over 15,500 participants. This was yet another indication of LaSalle's commitment to epic-scale running events within Chicago.

2. The information from Ms. Woods is derived largely from two presentations, including remarks and information-packet distributions, to the author's students during the classes of September 18, 2000, and September 29, 2003.

3. These are the people who drive "previously owned vehicles" rather than "used cars" and who entertain in their "great rooms" rather than their "living rooms."

4. REAL is an independent assessment group that provides objective data on the economic impact of institutions and events in the Chicago area. LaSalle has

commissioned assessments in the last few years (through 2000) after an original study was done in the mid-1990s.

5. A fifty-five-year-old woman who runs the race in 3:15 and places first in her division will contribute more than a thirty-two-year-old man who runs the marathon in 2:45 but is only in the top twenty of his division.

6. United Airlines sponsors the more modest Run for the Zoo 10K.

7. Dominick's withdrawal took place after this portion of the book was completed and could only be addressed during the copy editing. The grocery chain's representative stated on March 15, 2006, that the reasons were confidential and the firm was no longer able to continue its sponsorship.

8. Information from Mr. Fitzgerald is taken from his presentation to the author's students on September 26, 2003.

9. For a brief summary of some the acquisitions battles that led to this purchase, see the Wikipedia entry on Gatorade; http://en.wikipedia.org/wiki/Gatorade.

10. The Gatorade web site proudly features the institute; http://www.Gatorade.com.

11. Gatorade's current NFL contract extends through 2011; see "Gatorade Renews Sponsorship with NFL" on the NFL web site, http://www.nfl.com/news/story/7112505.

12. Information has been drawn from the author's interview with Mr. Zimmer and his presentation to the author's class on November 10, 2003.

chapter six: city government and sister agency support

Pages 111–16 and 119–21 are adapted from Andrew Suozzo's article, "The Chicago Marathon and Urban Renaissance," *Journal of Popular Culture* 36, no. 1 (Summer 2002): 142–59. The author gratefully acknowledges the *Journal of Popular Culture*'s permission to use this material.

1. By way of example, New York, Boston, Philadelphia, Miami, Nashville, Houston, Austin, Las Vegas, Phoenix, San Diego, Los Angeles, San Francisco, Minneapolis, Duluth, Columbus, Cincinnati, Detroit, and Washington, D.C., have marathons. This is but a short list that does not even begin to note the smaller cities and locales that also sponsor marathons.

2. See Jane Jacob's observations on sidewalk activity and pedestrian safety in *The Death and Life of Great American Cities* (New York: New Library Edition, 1993), 72–96.

3. This was a period of intense neighborhood development in which stadiums played a vital and sometimes conflictual part. See in particular chapter 6, "Lakeview," in Costas Spirou and Larry Bennett, *It's Hardly Sportin': Stadiums, Neighborhoods, and the New Chicago* (DeKalb: Northern Illinois University Press,

2003), for a discussion of the transformation of the Lakeview neighborhood that marks the northernmost reach of the Chicago Marathon course.

4. Kennedy noted 500 officers in 2000.

5. The author thanks Cindy Kaitcer for the information on CTA relations with the marathon.

6. Reithoffer, as noted earlier, is a real estate agent; Delort owns an auto repair firm.

chapter seven: charities

1. Chicago Marathon, "Charities," http://www.chicagomarathon.com/page_L2.aspx?subMenu=3&Page_ID=5&Nav_2_ID=4 (accessed August 4, 2004).

2. Interview conducted on August 5, 2004. The remarks that follow also come from that interview.

3. For a discussion of the Golden Bond scheme, see John Bryant, *The London Marathon: The History of the Greatest Race on Earth* (London: Hutchinson, 2005), 109–10.

4. There are certainly longer footraces, but none attract the attention or hold the mythological prestige of the marathon. When compared to the marathon, 50Ks and above contain minuscule fields, as indicated in chapter 1.

5. A fundraiser for Chicago House, an AIDS hospice, informed this author that when the AIDS ride disappeared, a $25,000 revenue stream vanished; there was simply nothing to replace the lost funds. It's hardly surprising that charities themselves are less concerned by the percentage of monies retained by the fundraisers than by the disappearance of substantial, irrecoverable funding once a source is eliminated.

6. In the November 2003 issue of *Running Times,* editor-in-chief Beverly noted that the article and related exchanges about a September letter on charity selection at the Boston Marathon ("Flowers and Flames," letter to the editor, *Running Times* [November 2003]: 6–8) "generated more mail than we've seen in years"; "Flowers and Flames," letter to the editor, *Running Times* (November 2003): 6.

7. This perception would probably not survive serious scrutiny today, as so many running clubs have evolved into social clubs more focused on cordial intragroup relations rather than being havens for competitive athletes. Parties, fun-runs, and simply options for broader networking are typical of such clubs, which sometimes boast about the number of marriages that have occurred among their members. Indeed, the clubs are often the modern equivalent of matchmakers.

8. Of course, this begs the question of the number of first-time marathoners not running for a charitable cause who return to their second marathon.

chapter eight: the media

1. For simplicity's sake, Kiser is described as working for the marathon. She and the entire marathon staff work out of an office at LaSalle Bank, which is, in turn, owned by ABN AMRO. Kiser and other staff members also make up the Shamrock Shuffle staff and the Standard Federal 10K (a Michigan race also owned by LaSalle ABN AMRO). In this world of overlapping corporate ownerships, accurately naming the employer is nearly a research project in itself.

2. For example, Jonathan Beverly, editor of *Running Times,* interviewed a Moroccan hopeful at the Chicago Marathon in French.

3. From Khannouchi's postrace remarks, it appears they did no such thing. Instead, he was applauded as a kind of favorite son.

4. Interview conducted on November 24, 2004, with e-mail updates for the 2005 marathon.

5. Mats are used to record data from chips at given distances throughout the race.

chapter nine: professionals and exceptional amateurs

1. The information from Rundell was not gathered during premarathon interviews; rather, it came from his presentation to the author's class in 2003.

2. A top Chicago area runner shared his anxiety about the now-defunct (alas) Trustmark Marathon (part of the Lake County races), which usually had a small field of around 600 runners. The runner in question had actually gotten lost on the course.

chapter ten: older runners

1. For a lively and lucid discussion of Dr. Fair's work, see David Leonhardt, "For Aging Runners, a Formula Makes Time Stand Still." *New York Times,* Science Times, October 28, 2003, pp. F1, F4.

2. Although Dunbar's experience does not correspond exactly to Paul Joseph and James Robbins's 1981 sociological study cited by Tim Noakes, her situation does relate to their observations. As Noakes indicates: "Finally, the greater the dissatisfaction with certain aspects of work (in particular, the potential it gave for self-development, self-involvement, or competition) the greater the tendency to rank running over work as the more important source of self-identity"; Timothy D. Noakes, *Lore of Running,* 4th ed. (Champaign, Ill.: Human Kinetics, 2003), 554.

3. In fact, she went on to complete the 2003 marathon.

4. That's probably not likely, however, because frequency of participation gives access to applicants for the New York City Marathon.

5. Paris is divided into twenty arrondissements, each of which has a separate mayor. These arrondissements correspond roughly to wards in the city of Chicago, and each mayor would be somewhat analogous to an alderman. Paris does have a mayor of the city as a whole; as of this writing, it was Bertrand Delanoë.

6. The author has chosen to include French runners not only for reasons of personal and professional ties to France, but also because for part of the Chicago Marathon's history, the French represented the largest number of foreign participants.

7. For a vivid account of this marathon, see Martine Segalen, *Les enfants d'Achille et de Nike* (Paris: Métailié, 1994), 154–62. Segalen describes the Marathon du Médoc in a way that indicates the current tendencies that are transforming the marathon into an event rather than a competition. She notes that "la performance est passée à l'arrière-plan et c'est vers la convivialité et la fête que les organisateurs ont orienté leurs efforts" (159). Author's translation: "Performance has moved into the background and the organizers have focused their efforts on conviviality and festival."

8. See chapter 6 for the author's discussion of Reithoffer.

chapter eleven: middle-aged and younger runners

1. This is not at all that far-fetched. The author knows a woman, the wife of an old high school running team member, who actually got her husband to go to Tuscany by pointing out to him that he could run in the Venice Marathon before heading to that region of Italy.

2. Eventually, Forcier did run the Boston Marathon, the qualifying time continued to elude him, but he was able to participate (and continues to do so) because of his charity fundraising efforts.

chapter twelve: charity runners

1. In 2004, St. Jude's took its fundraising to the Chicago lakefront with posters along the running trail that asked, "Need a reason?" Of course, Long, an Iowa resident, did not discover the hospital this way.

2. Interestingly, a professional will not hesitate to drop out of a race because of injury or, at times, when a race is just not going well. Economic interest compels professionals to spare themselves pointless harm.

3. Fred's Team, named for Fred Lebow, the New York City Marathon executive race director who succumbed to cancer, raises money to combat leukemia.

conclusion

1. Guttmann identifies seven interrelated characteristics of modern sports that interact systematically: secularism, equality, specialization, rationaliza-

tion, bureaucracy, quantification, and records. These have replaced earlier practices that he sees as more related to religious rights; Allen Guttmann, et al., *From Ritual to Record: The Nature of Modern Sports* (New York: Columbia University Press, 1978, 2004), 15–55.

2. Some charity runners not included in this book were unconcerned about their times (eight hours plus, which they insisted on defining as running) and seemed to feel that fundraising validated their performance. In fact, the moral aspect it provided clearly overshadowed any considerations typically associated with modern sport.

Paula Radcliffe set the women's world record time of 2:17:18 in Chicago in 2002.

bibliography

Barthelemy, Marianne. "Les Expériences multiples de l'endurance." *Sociétés* 64 (1999): pp. 43–49.

Berking, Helmuth, and Sighard Neckel. "Urban Marathon: The Staging of Individuality as an Urban Event." Translated by Mark Ritter. *Theory, Culture and Society* 10, no. 4 (1993): 63–78.

Beverly, Jonathan. "The Marathon Mystique." *Running Times,* July–August 2001.

Bingham, John. *No Need for Speed: A Beginner's Guide to the Joy of Running.* Emmaus, Penn.: Rodale, 2002.

———, and Jenny Hadfield. *Marathoning for Mortals.* Emmaus, Penn.: Rodale, 2003.

Bourdieu, Pierre. *Distinction: A Social Critique of the Judgments of Taste.* Translated by Richard Nice. Cambridge, Mass.: Harvard University Press, 1984.

Browning, Robert. "Pheidippides." In *The Works of Robert Browning,* vol. 9. New York: Barnes & Noble, 1966, pp. 221–29.

Bryant, John. *The London Marathon: The History of the Greatest Race on Earth.* London: Hutchinson, 2005.

Caro, Mark. "Big Race Is a Test For All." *Chicago Tribune,* Chicago Sports Final, North Edition, October 31, 1994, p. 1.

Cheung, Jeanie. "Record for Ndereba." *Chicago Sun-Times,* Sports, October 8, 2001, p. 84.

Chicago Marathon. "Charities." http://www.chicagomarathon.com/page_L2.aspx?subMenu=3&Page_ID=5&Nav_2_ID=4 (accessed August 3, 2004).

———. "History." http://www.chicagomarathon.com/page_L2.aspx?subMenu=3&Page_ID=3&Nav_2_ID=2&Page_Title=Race%20History (accessed August–October, 2004).

Connelly, Michael. *26 Miles to Boston.* Guilford, Conn.: Lyons Press, 2003.

Cooper, Pamela. *The American Marathon.* Syracuse, N.Y.: Syracuse University Press, 1998.

Daniels, Jack. *Daniels' Running Formula.* Champaign, Ill.: Human Kinetics, 1998.

Derderian, Tom. *Boston Marathon: The First Century of the World's Premier Running Event.* Champaign, Ill.: Human Kinetics, 1996.

———. *The Boston Marathon: A Century of Blood, Sweat, and Cheers.* Chicago: Triumph Books, 2003.

"The Marathon at Its Peak." Editorial, *Chicago Tribune,* October 19, 2002, p. 28.

Eitzen, D. Stanley, and George Sage, eds. *Sociology of North American Sport.* Madison, Wis.: Brown & Benchmark, 1993.

Fitzgerald, Matt. "Rethinking the Wall." *Running Times* (April 2005): p. 14.

"Flowers and Flames." Letters to the Editor. *Running Times* (September 2003): pp. 6–7.

"Flowers and Flames." Letter to the Editor. *Running Times* (November 2003): pp. 6–8.

Flora London Marathon. "Help the Hospices Official Charity." http://www.london-marathon.co.uk/iframes/news/main.htm (accessed September 1, 2004).

Freedman, Lew. "Beginner's Pluck? No, He's Good." *Chicago Tribune,* Chicago Marathon, October 13, 2003, p. 1.

———. "Encore Performance; Rutto Knows the Chicago Drill." *Chicago Tribune,* Chicago Marathon, October 11, 2004, p. 1.

Freescale Marathon advertisement. *Running Times* 321 (November 2004): p. 38.

Galloway, Jeff. *Marathon: You Can Do It!* Bolinas, Calif.: Shelter Publications, 2001.

Garcia, Marlen. "Ndereba Does Her Best." *Chicago Tribune,* Chicago Sports Final, North Edition, October 23, 2000, p. 3.

———, and Lew Freedman. "Chicago Marathon Bits; Fighting Fatigue—and Her Country." *Chicago Tribune,* Chicago Marathon, October 11, 2004, p. 3.

Gatorade. http://www.Gatorade.com (accessed March 8, 2006).

"Gatorade." Wikipedia entry, http://en.wikipedia.org/wiki/Gatorade (accessed March 8, 2006).

"Gatorade Renews Sponsorship with NFL." National Football League NFL News, February 23, 2004. http://www.nfl.com/news/story/7112505 (accessed March 8, 2006).

Ginnetti, Toni, and Larry Hamel. "Culpepper, Drossin Anchor U.S." *Chicago Sun-Times,* Sports, October 14, 2002, p. 92.

Guttmann, Allen. *From Ritual to Record: The Nature of Modern Sports.* New York: Columbia University Press, 1978, 2004.

———. *Games and Empires: Modern Sports and Cultural Imperialism.* New York: Columbia University Press, 1994.

Guttmann, Allen, Richard D. Mandell, Steven A. Riess, Stephen Hardy, and Donald G. Kyle. *The Erotic in Sports.* New York: Columbia University Press, 1996.

Hall, Tom. "The People's Race Turns 20." *Chicago Runner Magazine* (Fall 1997): pp. 14–19.

Hamel, Larry. "Khannouchi Blows Past His Record; Chepchumba Has a Dashing Sequel." *Chicago Sun-Times,* Late Sports Final Edition, October 25, 1999, p. 3.

———. "Long Run to Greatness: Marathon's Amazing Growth Is Right in Step with the Times." *Chicago Sun-Times,* Late Sports Final Edition, October 17, 1999, p. 29.

Hanc, John. "Walking the Walk." *Runner's World* (October 2004): pp. 84–89, 107–8.

Hanna, Julie. "Top Marathon Finishers Show True Grit." *Chicago Tribune,* Sports, October 26, 1992, p. 1.

———. "Brazilian, Finn Kick Chicago Marathon Weather." *Chicago Tribune,* Sports Final Edition, November 1, 1993, p. 11.

Hersh, Philip. "Amazing Finishes." *Chicago Tribune,* Chicago Marathon, October 8, 2001, p. 1.

———. "Civic Apathy Still Dulls Marathon's Luster." *Chicago Tribune,* Sports, October 29, 1988, p. 5.

———. "In the Long Run, He Puts U.S. 2nd." *Chicago Tribune,* Sports, October 6, 2004, p. 2.

———. "Like a Broken Record." *Chicago Tribune,* Chicago Marathon, October 14, 2002, p. 1.

———. "Marathons Need Finishing Kick." *Chicago Tribune,* Sports, October 30, 1990, p. 7.

———. "9th Chicago Marathon: Oct. 20, 1985 Series." *Chicago Tribune,* Chicago Marathon, September 27, 2002, p. 10.

———. "Problems Keeping Marathon on the Skids." *Chicago Tribune,* Sports, October 27, 1990, p. 5.

———. "Return to the Golden Days Firm Financial Footing Helps Chicago Draw Top Runners." *Chicago Tribune,* Chicagoland Final Edition, October 19, 1997, p. 12.

———. "Showing His New Colors." *Chicago Tribune,* Sports Final, North Edition, October 23, 2000, p. 1.

———. "Sorry, Marathon Means Running; Chicago Event Must Decide What It Wants to Be." *Chicago Tribune,* Sports Talk, October 14, 2001, p. 16.

———. "Thorns, Not Laurel Wreath, for Ch. 32's Race Telecast." *Chicago Tribune,* Chicago Sports Final, North Edition, October 31, 1994, p. 8.

———. "Top 3 Women's Finishers Gain Some Consolation." *Chicago Tribune,* Sport Notebook, October 31, 1988, p. 16.

———, and K. C. Johnson. "As Sponsors Desert Chicago Marathon, So Do Elite Runners." *Chicago Tribune,* Sports Final, North Edition, October 25, 1991, p. 1.

———, and Linda Young. "Marathon Notes." *Chicago Tribune,* Sports, October 30, 1989, p. 11.

Higdon, Hal. *Marathon: The Ultimate Training Guide.* Emmaus, Penn.: Rodale Press, 1999.

Hoban, Brom. "Paving the Way: Elgin's Dorothy Doolittle a True Pioneer of the Women's Marathon." *Austin American Statesman,* February 11, 2004, pp. D1, D5.

Hobsbawm, Eric, and Terence Ranger, eds. *The Invention of Tradition.* Cambridge: Cambridge University Press, 1983, 1988.

Jacobs, Jane. *The Death and Life of Great American Cities.* New York: The Modern Library Edition, 1993.

Johnson, K. C. "Chicago Marathon Can Bank on Sunny Forecast for Future." *Chicago Tribune,* North Sports Final Edition, November 1, 1994, p. 8.

———. "Marathon Director Waits in Wings." *Chicago Tribune,* North Sports Final Edition, October 12, 1995, p. 7.

———. "Silva Wins in, through a Breeze." *Chicago Tribune,* North Sports Final Edition, October 28, 1991, p. 11.

———. "'Sprint' Key in Marathon." *Chicago Tribune,* North Sports Final Edition, October 16, 1995, p. 1.

———. "Sutton Avenges Her Olympic Snub." *Chicago Tribune,* North Sports Final Edition, October 21, 1996, p. 12.

———, Philip Hersh, and Skip Myslenski. "Samuelson's Cramp Crimps Her 'Debut.'" *Chicago Tribune,* North Sports Final Edition, October 20, 1997, p. 6.

Kemp, Ian. "The Great Marathon Myth." http://www.coolrunning.co.nz/articles/2002a007.htmd (accessed October 20, 2004).

Kieran, John, and Arthur Daley. *The Story of the Olympic Games,* rev. ed. Philadelphia: J. B. Lippincott, 1961.

Kyle, Donald G., and Gary D. Stark. *Essays on Sport History and Sport Mythology.* College Station: University of Texas at Arlington by Texas A&M University Press, 1990.

Lawrence, Allan, and Mark Scheid. *Running and Racing after 35.* Boston: Little, Brown, 1990.

Lebow, Fred, with Richard Woodley. *Inside the World of Big-Time Marathoning.* New York: Rawson, 1984.

Leonhardt, David. "For Aging Runners, a Formula Makes Time Stand Still." *New York Times,* Science Times, October 28, 2003, pp. F1, F4.

Litke, James. "Sports News." The Associated Press, October 27, 1986, Monday, PM edition.

Lucian. "A Slip of the Tongue in Greeting." In *Lucian,* vol. 6. Translated by K. Kilburn. Cambridge, Mass.: Harvard University Press/London; William Heinemann, 1959, p. 177.

Mandell, Richard D. *The First Modern Olympics.* Berkeley: University of California Press, 1976.

———. *Sport: A Cultural History.* New York: Columbia University Press, 1984

Manier, Jeremy, and Julie Deardorff. "Marathon Death Stirs Questions." *Chicago Tribune,* North Sports Final Edition, October 16, 1998, p. 1.

McCann, Tom. "Stars, Strides, Sadness." *Chicago Tribune,* Metro, October 8, 2001, p. 1.

McClelland, Ted. "The Man Who Ruined Running." *Chicago Reader* 33, no. 45, sec. 1 (Friday, August 6, 2004): pp. 1, 18–19, 22–23, 25.

McDill, Kent. United Press International. October 21, 1985. http://web.lexis-nexis.com.ezproxy1.lib.depaul.edu/universe/document?_m=dc50ef9d1d7adbc14f0bd8927b5acd65&_docnum=4&wchp=dGLbV1b-zSkVA&_md5=7e9b22643552f3acd86523ce00e8e73 (accessed March 9, 2006).

Merle, Patrick F. "Big City Style: Culture and Competition from Coast to Coast." *Running Times* 320 (October 2004): pp. 38–39, 42, 44.

Mező, Ferenc. *Modern Olympic Games.* Budapest, Panonia Press, 1956.

Mondenard, Jean-Pierre. "The Death of Philippides, Nine Views of the Evidence." *Olympic Review* 257 (March 1989), http://www.aafla.org/OlympicInformationCenter/OlympicReview/1989/ore257/ore257s.pdf (accessed March 8, 2006).

Myslenski, Skip. "It Turns Out, Osoro's Run Isn't for Nothing." *Chicago Tribune,* North Sports Final Edition, October 12, 1998, p. 3.

———. "Sprinting, Struggling to Win, Kastor Survives Brutal Final 3 Miles." *Chicago Tribune,* October 10, 2005, p. 2.

———, and Jack McCarthy. "Kastor Rare U.S. Success." *Chicago Tribune,* October 10, 2005, p. 3.

Neumer, Alison. "Too Popular." *Chicago Tribune,* Red-Eye Edition, October 10, 2003, p. 27.

Nickel, Lori. "Evans Finds His Way in Marathon Briton's 2:08:52 Fastest since 1986." *Chicago Tribune,* North Sports Final Edition, October 26, 1996, p. 1.

Noakes, Timothy D. *Lore of Running,* 4th ed. Champaign, Ill.: Human Kinetics, 2003.

Paleologus, Kleanthis. "Marathon Man, the Historical Evidence." *Olympic Review* 261 (July 1989): 326–328, http://www.aafla.org/OlympicinfomrationCenter/OlympicReview/1989/ore257/ore257s.pdf (accessed March 8, 2006).

Pausanias. *Description of Greece.* 5 vols. Trans. William H. S. Jones. Vol. 1, *Attica,* New York: G. P. Putnam's Sons, 1918.

———. *Description of Greece.* 5 vols. Trans. by William H. S. Jones. Vol. 4, *Arcadia,* New York: G. P. Putnam's Sons, 1918.

"Pheidippides." Wikipedia entry, http://en.wikipedia.org/wiki/Pheidippides (accessed March 8, 2006).

Plutarch. *Moralia,* vol. 4. Translated by Frank Cole Babbitt. Cambridge, Mass.: Harvard University Press/London: William Heinemann, 1936.

Pope, S. W., ed. *The New American Sport History: Recent Approaches and Perspectives.* Urbana: University of Illinois Press, 1997.

Richards, Bob. "Charity Running at the LaSalle Bank Chicago Marathon—The Trend with a Cause." http://www.chicagomarathon.com/page_L2.aspx?subMenu=117&Page_ID=246&Nav_2_I_" 8/3/2004 (accessed August 3, 2004).

———. "Dos Santos Snow Job Plows Field." *Chicago Sun-Times,* Late Sports Final Edition, November 1, 1993, p. 2.

———. "Fellow Kenyans Can't Match Limo." *Chicago Sun-Times,* October 10, 2005, p. 114.

———. "Marathoner, 75, Has Old Age on the Run." *Chicago Sun-Times,* Sports, October, 11, 1995, p. 115.

———. "No Svet: Tomescu-Dita Coasts to Marathon Win." *Chicago Sun-Times,* Sports, October 11, 2004, p. 103.

———. "Zakharova Finally Catches Tomescu-Dita." *Chicago Sun-Times,* Sports, October 13, 2003, p. 92.

Robinson, Roger, and Jonathan Beverly. "The Greatest of These Is Charity: Considering the Future of Running and Charity Giving." *Running Times* (September 2003): pp. 14–21.

Roeper, Richard. "Tragedy No Indictment of Marathoner's Lifestyle." *Chicago Sun-Times,* Late Sports Final Edition, October 24, 2000, p. 11.

Rosenthal, Bert. "NYC Marathon/Bright." The Associated Press, October 26, 1984. http://web.lexis-nexis.com.ezproxy1.lib.depaul.edu/universe/doclist?_m=94456d817c9911f75db23d7f22f018b8&wchp=dGLbV1b-zSkVA&_md5=f33fe76ffaa6a9acfl1e3fcffb640a50 (accessed March 9, 2006).

Sears, Edward S. *Running through the Ages.* Jefferson, N.C.: McFarland, 2001.

Segalen, Martine. *Les enfants d'Achille et de Nike.* Paris: Métailié, 1994.

———. *Rites et rituels contemporains.* Paris: Nathan, 1998.

Serravallo, Vincent. "Class and Gender in Recreational Marathon Running." *Race, Gender and Class* 7, no. 2 (April 30, 2000): pp. 96–121.

Spirou, Costas, and Larry Bennett. *It's Hardly Sportin': Stadiums, Neighborhoods, and the New Chicago.* DeKalb: Northern Illinois University Press, 2003.

Suozzo, Andrew. "The Chicago Marathon and Urban Renaissance." *Journal of Popular Culture* 36, no. 1 (Summer 2002): pp. 142–59.

Treadwell, Sandy. *The World of Marathons.* New York: Stewart, Tabori & Chang, 1982.

Trinquesse, Vincent. "A Chicago, un francophile pas comme les autres." *France Amérique,* November 6–12, 2004, pp. 1, 17.

United Press International. October 22, 1984. http://web.lexis-nexis.com.ezproxy1.lib.depaul.edu/universe/document?_m=73ce930eec08509481 06d74e0a1ddhca&_docnum=4&wchp=dGLbV1b-zSkVA&_md5=f86af99c bac128981c46dbd66d26a412 (accessed April 22, 2006).

"What Killed Runner?" *Chicago Tribune,* Red-Eye Edition, October 14, 2003, p. 3.

Wilson, Terry. "Runner's Death Raises Question About Safety at Marathon." *Chicago Tribune,* Chicago Sports Final, North Edition, October 24, 2000, p. 5.

Young, Linda. "Weidenbach's Win Like Homecoming." *Chicago Tribune,* Chicago Sports Final, North Edition, October 30, 1989, p. 11.

Wong, Edward. "Greeted by Ennui on Streets of Paris." *The New York Times,* Sports, April 14, 2002, p. 10.

Ziehm, Len. "Cashing In on Fast Start." *Chicago Sun-Times,* Sports, October 26, 1992, p. 98.

———. "Chicago Marathon Gets 10–Year Deal from Its Sponsor." *Chicago Sun-Times*, Late Sports Final Edition, October 20, 1996, p. 36.

———. "Flaherty May Reveal Future of Marathon." *Chicago Sun-Times,* Sports, October 19, 1992, p. 100.

———. "It's a Time-Tested Marathon." *Chicago Sun-Times,* Late Sports Final Edition, October 29, 1993, p. 4.

———. "Kenya's Rutto Routs 'Em Again." *Chicago Sun-Times,* Sports, October 11, 2004, p. 102.

———. "Lemettinen Left All Alone, Wins Women's Race." *Chicago Sun-Times,* Late Sports Final Edition, October 16, 1995, p. 80.

———. "Stunning Victory for Pacer Kimondiu." *Chicago Sun-Times,* Sports, October 8, 2001, p. 85.

Zorn, Eric. "Fat Jack Is Gone." *Chicago Tribune,* Chicago Metro, October 13, 1998, p. 1.

———. "Finish Line Visible for Marathon Epic." *Chicago Tribune,* Chicago Metro, October 15, 1998, p. 1.

———. "Fools Like Me Shuffle toward Date with Destiny." *Chicago Tribune,* Chicago Metro, March 23, 1998, p. 1.

———. "Fools Rush In . . . and Slog Out." *Chicago Tribune,* Chicago Marathon, October 12,1998, p. 1.

———. "In the Long Run, Victory Is Where You Find It." *Chicago Tribune,* North Sports Final, July 28, 1998, p. 1.

———. "Marathon Looks Like a Peak on the Way to Over-the-Hill." *Chicago Tribune,* Chicago Metro, January 6, 1998, p. 1.

———. "Marathon Success Depends on What You Have in Mind." *Chicago Tribune,* Chicago Metro, September 24, 1998, p. 1.

———. "Marathon Training a Longer Road Than the Race Itself." *Chicago Tribune,* Chicago Metro, April 28, 1998, p. 1.

———. "Oprah's Mark Puts Marathon within Our Reach." *Chicago Tribune,* Chicago Metro, October 5, 1998, p. 1.

———. "They Follow the Fleet for These Amateur Runners." *Chicago Tribune Magazine* (October 4, 1998): p. 12.

———. "This Fool Trains as Skeptics Run Their Mouths." *Chicago Tribune,* Chicago Metro, February 5, 1998, p. 1.

———. "Toni's Syndrome Strikes Foot Fears in Foolish Hearts." *Chicago Tribune,* Chicago Metro, June 9, 1998, p. 1.

———. "With Miles to Go Before We Sleep, the Ranks Thin Out." *Chicago Tribune,* North Sports Final, July 27, 1998, p. 1.

lecture sources

Dilbeck, Michael. Chicago director of Walk the Talk Productions, the National AIDS Marathon at the Chicago Marathon, September 17, 2003.

Fitzgerald, Don. Former vice president of marketing for Dominick's Finer Foods, the food industry and the marathon market, September 26, 2003.

Kaitcer, Cindy. General manager, marketing and advertising, Chicago Transit Authority (CTA) and the Chicago Marathon, October 17, 2003.

Kennedy, David. Former sports director, Mayor's Office of Special Events, the city and the marathon, October 3, 2003.

Patt, David. Former CEO, Chicago Area Runners Association, Chicago area running, the marathon, and the broader gamut of races and running clubs, October 22, 2003.

Pinkowski, Carey. Executive director, LaSalle Bank Chicago Marathon, September 15, 2003 (and earlier).

Reithoffer, David. Frontrunners' aid station director and French recruitment coordinator, volunteer participation in the marathon, and international recruitment, September 22, 2003.

Richards, Bob. Former editor, *Chicago Amateur Athlete,* sports journalism, October 1, 2003.

Woods, Kim. Former senior vice president and director of internal communications, ABN AMRO, and former managing director of the LaSalle Bank Chicago Marathon, a corporate perspective, September 18, 2000, and September 26, 2003.

Zimmer, David. Owner, Fleet Feet, a small-business perspective on the marathon and involvement in area running, November 10, 2003.

interviews

Bravo, Jacques. Mayor, Paris, ninth arrondissement, April 9, 2003.

Campbell, Michael. May 20, 2002.

De La Cerda, Peter. October 6, 2001.

Deloit, Gérard. July 10, 2002.

Ducham, Jane. August 23, 2003.

Dunbar, Jo. May 30, 2002.

Foot, Jay. CBS executive producer, 2003 and 2004 productions of the Chicago Marathon, November 24, 2004. E-mail updates for 2005 marathon.

Forcier, Gary. May 21, 2001.

Forcier, Kathy. May 21, 2001.

Glazier, Marta. Respondent to questionnaire, August 13, 2003.

Gonzalez, Richard. May 22, 2002.

Humphrey, Luke. October 9, 2004.

Jones, Rex and Tracy. August 12, 2003.

Kaplan, Lisa. Former community relations and special programs director for the Chicago Marathon, August 5, 2004.

Kiplagat, Lornah. October 5, 2001.

Kiser, Elizabeth. Communications manager, LaSalle Bank Chicago Marathon/ABN AMRO, August 26, 2004.

Lample, Debbie. Chicago campaign manager for Team in Training, August 10, 2004.

Long, Mark. August 21, 2003.

McKenzie, Pat. May 30, 2002.

Nishi, Mike. Chicago, September 8, 2004.

Ouaadi, Mohamed. October 5, 2001.

Pinkowski, Carey. Executive race director, LaSalle Bank Chicago Marathon, August 4, 2001, and August 9, 2003, and numerous discussions.

Platt, Shawn. First vice president and director of public relations, LaSalle Bank ABN AMRO, October 19, 2004.

Reithoffer, David. April 21, 2002, and numerous discussions.

Rogers, Curtis. May 29, 2002.

Russell, Blake. October, 9, 2004.

Schulz, Melissa. August 21, 2003.

Tanner, Dorothy. April 25, 2002.

Tanui, Moses. October 5, 2001.

Tergat, Paul. October 5, 2001.

Aid Station Captains' Interviews

Cheung, Celia. June 16, 2001.

Gomez de la casa, Bernardo. June 13, 2001.

Lyles, Bernard. June 10, 2001.

Onines, Pat. June 6, 2001.

Oppenheim, Paul. June 7, 2001.

Schulman, Stewart. June 8, 2001.

index

Andrew Suozzo is a professor of modern languages at DePaul University. He is the author of *The Comic Novels of Charles Sorel* and coauthor of *Teaching French Culture: Theory and Practice.* Suozzo, an experienced marathoner, has taught courses on the Chicago Marathon and lectured on marathon running in the United States and abroad. He won the Russel B. Nye award for his article "The Chicago Marathon and the Urban Renaissance."

The University of Illinois Press
is a founding member of the
Association of American University Presses.

Composed in 9.5/13.5 ITC Stone Serif
with Folio display
by Jim Proefrock
at the University of Illinois Press
Designed by Dennis Roberts
Manufactured by Sheridan Books, Inc.

University of Illinois Press
1325 South Oak Street
Champaign, IL 61820–6903
www.press.uillinois.edu